"HILARIOUS."
Newsweek

"Uproariously funny . . . Zany . . . The dialogue is hilarious and the shopping scenes are absolutely, you should pardon the expression, priceless."
San Diego Tribune

"Absolutely hysterical . . . Rudnick uses every trick in the book to lovingly and satirically portray one of our most popular national pastimes. . . . Delightful."
Chicago Sun-Times

"Rudnick pulls off a comic coup: He's biting and kind in the same breath. . . . Exuberantly funny from first page to last."
Philadelphia Inquirer

"A witty, spirited look at the shop-till-they-drop crowd."
New York Magazine

"I would urge readers to come upon the chapter at the dressing room at Loehmann's in private, because they are bound to giggle, laugh, and finally fall off the chair."
WENDY WASSERSTEIN

Also by Paul Rudnick
Published by Ballantine Books:

SOCIAL DISEASE

I'LL TAKE IT

A novel by
Paul Rudnick

BALLANTINE BOOKS • NEW YORK

For the Klahr sisters,
Lillian, Hilda, and Selma

Copyright © 1989 by Paul Rudnick

All rights reserved under International and Pan-American
Copyright Conventions. Published in the United States by
Ballantine Books, a division of Random House, Inc., New
York, and simultaneously in Canada by Random House of
Canada Limited, Toronto.

Library of Congress Catalog Card Number: 88-46160

ISBN 0-345-36225-X

This edition published by arrangement with Alfred A.
Knopf, Inc.

Printed in Canada

First Ballantine Books Edition: May 1990

15 14 13 12 11 10 9 8 7 6

1

Joe Reckler was dreading the whole idea. A week earlier, Joe's mother had phoned him and demanded that he accompany her on a week-long car trip through New England. It was October and Mrs. Reckler wanted "to see the leaves change." Also along for the ride, packed into the Reckler Oldsmobile, would be Mrs. Reckler's two older sisters, Joe's Aunt Ida and Aunt Pola. Joe fervently believed that this trip could kill him. Under "Cause of Demise" on Joe's death certificate, the coroner would scribble "Traveling with his relatives," and everyone at the morgue would nod, and understand.

Joe loved his relatives, most assuredly; it was just that he was twenty-six years old, and he didn't long to abide in a small, enclosed space with the Esker sisters for an entire week. Still, Joe had agreed to make the journey; something in his mother's voice, an urgency, had persuaded him. That, and the fact that if he refused to go, his mother would never let him forget the trespass. A week of agony seemed preferable to a lifetime of guilt and accusatory glances and mentions of "the trip that Joe was too busy to go on with his own flesh and blood."

Joe was now wandering restlessly through his Manhattan apartment, waiting for his mother to arrive from New Jersey and buzz his doorbell from the street. He lived in a miniature one-bedroom apartment in the East Village, a rental on the second floor in the rear of a brownstone. The apartment overlooked a courtyard and the back of the brownstone across the way. Joe's apartment reminded everyone of Jimmy Stewart's digs in *Rear Window*, except that while Jimmy Stewart, laid up with a fractured leg, had used his binoculars to ogle murderers and lonely, disrobing maidens, all Joe had ever glimpsed was a fully uniformed flight attendant watering his plants.

Joe's apartment resembled a crowded furniture storeroom. He regularly plundered the city's better junk shops for a style of furniture he had dubbed "theatrical gothic." Everything was dark oak and ornately carved, moody with roaring lions' heads and medieval turrets and gnarly claw feet. Joe felt he was living in a summer-stock set for a thirties murder mystery. Only revolving secret panels and a tarnished suit of armor were missing, and perhaps a cameo appearance by Vincent Price. Joe did not care for modern furnishings, for low foam couches and butcher block and canvas-backed directors' chairs, all of which he felt lacked spice, and history.

The doorbell buzzed. Joe buzzed back, opening the front door a flight below. Joe knew that if he let his mother buzz more than once she would take it as a sign that he was doing something he was ashamed to have her see, something bizarrely sexual or, far worse, something like shoving dirty laundry under the bed.

"So what were you doing?" asked Mrs. Reckler as Joe opened the door.

"Nothing," said Joe, kissing his mother. "Just don't go in the bedroom."

"I have no intention. Why shouldn't I go in the bedroom?"

"Mother," said Joe, rolling his eyes as only he could. "I was joking."

"Ha ha," said Mrs. Reckler, taking a quick peek in the bedroom. "May I sit down?"

"No," said Joe, sitting on his tufted red leather couch, a hefty Victorian barge.

"Wiseguy," said Mrs. Reckler, sitting on the matching tufted red leather wing chair.

Joe and his mother looked at each other, both waggling their eyebrows. They smiled. The Recklers loved each other so much that it embarrassed them both. Joe thought that his mother was the best in the world, he felt so lucky. Mrs. Reckler lived for the son she knew was handsomer and smarter than any child on earth. The Recklers expressed their love not openly but through other, equally satisfying channels. They nagged one another and teased and traded patter; they took a prickly delight in each other's presence.

Joe and Mrs. Reckler were unmistakably mother and son; they shared the same nose, a prominent, distinguished beak. Joe had a lantern-jawed, horsey face and a full head of thick, shaggy dark-brown hair. Joe's appearance suited his furniture; he looked like a young, amiably sloppy Sherlock Holmes. Today he wore jeans, Converse basketball sneakers, and a fluid, scarlet gabardine shirt (Joe's favorite color was red, a choice that he hoped reflected a torrid persona).

Mrs. Reckler was becomingly plump, with strong peasant features. Her round, careworn face and bright brown eyes would have looked entirely appropriate gazing out from beneath a stylish babushka. She wore her hair in a coiled bun at the nape of her neck, a style favored by both Mrs. Reckler and her sisters. She had a crush on imperious, independent beauties like Louise Nevelson and Martha Graham, so she went for oversize ethnic jewelry and rich, dramatic fabrics. Today she wore a loose woolen dress in a bold houndstooth check, with heavy amber beads and chunky gold earrings. She also carried a large handbag of butter-soft beige kid, a simple rectangle with a gold clasp.

"Do you like this?" Mrs. Reckler asked her son, holding up the bag.

"It's beautiful. How much?"

"Oh shut up. That's not what's important. I needed a bag. $22.50, reduced from $60, Bamberger's, and it's Italian. Pish pish."

Joe nodded approvingly, at the quality of both the bag and the bargain. Bargains were a great Reckler tradition. Even if the bag had been hideous or poorly sewn or ripped, the bargain was sufficient to endorse the purchase. The bag was lovely, so the savings created a rapture. A well-made, well-designed, imported handbag in a useful color at almost 60 percent off demonstrated, as far as either Reckler was concerned, the existence of God.

"So what's new?" asked Mrs. Reckler, inspecting the apartment from her chair. "Look at all this stuff. You're a loon. So what have you bought and not told me about?"

"Nothing. Just this little table," Joe said, indicating an end table, a metal contraption cunningly painted to resemble a stack of hand-tooled-leather-bound antique books.

"Oh my God," said Mrs. Reckler. "You know, I almost bought this exact table. Daddy and I went to Short Hills a few Sundays ago, and I saw this table in a store and I wanted it, but it cost too much and I didn't know where I would put it."

"Really? You know, I saw it at Bloomingdale's, and I kept going back to visit it, for months. I couldn't decide if it was ridiculous or if it was wonderful, and I finally just gave in." Visiting hotly desired objects in stores was another invincible Reckler sacrament. The Recklers visited things so that the things would feel cherished. The Recklers knew that, at any moment, an item might shudder, gulp, and go on sale. If they visited the item frequently enough, if they were vigilant, they might well arrive at the very instant that the price was being slashed by a third, and then they could kidnap the chair or jacket before anyone else could pounce. If you visited a beloved something at a store with sufficient dedication, you earned it. The item was not purchased but awarded.

"It's beautiful," said Mrs. Reckler, stroking the little table. Mrs. Reckler did not really share her son's taste, finding it a bit over the top, if not downright silly, but she appreciated it. Visiting her son's apartment, she always felt she was browsing through some enchanted flea market. "If I was your Aunt Pola," Mrs. Reckler commented, with regard to the table, "I would ask how much you paid for something like this."

"It's a good thing you're not my Aunt Pola."

"Very funny. I don't care what you spent, it's your money to throw away. Believe me, I could care less. I just want to see the price difference between the store I saw it in and Bloomingdale's. So I'll know if I could have had a bargain."

"Forget it." Joe never told his mother what he spent on things; this made him feel adult, the master of his financial destiny. Also, living in New York, he tended to pay atrociously high prices for things, and being a Reckler, he was suitably ashamed.

"Do we have to go on this trip?" Joe asked, lying full out on the couch, in Camille-like despair, trailing a pale hand on the Oriental rug.

"Yes, you just be quiet. We're going to see the leaves change. It's going to be gorgeous."

"We're not going to see the leaves change, we're going to see the leaves die. When they turn orange and red and yellow it means they're rotting and about to fall off. This whole trip is morbid. It's a leaf funeral."

"Well, you're going, so get used to the idea." Mrs. Reckler had been Joe's mother a long time; she was used to his intransigence.

"I don't feel well," said Joe, resting his head swanlike on his shoulder. "I have a stomachache."

"I'll give you a stomachache," said Mrs. Reckler. Then she became concerned. "Does your stomach really ache? What did you eat? Have you taken anything for it?"

"*Mother.*" Faking terminal illness had not worked since the third grade, when Joe had employed a ghoulish repertoire of hacking coughs, unearthly moans, and strange, indeterminate swellings, all in an effort to avoid elementary school quizzes on the boyhood of Thomas Alva Edison. Joe knew he was going to go on the trip through New England; he just wanted to make sure his mother appreciated the unparalleled enormity of his self-sacrifice.

"I'll just use your bathroom, and then we'll go," said Mrs. Reckler. "Can I go in there? Is anything crawling?"

"Go find out. Live dangerously."

"Uch," said Mrs. Reckler, shaking her head over her son's foolishness. She journeyed to the bathroom, with an attitude that suggested a need for a pith helmet, a vial of snakebite serum, and a well-honed machete.

"Your cleaning person has been here," Mrs. Reckler said, returning to the living room. "I'm impressed." An out-of-work actor cleaned Joe's apartment, so he was referred to as the cleaning person.

"Maybe I cleaned my bathroom," Joe protested. "Why do you assume it's my cleaning person?"

"Because I'm your mother, dear."

"Do you wish I was a cleaning person? Then would you be proud of me?"

"No. I just want you to be a clean person; is that too much to ask? Were you brought up in a dirty home?"

"No, but we always had a cleaning lady. If you had wanted me to be naturally clean, you should have cleaned the house yourself. But you had Mrs. Dunn, so I assumed that the point of life was not to be clean but to make enough money to hire a cleaning person. That is what you taught me, by example. That is how I was stunted and morally crippled."

"Let's go. Do you need to use the bathroom?"

"Mother, if I needed to use the bathroom, don't you think I would just go use it? It is my bathroom. Why would I need to announce it? If I truly needed to use the bathroom, do you think I would have forgotten and needed you to remind me? What do you think happens when you're not here?"

"I don't know, and I don't want to know. Get your things and don't be fresh."

Joe did have to use the bathroom, but he now refused to; he would rather have died.

"Did you know about this garage?" Mrs. Reckler asked her son, as they climbed into the car at a nearby parking facility, an echoing underground cavern. "It's so convenient, I have to tell your father. Has it always been here?" A parking space in the city was another Reckler grail. Locating an available parking space on the street was the equivalent of a miracle healing; a convenient, inexpensive parking garage was the next best thing. When Joe was little, he had assumed that finding parking was the sole reason his family visited Manhattan; his parents had taken such scientific joy in the hunt. After seeing a hit Broadway play or musical, his parents would first discuss the quality of their parking experience, with an enthusiasm often lacking in their treatment of the theatrical event.

"Your father had the car washed, and then he vacuumed it with the Dustbuster," Mrs. Reckler told Joe. "Doesn't it look nice?"

"It looks lovely. I could eat off it."

"Very nice. If you're going to keep talking that way, you can just stay home."

"Promise?"

"No. For talking that way you're being punished, you're coming on the trip."

Joe settled into the front seat beside his mother. Much of his childhood had been spent in this very car, a 1972 Oldsmobile Cutlass, pale yellow with a pebbly Harvest Gold vinyl roof. Joe relished the heavy crunch of the car door as he slammed it. He inhaled the familiar aroma of vinyl, old Life Savers, and his mother's Chanel No. 5. When Joe was a child he had normally sparred with his older brother in the back seat. Driving in from New Jersey, they had especially liked to tangle over whose feet had first crossed the state line, a border striped on the tiled walls of the Holland Tunnel. Sitting up front made Joe feel important, ennobled, on a par with the driver. Joe yanked and locked his seat belt as his mother slicked her hairline in the mirror clipped to the back of the fold-down eyeshade.

"We have gas," said Mrs. Reckler, checking the gauge. "We have maps, we have sucking candies, we have the charge, I hope you packed a sweater in case it gets chilly, all right, we can go."

This recitation stirred Joe; he knew that the universe could be conquered with just these items. His mother started the car, and Joe made the definitive Reckler hand gesture: he lightly touched the padded vinyl dashboard with the fingertips of his right hand. Whenever Joe's father was driving, and Mrs. Reckler decided he was going too fast, she put her hand on the dashboard. She somehow imagined that this gesture would immediately stop the car and avert a highway collision. Joe made this gesture without thinking, as a good luck charm.

Aunt Ida and Aunt Pola lived out on Long Island; Mrs. Reckler headed uptown to the Queensboro Bridge. Mrs. Reckler had been raised in Queens, an outlying borough of New York, so she knew the city well. While Joe was growing up, his mother had often brought him on the train into Manhattan, for shopping and the Metropolitan Museum and matinees. She had made certain that her son appreciated the glory of New York. The Recklers' early excursions had filled both mother and son with excitement, with a liberation from their suburban routine, with a respite from sunlit, trafficless streets and sleepy backyards. Their stolen afternoons in Manhattan had allowed Joe and his mother a sense of the glamorous, overwhelming possibilities of life. This exhilaration now returned as Mrs. Reckler steered the car along Union Square.

"You know where we are," said Mrs. Reckler, with a pang. "It's all gone. Klein's."

Joe was jealous of his mother for having lived during Klein's heyday. "Klein's was the biggest department store in the city," Mrs. Reckler recalled. "I think even bigger than Macy's. I'd take the subway with my friend Lenore Waxman, and we would go to Klein's basement to buy underwear. Everything was out on tables, and the women would fight. When I was sixteen, I once bought two blouses for fifty cents each. I was so excited I went to a phone booth and called my sisters and told them. I couldn't even wait till I got home. Even my mother went to Klein's, and she hated coming into the city. Now it's all gone.''

Joe sighed. He had been raised on tales of Klein's; he thought of the store as mythical, a raw, heady form of retail, a hands-on jubilee. Shopping since Klein's had closed struck Joe as a coldwar phenomenon, somewhat bloodless when compared to the joyous, frenzied wrangling of an earlier era. By the time Joe had moved to Manhattan, four years earlier, all that remained of Klein's had been some barnlike shuttered buildings and a huge unlit neon sign, incorporating a mammoth protractor, that read KLEIN'S ON THE SQUARE. When even these remnants had been demolished, Joe had seriously considered trying to salvage the battered, rusting sign for his apartment. He had wanted to retrieve it for his mother's sake, as if bringing her the Golden Fleece.

Macy's and Gimbel's occupied only a minor rung in the Recklers' shopping pantheon; they were considered too obvious, although Joe always watched the Macy's Thanksgiving Day Parade on television. He ranked it above the Rose Bowl and Orange Bowl parades. Those processions were followed by football games; the Macy's parade concluded with a padded actor ho-ho-hoing as Santa aboard a mechanized sleigh, heralding the advent of the Christmas shopping season. Joe couldn't even think about the Christmas shopping season; he would get too tingly. Besides, Mrs. Reckler frowned on any passionate mention of Christmas. ''We are Jewish,'' she always reminded Joe. ''And we have Chanukah.''

Christmas had always worried Mrs. Reckler. She had feared that Joe and his brother might be jealous of their Christian schoolmates, coveting their mistletoe and greeting-card-bedecked mantels and those infernal tinseled trees. The family living directly across the street from the Recklers had been a real Christmas tribe; they had wrapped their house in yards of rainbow-colored, twinkling bulbs, and their every doorknob had worn a hand-crocheted cover with Santa's ruddy face.

The Recklers were far from Orthodox Jews. Mr. and Mrs. Reckler insisted on upholding Jewish traditions not out of deep religious fervor but as a means of honoring their own beloved parents and forebears. Celebrating Chanukah was a form of pride. The Recklers rarely attended temple, but they refused to hang even the plainest wreath on their door. Mrs. Reckler disliked the shopping marathon of the Yuletide season. She felt that the Christian legions clogging the stores were dilettantes, amateurs; real shoppers knew no season.

Joe had always welcomed the Christmas season and still did. He considered Christmas to be an invocation to shopping, a shopping feast, the antithesis of gloom. He awaited the cardboard snowmen in shop windows and the neon bells pealing from lampposts and strung on armatures stretching across streets. It all seemed a celebration not of Christ's birth but of shopping, of the fine American sport of browsing and buying and giving and getting. Joe was solidly in favor of the commercialization of Christmas, the more rubber holly the merrier. Joe had never minded that his own home had gone undecorated; he had admired his parents' religious convictions. He had known they were right. Besides, the rest of the world provided plenty of felt elves and spray-on snow and battery-operated reindeer.

Joe liked Chanukah because, like Christmas, it was an occasion for gifts and Scotch-taped wrapping paper and pretied bows purchased twelve to a pack. Chanukah vexed Joe for only one reason: it came in December. Joe's birthday was December 29. The greatest terror of Joe's life was that people would offer him a single gift to cover both holidays. People with birthdays in June received two proper Himalayas of packages, one in winter and the second in summer. Joe always wondered and grieved that he might never receive his full due and that justice would crumble.

Still, Joe was tickled at having a December birth date. When he was very young, Joe had assumed that the world's

Christmas and Chanukah fuss was all in honor of his birthday. He secretly still believed this.

"Are you hungry?" Mrs. Reckler asked Joe, driving up Park Avenue, past the Seagram Building and the other boxy chrome-and-glass behemoths. Joe and his mother liked this area, because it was so clean and sparkling and lofty, with its corporate Triumph of the Will architecture. Park Avenue was a dream of New York, but there were few stores. Park Avenue glitters, but it lacks humanity; stores are humanity's essence.

"I want a brownie," Joe decided.

"A brownie?" said Mrs. Reckler, trying to decide whether she should scold her son for this sugary, unhealthy desire. "Wouldn't you like something more substantial? Would you like a waffle?"

"It is three o'clock in the afternoon," said Joe. "It is not waffle time. It is brownie time."

"All right," said Mrs. Reckler. A brownie would at least be nourishment, she reasoned, and maybe she would have a bit, just a corner maybe.

Mrs. Reckler and her son shared a passion for sweets that bordered on the devout. Nothing fancy, never powdery Peruvian truffles or white chocolate mousse or flan; Joe felt that these were desserts for people who didn't really like dessert, who found dessert immature. Joe equally despised the concept of carrot cake; carrot cake, as far as Joe was concerned, was a vegetable, not a dessert. Mrs. Reckler and Joe had spent much of Joe's childhood wheeling wire carts through the spacious supermarkets of New Jersey, admiring things like Drake's Yodels and Hostess Twinkies and Mallomars and Ring Ding Jrs. "I don't know why you like this garbage," Mrs. Reckler had always said as Joe piled the cart with valueless calories. But in the car on the way home, both mother and son had always dug in, seduced by bouncy yellow sponge cake and jet-puffed pink marshmallow and tunnels of creme filling.

It pleased Joe to share junk food with his mother. Mrs. Reckler's fondness for childish treats impressed him deeply. There was an intimacy to their snack sessions, an equality.

Joe loved his mother because she ate what she pleased, no matter what anybody thought. Mrs. Reckler agonized over her subsequent weight problems, but Joe thought she looked great just as she was. Mrs. Reckler's yielding to temptation was among her most precious gifts to her son. She had showed him the way, she had taught him to relish happiness.

Joe had existed since childhood solely on sweets. Denial made no sense to him; if dessert was the best part of the meal, why not make it the meal? Forcing down steak or peas while dreaming of chocolate-chip cookies struck Joe as unnecessary masochism. His friends found it hard to believe that Joe dined only on sugar. They imagined that when he was alone, he secretly gobbled celery and ground round. But they were mistaken; Joe liked candy and cake, so that's all he ate. This behavior tormented Mrs. Reckler, who was concerned for her son's health, but Joe remained remarkably fit. Mrs. Reckler secretly envied her son, who fulfilled one of her own most cherished fantasies: to be locked overnight in a bakery.

"Where are good brownies?" Mrs. Reckler asked, as she paused at a stoplight.

"Bloomingdale's," said Joe without hesitation.

3

Like an obedient hound, the Reckler Oldsmobile noted the word "Bloomingdale's" and immediately lunged in the correct direction.

Bloomingdale's is the purest embodiment of shopping; Bloomingdale's understands shopping. Tiffany's is about status and a signature azure box. Macy's connotes sheer volume. Only Bloomingdale's knows that in the modern world, people don't really need anything. They need to shop.

Mrs. Reckler shopped at Bloomingdale's as if the Reckler family owned the store. She felt a complete familiarity with the premises, a natural right to be there. Mrs. Reckler's sister, Joe's Aunt Ida, had worked as a Bloomingdale's salesgirl during the Depression. Ida was now a librarian with a Master's Degree, yet she would proudly recall her days hawking housewares and notions as a teenager; Ida, so family legend had it, had occasionally made out her receipts in Yiddish. The Esker sisters felt that Bloomingdale's represented the best of the Jews: quality without pretension, with a dash of show biz.

Whenever Joe was broke he would hike uptown to Bloomingdale's. Joe was listed on his mother's charge account as an "Authorized Shopper." This meant he could charge things to the Reckler account, without owning a card himself. Joe would ride the escalator to the Credit Department, where a clerk would check the files and issue Joe a temporary card good for the day. Joe would stalk the store, charging fudge brownies and butter-drenched croissants and half-pound bars of Swiss chocolate; this was food, a staple, so Joe never felt he was abusing his parents' generosity.

Joe's favorite expression in the world was "Authorized Shopper." He considered it in every way the equivalent of the phrase "Licensed to Kill." Being an Authorized Shopper on his parents' charge made Joe feel truly part of a dynasty, as if a torch had been passed. Joe had not applied for any other charge accounts; if he had, he would have bankrupted himself and his family within a weekend.

Mrs. Reckler parked the car at a familiar garage. She felt as if she were leaving her steed at the stables on the grounds of her estate. Bloomingdale's occupies a solid city block, staking out East Fifty-ninth Street to Sixtieth between Lexington and Third avenues. The store's exterior is nondescript; like all stores, Bloomingdale's devotes its energies to the indoors and to man-made wonder. Entering the establishment, from a revolving door on Fifty-ninth, the Recklers reeled, affected not by any single display but by a general dazzle, a sparkling hullabaloo of black glass and shiny brass trim, by the shimmering waterfall of merchandise that crashed deliriously over their heads. There were billows of silk, teetering pinnacles of Lord-knows-what, acres of glinting countertops, and everything howled, "Look at me first!"

Joe and his mother began their excursion with a few moments of wandering, acclimatizing themselves, getting their sea legs. They strolled the main floor and looked at everything. This was the cardinal rule of Esker shopping: You never know. If you don't keep an eye out, you might miss something wonderful.

Gradually the specific departments came into focus. Now the Recklers were ready; now they could commence some hard-core browsing. They circled a jewelry counter, fondling the necklaces dripping from a Lucite display stand. Mrs. Reckler pulled on a bracelet, a simple inch-thick band of heavy gold.

"I like it," Joe decreed. "Buy it."

"I wish I had your money," Mrs. Reckler replied, always her opening parry.

"How much?" asked Joe.

"Too much," said Mrs. Reckler, turning the tag.

"How much?"

"It's ridiculous. I don't need another bracelet, even if it is gorgeous and looks perfect with this dress. Listen, for $275 I can buy ten bracelets." Mrs. Reckler firmly returned the bracelet to the Lucite stand.

"Mom, that's not much, not for gold. It's classic; you'll always wear it. It's worth it; buy it."

"No," said Mrs. Reckler, wanly. "Your father would kill me. If I brought this home he'd say, 'But you already have a bracelet.' It is beautiful, though, so you visit it for me. And when it's ten dollars, you can buy it, for Mother's Day."

"You're crazy," Joe insisted. He liked to make his mother do nice things for herself. *"Buy it."*

"Shut up. Let's go."

Mrs. Reckler moved on to the makeup and perfume counters that covered much of the store's ground floor. Every cosmetics and fragrance mogul had been allotted a nook, a few square feet in which a customer might be lured by the severe black-and-white hauteur of Chanel, by the sultry high-gloss musk of Saint Laurent's Opium line, by the hypoallergenic common sense of Clinique's pressed powders. These counters formed a Kabuki bazaar, a maze consecrated to the purportedly feminine arts, to shading and blushing and concealing and smelling sweet, or bawdy, or like a mandarin orange. Each brand name had hired a separate sales crew, women in official smocks, trained to daub and blend and spritz. These women were more than mere employees; they were gum-popping handmaidens of beauty.

Mrs. Reckler headed for the serene pale blue packages of the Estée Lauder corner, for her yearly acquisition of a gift pack. Once each year the Estée Lauder company, as a promotion, offered a complimentary zippered plastic pouch holding tiny samples of Lauder products, all free with any legitimate purchase. Mrs. Reckler bought a small size of Youth-Dew moisturizer and received, as her bonus, a sample of Estée's New Romantics Cinnabar lipstick, an inch-high bottle of White Linen splash, a packet of EyeZone controlling gel, and a mascara wand. This was a ritual purchase. Mrs. Reckler often did not use many of the free goodies because she thought they were absurd colors or just not her. Still, her gift pack always made her feel canny, due to the savings involved, and rich, as socialites everywhere swore by Estée Lauder treatments. Mrs. Reckler approved of Estée Lauder, because it was rumored that the cosmetic magnate's real name was Esther. Elizabeth Arden's real name was most likely Elizabeth Arden.

"Do you want the Aramis gift pack?" Mrs. Reckler asked her son. Aramis was the Estée Lauder men's line. The gift pack included basically the women's products but sold under hypermasculine names, like Lab Series or Dual Action Face Scrub. Joe suspected that sooner or later, Aramis would merchandise lipstick for men under the brand name Lip Dirt.

"Come on, I'll treat you," said Mrs. Reckler. "I'll buy you aftershave, or the soap-on-a-rope."

"Mother," Joe groaned. Once every year, for Chanukah or his birthday, Mrs. Reckler bought Joe a bottle of designer-label aftershave and a matching soap-on-a-rope, a bar of heavily scented soap dangling from a nooselike circle of cottony twine. Joe was never sure if this concoction was intended to be conveniently draped over a showerhead or worn as a pendant. Either way, Joe preferred Dial or some other ropeless supermarket soap. He would never use his mother's gifts; the glossy gift boxes would accumulate in his bathroom, and every few years he would throw them out.

"Mother," Joe repeated. "I never use soap-on-a-rope or aftershave, you know that. I hate soap-on-a-rope and aftershave, and I refuse to smell like Aramis."

"You love it," Mrs. Reckler insisted, handing the salesclerk a soap-on-a-rope package. Mrs. Reckler wanted the sort of son who used soap-on-a-rope and aftershave, a decent, briskly scented American boy. If Joe refused to cooperate, she would just ignore him. The salesclerk handed Mrs. Reckler her charge and an eyeshade-green paper bag containing the soap-on-a-rope and the Aramis gift pack. Mrs. Reckler tried to give the bag to Joe.

"I don't want it. Forget it."

"Then I'll keep it," said Mrs. Reckler, tucking the paper bag into her purse. In a few months, at Chanukah, she would wrap the products and give them to Joe as a gift, just to watch him roll his eyes. Now she had accomplished two bargains and the repeated torture of her child; Mrs. Reckler glowed. She had bought things, small things, beginning purchases. She had gotten her feet wet.

"I need a nightgown," Mrs. Reckler announced. "Do you want to help me look for a nightgown?"

"No, I want to go look at sweaters."

"All right. Where shall we meet?"

"Back here in half an hour?" Joe suggested.

"Forty-five minutes," Mrs. Reckler said. "I need a nightgown very badly."

The Recklers both checked their watches, or rather Mrs. Reckler checked her watch and Joe stared at his bare wrist. Joe hated watches. He felt only pedants and prissy types wore watches. He was also convinced that a watch was too practical to be worth shopping for. Buying a watch did not count as a shopping experience; it was akin to investing in a garbage disposal. During the brief spells when Joe had worn a watch, he had changed his watchband almost daily, from lizard to ribbon to embossed cowhide. Shopping for watchbands was delightful.

"Four o'clock, right here," Mrs. Reckler said.

"Roger," said Joe.

Mrs. Reckler visited her bracelet. She touched it, slipped it on, and once again concluded that purchasing such a stunning, costly item was ridiculous. She rode the escalator to the lingerie department and quickly bought two nightgowns. She allowed herself to buy two because these were utilitarian, humdrum purchases and to make up for not buying the bracelet.

Mrs. Reckler toured the various dress departments, from The Young EastSider to the Coat Corral to Better Loungewear, but she was not particularly motivated. Mrs. Reckler knew her own taste; either something was right or it wasn't. Mrs. Reckler liked clothes, but she was far too sensible to fall prey to fashion's allure. She was perfectly content to thumb through *Vogue* or *W* at home. Extravagant clothes always struck her as pretty but essentially unwearable. Even as a girl, Mrs. Reckler had stuck to handsome, simple dresses in sturdy fibers and deep, appealing colors.

Mrs. Reckler rarely bought clothes at department stores for another reason: she couldn't bear to pay full price. Whenever Mrs. Reckler paid full price for a garment, she invariably returned it or shunted it to the back of her closet, as her secret shame. She knew that if her sisters ever discovered that she had paid retail, they would cluck and exchange disbelieving glances and consider having their baby sister institutionalized.

Mrs. Reckler also didn't like buying clothes because she was forever on a diet, or planning to go on a diet, perhaps the popcorn and Tab regimen recommended by a supermarket tabloid or the Beverly Hills Grapefruit Plan or Dr. Rowayton's High-Fiber Pounds-Away System. She was always about to drop down a size, so any purchase would quickly become obsolete. Mrs. Reckler did worry about her weight, the way the magazines warned her to, but in her heart she acknowledged a pleasing truth: she vastly preferred Drake's Yodels to even the most sumptuous Givenchys or Saint Laurents.

Mrs. Reckler considered buying underwear or a robe, but decided that the whole idea was too leaden for words. She was at Bloomingdale's, not a hardware store. She gave in, as she always did, and headed for Housewares.

Mrs. Reckler lived for housewares, for welcoming paper-lined cupboards of stacked china and antique silver ladles and eccentric crystal vases and crisply folded linens. She had grown up in a home with only meager supplies of these items, and she had coveted them. She never had to fret over correct sizes when comparison-shopping for stainless; everything fit. She never had to be concerned that she already had a tablecloth. She believed that every citizen was entitled to as many tablecloths as she liked.

Mrs. Reckler was no domestic drudge; she had never longed to be a housewife. She had always worked. The thought of afternoons passed with blaring soap operas and other bustling suburban moms and their bawling infants had always struck her as perverse. If it was wildly fulfilling to be a housewife, men would be housewives, they would battle for the privilege. But Mrs. Reckler loved making a home. She treasured the security of nice things and sparkling glassware and a pretty table set just so. This was her vanity, her pride. She wanted everyone to say, That Hedy Reckler, where does she find the time? Everything looks so lovely!

Mrs. Reckler invaded the bedding area, assessing the latest patterns and tints from Wamsutta, Cannon, Fieldcrest; these were her Valentino, her Gable, her Astaire. Mrs. Reckler did not acquire any sheets for herself; she would wisely hold off until the January white sales. Some ugly Perma-Prest fitted sheets were on sale, even in October; Mrs. Reckler charged a set for her son. Mrs. Reckler did not deliberately buy appalling sheets for Joe; she just decided that boys didn't care about what color they slept on. She knew that Joe did, but he shouldn't. And besides, she suspected that Joe rarely changed or laundered his sheets. Now at least his bedding would be clean, if orange-and-brown plaid.

Mrs. Reckler mooned over recarpeting her bathroom. Her bathroom required only a few square feet of pile, so she changed it yearly, without too much guilt (she drew the line, however, at the tackiness of a matching toilet seat cover and Kleenex caddy). She worked her way along the walls displaying mounted place settings of flatware and the shelves stacked with stemware, from wine goblets to champagne flutes to tumblers. In each area she selected a pattern or a size, priced the individual items, and scribbled the accompanying code numbers on a slip of paper, in case she someday located a wholesale outlet.

Mrs. Reckler gradually refurbished her entire home without buying a thing; in her mind she spent thousands. Joe had once spied on his mother as she shopped for housewares. He had watched her heft forks, because a weightier fork is superior. He had watched her plink crystal with a fingernail, because fine lead crystal gives a bell-like ring. He had watched her place her hand behind a dinner plate as she held the plate up to the light; bone china is nearly transparent. Joe respected his mother's absolute mastery of housewares. She had reminded him, in her patience and ardor, of Madame Curie.

Joe had no personal affection for housewares; he considered housewares too useful for pleasure. Funds were better lavished on red cotton turtlenecks or an inviting stack of the week's magazines. While Joe's apartment was jammed with outlandish furniture, his kitchen boasted only two glasses and four white plates, all contributions of his mother. Joe lived alone, so he used only one of the glasses, and he ate off paper plates, or a paper towel spread across an album cover. As far as Joe was concerned, the less cleanup the better. He had finally gotten into the habit of trundling the garbage down to the curb; whenever he did this he somehow expected a Nobel Prize.

Joe resented every penny he had to allot toward rent, Con Edison, shampoo, or other bare-bones essentials. He much preferred more personal purchases, expenditures he liked to think of as Art. Perhaps in reaction to his mother's careful spending, Joe had no head for money. He refused to carry a wallet, as he deplored the bulge it caused in his rear pocket.

He stuffed his bills and coins into his front pants pockets. Whenever he had to pay for anything, the money spilled out, as if it were his allowance.

Joe had once maintained a checking account, but he had closed it after bouncing countless checks. He had grown savvy to his own shortcomings. Joe had always been stymied by math. A balanced checkbook, let alone a tax return, was light-years beyond him. Using sound Reckler reasoning, he hired people to add and subtract for him. His accomplished, stringent accountant was suitably appalled at Joe's financial habits.

Joe loved shopping for clothes and had an addiction to costuming himself. Clothing was the most benign self-indulgence. Shopping for clothes felt like sex, with a comparable cycle of foreplay, orgasm, and afterglow. If Joe had smoked, he would always have languorously puffed a cigarette after hitting the menswear departments.

Joe hunted for clothes as he would for a lover. When he saw something he fancied, he suffered physical need, irrational longing, the if-I-can't-have-you-I'll-die-I'll-just-die syndrome.

Joe patrolled each of Bloomingdale's designer boutiques and eyed each label. He avoided the John Talley section; Joe interpreted John Talley as anti-Semitic. Talley's real name, so scuttlebutt had it, was Tishman; he was clearly ashamed of his ethnic roots, Joe assumed. All of John Talley's output aped the Waspy Connecticut styling of Brooks Brothers. The Talley ads trumpeted "an heirloom elegance." Joe found this all hideously white supremacist. Every John Talley item was embroidered with a tiny trademark huntsman astride a rearing stallion. Joe considered this emblem to be the moral equivalent of a swastika. Joe could never quite determine who the Sandinistas were and whether they were good or evil, but he became fiercely political when it came to designer labels.

Joe flirted with Perry Ellis and teased Calvin Klein mercilessly (Joe approved of Calvin for retaining his Klein). Joe toyed with buying something Japanese, some impossible poncho-like item of raw hemp, just so he could hear his mother describe the piece as a *shmatte*, a rag. Joe tried on a slimly cut cashmere Armani blazer, daydreaming himself a pricey Roman gigolo. He sampled at least four black leather jackets. Scowling rebelliously, he polished his best James Dean pout in the full-length mirror.

Joe acted as if he already owned everything in the store, as if Bloomingdale's were his multistory closet and he was simply deciding what to coordinate that day. Then he glimpsed the sweater, winking from a low glass display case. Joe's heart pounded recklessly and his throat constricted, urging him on. He stumbled across the store, frantically selecting an opening line, wondering if he should offer a bouquet. Joe had fallen in love with a Missoni.

He had the salesclerk unlock the case and hand him the sweater. Joe had to hold the garment, to protect it, to make certain that a more wily suitor wouldn't seduce the only one left in Joe's size and flee. Shopping made Joe violently territorial. Joe knew that he had to have the sweater or he would perish, that if he didn't buy it he would be unable to concentrate on anything else for months, that the sweater would haunt him. The Day I Didn't Buy the Missoni would become the date marking his decline into madness, blank-eyed disillusion, certain death.

Joe stepped back. He recognized his convulsive infatuation, he struggled for self-control. He flipped the price tag: $1,250.00. A stumbling block, a definite obstacle to contented matrimony. Joe couldn't spend that kind of money, even if he had it. The figure was obscene; you could undoubtedly feed an African village for a year, plus vaccinate everyone against typhus and build the cinderblock schoolhouse, all on the cost of one Missoni pullover.

Joe knew that he would have to talk himself out of the sweater, he would have to break it off, cleanly, responsibly, and go on with his life. It's not really that hot a sweater, he lectured himself. It's too many colors, it's too bulky, it would look lumpy under a coat. It's so obviously a Missoni, everyone would know, and he'd feel unconscionably trendy. No, the sweater was definitely hopeless, a major error, a feelingless cad. Next, please. Joe convinced himself that even if the sweater cost two dollars he wouldn't go near it. Yuck, Joe told himself, what sort of a total geek wears a Missoni sweater?

For both Joe and his mother, shopping entailed a stream-of-consciousness dialogue with any possible purchase. This was why neither Joe nor Mrs. Reckler had ever required the services of an analyst. If they were blue or confused or lonely, they worked it out with the sale rack.

Joe exhausted the menswear enclaves. He escalatored to the basement gourmet shop to lasso the brownies. He bought two and then returned for a third, which he and his mother could split. This was gluttony, but by dividing the purchase into two trips Joe felt he had proved himself properly tortured over the sin.

Joe rendezvoused with his mother back at the Estée Lauder counter. Mrs. Reckler was lugging a large brown paper shopping bag with handles.

"What did you buy?" Joe asked.

"Two nightgowns for me and sheets for you, so don't say I never buy you anything."

"Thank you," said Joe sincerely. Joe wasn't too thrilled about getting sheets, but he liked getting a gift.

"Did you buy anything?" Mrs. Reckler asked.

"A new car."

"Don't be fresh. Didn't you find anything?"

"Nah. All the fall things are gross."

"Joseph. All the fall things cannot be gross. Every item of men's clothing in this store cannot be gross."

"It's true. It's the new look: this fall everyone's dressing gross."

Mrs. Reckler rolled her eyes; she grabbed a sample spray bottle of men's cologne from the counter and sprayed it on Joe's neck before he could jump out of the way.

"Mother!"

"I just want you to smell nice, in case people think you're my son."

"Great. Now I *smell* gross."

Mrs. Reckler picked up a tester bottle of an Estée Lauder fragrance and spritzed it on the inside of her wrist. She waved her arm, so the perfume would dry. She sniffed her wrist and then held her wrist out for Joe to evaluate. He sniffed.

"Very nice," Joe said. "Why don't you buy some?"

"Estée Lauder doesn't need my money. Maybe next year she'll put some in the gift pack."

The Recklers retrieved their car and set out for the Long Island suburb of Roslyn, where they would spend the night at the home of Aunt Ida. Aunt Pola would hook up with the expedition in Roslyn, and everyone would depart the next day for New England.

Mrs. Reckler was a steady, practiced driver. Suburban mothers are forced to develop impeccable driving skills. Mrs. Reckler had spent many years chauffeuring her sons to guitar lessons and Cub Scout jamborees and movie triplexes. Still, Mrs. Reckler did not really like driving. She worried about collisions and engine trouble. She felt burdened, embedded in so much technology. So usually, Mr. Reckler took charge of the family Oldsmobile. Joe enjoyed the novelty of having his mother drive on the Long Island Expressway. It was like watching her sky-dive or hunt big game.

"Mom," said Joe, catching a glint of gold at his mother's wrist. "Did you buy the bracelet?"

"No, I did not. I told you, I can't afford it. Your father would have a conniption fit."

"But Mom—isn't that the bracelet? On your wrist?"

"Yes," said Mrs. Reckler, matter-of-factly.

"Mom," said Joe, sighing. "I thought you were going to stop."

Mrs. Reckler had been stealing luxury goods for as long as Joe could remember. He had first caught her at it when he was five years old. Joe had been idly rifling the Danish Modern bureau in his parents' bedroom, and he had come across a handsome, felt-lined mahogany case. The case had contained a full set of sterling-silver flatware, service for twenty, in the Autumn Crescendo pattern.

"Mommy, did you buy this?" the five-year-old Joe had asked his mother.

"No, dear," Mrs. Reckler had replied. "We can't afford things like that. We're not made of money."

"But Mommy, where did it come from?"

Mrs. Reckler had picked up her son and sat him on the big, beautifully made double bed. She had gazed at him adoringly and smoothed his hair.

"Honey," she had said. "I love you so much. And I love your father and your brother. And I want all of you to have only the nicest things. And I was at the store and I saw that silver, and it was so gorgeous. I loved that silver, and we need flatware; we only have everyday things. If you really love something, and it loves you back, then you're allowed to have it."

This explanation had impressed young Joe no end; it had also solidified his worship of his mother. Joe had never told anyone about his mother's theft or her subsequent crimes. He knew it was their secret, that only the two of them had the proper appreciation of shopping and its logical progression into grand larceny.

Joe's mother had remained strict with her younger son. She had kept the family on a tight budget. Joe had known that his mother heisted only things she was truly infatuated with, goods that cried out, that demanded to be stolen. Over the years, Mrs. Reckler had conducted turbulent love affairs with a complete boxed set of Gilbert and Sullivan recordings, a Steuben crystal punch bowl, a home computer for Joe's father, an antique Tiffany stained-glass lampshade, a Water Pik, and on one memorable occasion, eight rolls of a vinyl wall covering used to complete a kitchen redecoration.

Joe had no idea of how many items his mother had snatched overall. He had only recently begun to worry about her thefts, to fear that she might be caught and imprisoned; he could not bear the thought. When Joe had returned home for a Passover Seder six months earlier, he had taken his mother aside. She had shown him ten rose-colored damask napkins she had just acquired via her capacious handbag. Joe had made his mother swear she would never steal anything again.

"Mom," Joe said, as his mother navigated the expressway. "You promised. I don't want you stealing anything, not anymore. I'm not home to watch out for you; you could get into terrible trouble. And besides it really isn't the most incredibly nice thing to do. I know that you only took things so that we would have a nice home, and to impress Aunt Ida and Aunt Pola, but your children are grown now, your home is all done. I feel terrible, thinking about my own mother running around shoving things in her pocketbook. And besides, you promised me you'd stop, and you went back on your word. I'm very disappointed."

Joe hoped his tone was suitably solemn, even rabbinical. He wanted to function as his mother's stern parent. He shook his head, sighed heavily, and clicked his tongue for additional chastising emphasis. "Really, Mother."

"Joseph," Mrs. Reckler began, "I know I promised, and I'm sorry. But we're going to see my sisters, and this bracelet does go perfectly with my dress."

"That's not good enough, Mother."

"And, Joseph, if you're going to take that tone with me, I suggest you take the price tag off that sweater you're wearing. That Missoni sweater. I thought you said that everything at Bloomingdale's was gross."

6

"**Mother,**" **Joe** said impatiently. "This sweater costs $1,250. Even on sale it would still be at least $900. That's obscene. I would never pay that kind of money for a sweater. But it's gorgeous, and it has a lot of red in it, and that's my color, and I knew it would look great on me. It's a perfect sweater. And winter is coming and I need to be warm and all my other sweaters are old and I've worn them and all my friends are getting sick of seeing them. And this is a Missoni, which means it's very well made, and okay, I would rather die than be the kind of rich geek who buys $1,250 Missoni sweaters. But I didn't buy it, so it works out fine."

Joe felt wounded by his mother's scolding. After all, he almost never stole sweaters or any objects at all. Joe was a pickpocket.

Joe's parents had raised him to appreciate the value of a dollar. When Joe was thirteen he had been forced to pursue an after-school job, shelving books at the local public library, pushing a wooden cart and learning the Dewey Decimal System. Every summer he had been required to work as well, as a harried junior counselor at a day camp, organizing Wiffle ball tournaments and teaching lanyard technique. All of this early gainful employment had taught Joe one thing: he would rather die than have a job.

The notion of laboring nine to five literally sickened him;

it just wasn't Joe Reckler. At Yale he had tried to settle on a career but nothing enticed him. Joe's first priority involved sleeping late, at least until noon. Maintaining this schedule was all that really obsessed him. Being a Reckler, Joe also wanted nice things and the opportunity to shop. After sleeping late, Joe's most pressing ambitions involved sweaters.

Joe wished he had a trust fund or some form of independent wealth, but the Recklers were far from rich. During his first year out of school, he had relied on his parents' handouts for rent, Snickers bars, and the phone bill. The Recklers had been more than generous, but they had warned Joe that his stipend could not continue indefinitely. Their pertinent phrases had included "We're not a money tree," "This isn't the gravy train," and "We're not your personal bankers."

Joe had understood completely. He had dreaded placing those agonized late-night phone calls to beg for additional checks. He had hated having to coax a piteous sob into his voice. Joe loved his parents, and he did not feel that they owed him a living; still, Joe felt that *someone* owed him a living. He didn't need a professionally typeset résumé or an Old Boy Network or an MBA. All Joe required for personal happiness was a little ready cash.

During his childhood, Mrs. Reckler had been insistent that Joe master a musical instrument, to encourage discipline and cultural enrichment. Joe had moped and whined through years of piano, clarinet, and oboe lessons. His final attempt, in high school, had been the glockenspiel, a sort of mobile xylophone worn on a strap and carried in a marching band. While Joe had never progressed beyond amateur standing at any of these instruments, he had developed a certain manual dexterity, a light-fingeredness. He found that he could pluck a wallet from beneath a pedestrian's blazer with astonishing grace. He could apprehend women's handbags with equal, Brahms-inspired ease.

Joe did not steal from just anyone. He selected his targets with great care and a well-honed ethical sense. Joe stole only from people who deserved to be relieved of their cash, from people who were just asking for it. Joe could spot an especially unctuous corporate attorney at ten yards. With his eyes shut he could sense the nearby sadism of a Park Avenue oral surgeon. Joe was in essence a postmodern Robin Hood: he stole from the rich and gave to himself.

"Don't you like my sweater?" Joe asked his mother. "It's a Missoni."

"It's beautiful. It looks very nice on you, you rotten kid. And on second thought, leave the tag. For Aunt Pola."

Mrs. Reckler grinned; so did Joe. When Joe had first begun to pay his own bills, the Recklers had been curious. Their son, as far as they knew, had no aptitude for anything. They knew that Joe was bright and well mannered, even if he did have a fresh mouth, but they had always worried over his lack of anything remotely resembling a skill. When asked, Joe had told his parents he was free-lancing. Pressed further, he had claimed he was working at home. When truly interrogated, he had informed his parents that he was writing a screenplay for which a film studio was advancing him a small fortune. Joe had been polishing that screenplay for almost four years now.

Mrs. Reckler had come to realize the true source of her son's income. She had caught Joe carrying an expensive Mark Cross evening bag, and she knew that he considered Mark Cross to be the Krupp of Fifth Avenue.

Mrs. Reckler would have preferred that her son be a gifted neurosurgeon or a tenured art history professor rather than a pickpocket, but she was a terrific mother, and she desired her son's happiness, not her own. And secretly, she was very proud of Joe. Joe had always been her favorite, and his choice of career had confirmed their special understanding. Joe was his mother's son.

Both Mrs. Reckler and her son wanted proper bourgeois lives. They leaned toward aggressive air-conditioning and fresh lilacs and regular expeditions to Bloomingdale's. They also yearned for something less acceptable, some spark of rebellion, some wild card. Crime had admirably satisfied this yearning. Mrs. Reckler and Joe were the most frankly bourgeois crooks imaginable. They were that unheard-of anomaly, nice people with sticky fingers. Seat-belted into their Oldsmobile, on their autumnal trek to see the leaves change,

Mrs. Reckler and Joe were Bonnie and Clyde Goldberg, Ma Parker and her Yale boy, the most suburban criminals on the block. Besides, they were not really thieves; thieves, Mrs. Reckler had once informed Joe, were people who took color television sets to buy heroin. Mrs. Reckler and Joe were not thieves; they were merely people who shopped without money.

"If your father sees that sweater," Mrs. Reckler warned Joe, "you tell him it cost twenty dollars."

Joe's father was very much on Mrs. Reckler's mind.

"Your father," Mrs. Reckler began, as she swerved onto the Roslyn exit ramp. "You know, he wanted to come with us. But I said, Saul, you want to drive through New England with me and my sisters, and our terrible child? And he said sure. So I said, Saul, you're retired. Stay that way."

Mr. Reckler had been retired for a year now, and he was having a remarkably good time.

"Other men, when they retire," Mrs. Reckler commented, "they're not so happy. They have adjustment problems, with a whole day to fill. But not your father. He has his crossword puzzle book and his new hearing aid. He's very happy. I asked him, I said, Don't you miss going to work? He said not at all."

"He's a bum," Joe said approvingly.

"Like some other people I could mention. Why am I the only one who likes to work? I don't see how you can stand it, just sitting around all day."

"I don't just sit around all day," Joe insisted. "I sleep."

"Wiseguy. But I didn't want your father on this trip. He's had two heart attacks. He doesn't need any more stress."

In his final years of employment, Mr. Reckler had suffered two coronaries. Thanks to medication, an exercise bicycle, and a bland diet, he was doing fine. Joe had read that heart disease could run in families. This information allowed Joe to consider his own lifestyle a necessary precaution. He had a medical excuse for not doing anything.

"After this trip," Mrs. Reckler continued, "I am never going to take anything, not ever again, you'll be pleased to know, Mister Nudge. After this trip it's all over, that's it, no more. *I'm* retiring."

"Why? Why should I believe you?"

"Because there's only one more thing I want. And it's not just for me, it's for all of us."

"What?"

"A new living room. I haven't changed anything in there since you went away to Yale. Now your father's home all day and I'm embarrassed to have him sit in that dump. I can't even look in there. I close my eyes. And of course we don't have the money. I haven't even mentioned it to your father, I don't want him to feel guilty for being retired. But it isn't fair. Your father worked very hard for over forty-five years, I've worked very hard for over thirty-five years, and we still don't have the money. We have to watch every penny, or we'll end up in the poorhouse. I don't know what went wrong. You should be taking care of us in our old age."

"Dream on," said Joe.

"I will, I assure you. But I can't stand it, not one more second, those lumpy old couches and that shiny rug. I was embarrassed to have Mrs. Dunn clean in there. So I figured it out, I made a list. First I want to have the whole downstairs repainted, just to freshen things up. Then it's new couches, maybe leather like yours, a comfortable chair and an ottoman, new wall-to-wall or maybe a nice Oriental, and then a table or two, and lamps. I went to the stores and I added it up. I can do everything for $10,000—isn't that awful? For $10,000, once upon a time, you could practically buy a whole new house, and now it's only redecorating the living room. It makes me physically ill, but it has to be done. I can't have people to the house, especially not my sisters. I'm so ashamed. So we're going to rob L. L. Bean.''

There was a pause as Joe considered this information.

"What do you mean, 'we'?'' Joe asked finally.

"I need your help. I'm sorry, but you'll just have to get up early. I read in the *Times*, over the past ten years L. L. Bean's business has gone sky-high, it's quadrupled. Believe me, they're loaded; they don't know what to do with all the money. I've ordered things from the Bean catalogue for years; I'm a very loyal customer. It's like a rebate. It's only $10,000, they'll never miss it. They won't even know it's gone. The store is in Freeport, up in Maine, do you remember? How old were you the last time we drove up that far? It's a beautiful building—I hear they've expanded—and it's open twenty-four hours a day. It's very convenient.''

"L. L. Bean?'' Joe repeated, still extremely doubtful. L. L. Bean was a legendary store, famed for its rugged hunting gear, its waterproof thong-laced moccasins, and its toasty Hudson's Bay blankets. Like most Americans, Joe had ordered from the sacred L. L. Bean catalogue many times, eagerly receiving cartons of hearty chamois shirts and thick "wool ragg'' hiking socks. Visiting the store in person, let alone robbing it, struck Joe as baroque. "Mom . . .'' he began skeptically.

"Don't 'Mom' me; it's not open to discussion. We need the money. I wish I could do something about the kitchen—the linoleum is peeling, the toaster oven is on its last legs—but I don't want to overdo it. If I started thinking about the whole house, we'd be visiting Chase Manhattan, not just Bean. But this is why your father isn't coming on this trip. He'd notice something, he'd ask a question. After all these years I don't need my husband to know I'm . . . a person who takes things.''

Mr. Reckler never suspected his wife's less-than-legal activities. Whenever she brought home a new electric yogurt maker or imported Italian tapestry bedspread or antique porcelain canister set, he assumed she had charged it. Mr. Reckler never rigorously followed his family's purchase patterns because he was not a shopper. He was proud of his well-dressed wife and his attractively appointed home, but he had no grasp of how these phenomena occurred. He paid the bills happily, without checking the figures. As far as Mr. Reckler was concerned, his wife and children deserved anything they wanted.

Mr. Reckler never participated in his family's pilgrimages to the mall, or at least not in the shopping aspect. Mr. Reckler would sit contentedly on a slatted wooden bench beside a poured-concrete planter in the air-cooled plaza, enjoying what he called "the passing parade" while he waited for Mrs. Reckler and Joe to exhaust themselves. Mr. Reckler admired his wife's stamina and taste, but he never felt the urge to accompany her on a spree. This attitude occasionally annoyed Mrs. Reckler. "Saul," she would say. "Please. You need underwear. You need a sports jacket. Here's the charge, don't look at the prices, just buy yourself something. Just *go*."

Once when Joe was in grade school, his mother had exploded over the sorry state of his father's haberdashery and his unwillingness to replace it. All of Mr. Reckler's T-shirts and briefs had become full of holes. Mrs. Reckler had decided to take steps. She had assaulted her husband's underwear drawer with a pair of shears. Then she had strode through the house wearing the shreds of Mr. Reckler's underwear around her neck. Joe and his father had laughed uproariously at this wrathful crusade. Mr. Reckler had then asked his wife, in all seriousness, "Honey, is something bothering you?"

"Your father is a saint," said Mrs. Reckler, pulling into Aunt Ida's driveway. "I bought him a new puzzle book, and there's food in the freezer; he'll be fine. We'll do L. L. Bean."

"But, Mom, have you ever robbed a store before? I mean, of big money?"

"No, of course not; what do you think I am? I work all day—do I look like I have the time for such nonsense, such *mishegoss*? No, I had to wait for my vacation. My one week off, and I'm robbing Bean. But the leaves will be nice."

"But Mom, when and if we rob L. L. Bean, what are we going to do with Aunt Ida and Aunt Pola?"

"We're robbing Bean, no whens or ifs. I've planned it all out; I've made lists. I don't sit around all day on my behind like some people I could mention. We'll send Aunt Ida and Aunt Pola to Waterville for the day, to the Hathaway shirt outlet; they'll be very busy. Uch, if they knew . . . I'd die. I would die."

Mrs. Reckler stopped the car. She looked straight ahead.

"You know, the things we do, you and I, it doesn't bother me, it really doesn't. I'm a terrible person and an unholy mother, but the living room will be lovely. And I really think we're both very nice, I do."

"*I'm* very nice," Joe agreed.

"You, you're a good-for-nothing, you're God's judgment on me, but I love you very much, why I'll never know. But if my sisters ever found out about . . . you know what, I would kill myself, from the nearest bridge. They think I'm a nice woman. They think we live well. If they knew . . . Well, we just won't think about it. That's what our family is very good at, not thinking about things."

"Exactly," said Joe happily. "I think it's a gift."

"You would. And when we get to Maine, everything will be fine."

Mrs. Reckler knocked on the dashboard and then realized it wasn't wood. Her arm wavered, aiming to land on something wooden in a vehicle composed only of metal, glass, and vinyl. Finally she rapped twice on her son's head.

"Knock on wood," said Mrs. Reckler.

8

"**Look who's** here!" said Aunt Ida, opening her screen door and wiping her hands on her yellow-and-white-checked apron, which she had stitched from two dish towels.

"Look who's here!" replied Mrs. Reckler, heading across the brief expanse of lawn to greet her sister.

Aunt Ida lived in one half of a two-family home that had a sloping, shingled roof, like a cottage, and was divided almost eerily in half, with two front doors side by side, two chimneys, identical azaleas blooming in matched brick-bordered flower beds, two of everything. It was just like Aunt Ida to live in a two-family house. She was extremely self-effacing; half a house was more than enough.

"Look who's here!" Joe added, kissing his aunt.

"You look wonderful!" said Mrs. Reckler.

"I look wonderful!" Aunt Ida replied, scoffing. "*You* look wonderful, the two of you!"

This gush of compliments and denials continued for several minutes, accompanied by hugs, pats, and cackles. Whenever Mrs. Reckler and one of her sisters got together, they always sounded like a mob scene. They celebrated one another and the fact of their meeting. Joe loved hearing this sisterly cacophony. It reminded him of a flock of happy, gossipy birds, singing and pecking at each other.

35

"Come in, come in," said Aunt Ida. "Don't stand around outside; the neighbors will talk."

"Let them talk," said Mrs. Reckler, and then, confidentially, "Do they really talk?"

Joe wondered what these neighbors talked about; what scandal could they conceivably pluck from his arrival with his mother in an Oldsmobile? Joe realized he was being obtuse. "The neighbors" was a metaphysical concept in his family, referring to Other People, to Those Who Will Notice If You Don't Have On Clean Underwear, to Those Who Will Know Our Shame and Prevent Us from Showing Our Faces in Public Ever Again.

"Here, we brought you a little something," Mrs. Reckler told her sister, as everyone pushed into the house. Mrs. Reckler handed her sister a white cardboard bakery box, tied with twine and rattling with waxed paper and Bloomingdale's cookies. These were not real cookies, Oreos or Chip-A-Roos; these were ceremonial cookies, thin slivers shaped like leaves, coated on one side with layers of green mint creme and bittersweet chocolate. The box also included disturbing Greek inventions involving chopped dates and walnuts wrapped in tubes of flaky dough. Joe was never tempted by these treats; in fact, he had never seen anyone actually eat such things. Expensive, preferably foreign baked goods showed that you cared and that you had spent money. Such cookies were ambassadorial, a token from the Three Wise Men.

"Oh, look," said Aunt Ida, opening the box. "So beautiful; you spent a fortune. I can't eat these, you keep them, you're crazy."

"You're insane," said Mrs. Reckler. "These are your cookies. Eat them."

"You eat them," insisted Aunt Ida. "They're too nice for me. Joe, have a cookie."

"Don't you touch them," Mrs. Reckler warned Joe, shoving the box back into her sister's hands. "Ida, have a cookie."

"I'll have a cookie," Aunt Ida conceded, taking the box. She quickly closed the flapping lid and retied the string. "I'll save them for company."

"And what are we?" asked Mrs. Reckler. "Chopped liver?"

Everyone laughed at this ancient retort. "I have some liver," Aunt Ida then admitted. "Are you hungry?"

Aunt Ida led Joe and Mrs. Reckler into the kitchen, always the hub of any Esker household. An Esker living room was kept pristine, vigilantly vacuumed and dusted, for "company." The kitchen was where mere family members might cavort and spill diet soda and attempt conversations over the maniacal chug of the dishwasher. Esker kitchens were always sun-filled and bright; Aunt Ida's was painted with canary-yellow enamel. Decorative floral plates hung on the walls from wrought-iron hooks, and the linoleum was the traditional black-and-white checkerboard.

The glass-topped, wrought-iron kitchen table was covered with a yellow seersucker tablecloth and the prodigious buffet Aunt Ida had been slaving over since early in the day: a ceramic mixing bowl of homemade potato salad, a burly pound cake set atop a doily and dusted with confectioner's sugar, two wicker baskets of warm crescent rolls, a rotating lazy-Susan platter of cold cuts preserved beneath Saran Wrap, glass pitchers of iced tea, milk, and orange juice, and much, much more—enough food for at least a week's menus. Utensils and yellow paper napkins were fanned out beside a tall wooden pepper mill, squeeze bottles of catsup and mustard, and a potted geranium. Joe recognized the spread as similar to those his mother devoted her mornings to when relatives were due. With Mrs. Reckler and her sisters, food was currency, and excess always indicated devotion.

"Have something," said Aunt Ida. "After all that driving, you must be hungry."

"I can't eat a thing," said Mrs. Reckler. "Ida, you shouldn't have done this. I'm very upset. Look at all this food. Who were you expecting, the army and the navy?"

"Oh shut up," said Aunt Ida. "What're you talking? If you don't want to eat, don't eat, no one's forcing you. You won't hurt my feelings."

"I could kill you," said Mrs. Reckler. "You always do

this. I want you to wrap all of this up and freeze it. Give it
to Danielle.''

Danielle was Aunt Ida's daughter, Joe's cousin. Danielle
was a beautiful girl, currently teaching learning-disabled students in Bayside, a nearby Long Island community. Danielle
had earned Joe's undying respect through a simple but sig-
nificant act. Two years earlier, she had been engaged to a
handsome, personable Jewish medical student, and she had
broken the engagement. Danielle had decided that she just
didn't love the young man. Halting a betrothal to a Jewish
premed, ''with a brilliant future ahead of him,'' was considered, by certain outlying members of Danielle's family, to
be immediate grounds for a competency hearing.

Mrs. Reckler and Aunt Ida had supported Danielle's decision, albeit wistfully. They trusted Danielle's instincts in
the matter. Mrs. Reckler and her sisters were all progressive
mothers. They had encouraged their children to be curious,
brave, and independent. These children had obligingly grown
into curious, brave, and independent adults. Mrs. Reckler
and her sisters occasionally found this most distressing.

''Danielle doesn't need my food,'' Aunt Ida insisted.
''She's a grown girl, she has her own place, she buys her
own food. Besides, I filled her freezer on Tuesday; I had
leftovers. Eat.''

''So you'll freeze for yourself,'' Mrs. Reckler said.
''Where's the aluminum foil? I'll help you. After our trip,
you'll have nice lunches just waiting for you.''

Mrs. Reckler and her sisters rated the freezer as a civiliz-
ing advance running slightly ahead of fire, the wheel, and
the flush toilet. Capacious General Electric freezers allowed
the sisters to create constant banquets, encompassing far
more produce than anyone could eat. These feasts could be
stored in tinfoil bricks and neatly labeled Tupperware for
eons. In this manner, the sisters were always prepared, secure. They had hostess insurance in case people dropped in.
The sisters invoked their freezers in a mode similar to the
stockpiling of nuclear weapons by superpowers. Nothing in
the freezers was ever used, but it made the sisters sleep easier, just knowing it was there.

"I can't eat any of this," said Mrs. Reckler, beginning to nibble the cinnamon topping off a crumb cake. "I just started my diet."

"Oh?" said Joe, recalling his mother's recent acceptance of a brownie.

"Shut up," said Mrs. Reckler. "I started it in the car. I started my diet as we were coming up the walk."

Everyone laughed. "But you're right," said Aunt Ida. "I can't eat anything either. I've been on a diet all week."

"Ida," said Mrs. Reckler, "you're my sister and I love you dearly, but if you tell me you're on a diet one more time, I'll bash your brains in. You're a stick."

"What?" Aunt Ida protested. "What're you talking?"

Mrs. Reckler was right; Aunt Ida was blissfully slim. Aunt Ida was one of the most truly chic women Joe had ever seen. She never wore particularly fashionable or expensive clothes, but she had a natural elegance. "Ida could always wear clothes," Joe's mother had once explained. "She's always been beautiful." Aunt Ida had a narrow, oval face marked by the same tenderness as her sister's. With both women, the years had burned off any trivial prettiness, leaving a sweeter beauty, an openness, faces that told of worry and hard work and helpless laughter.

Aunt Ida wore her hair pulled taut in a bun, like her sisters', and she kept her eyeglasses on a chain around her neck, so she wouldn't misplace them. Today she was wearing her handmade checked apron over a plain cornflower-blue linen sheath with a matching belt; the outfit came off as pure Dior. Aunt Ida's eyes tended to dart, looking after her guests. She was also fond of crossing her arms and rubbing her elbows, as if this gesture would cause a genie to materialize and supply more breadsticks and maybe a nice kugel.

"This is delicious," said Mrs. Reckler, breaking off another ragged chunk of coffee cake. "Did you make this?"

"Lorenzo's Bakery, around the corner," said Aunt Ida, helping herself to a pinch of crumb topping. "That's my recipe."

People in Joe's family rarely took a plate, filled it with food, and ate at a table, using a knife and fork; such a game plan would involve admitting that you were eating. Mrs. Reckler and her sisters liked to nibble, to pick, to decimate an angel-food cake or a Thanksgiving turkey bit by bit, so they could pretend they were eating only crumbs, air. In this manner their extraordinarily elastic diets would remain, on some Zen level, intact. They also could convince themselves that they were leaving the food for others, who deserved it.

"You know what we should do?" Mrs. Reckler suggested, splitting a roll in half. "We'll freeze everything and Federal Express it out to Kurt, that's what we'll do."

Kurt was Aunt Ida's handsome son, who was a heart specialist at a hospital in Monterey, California. Kurt was bearded and genial; Joe liked Kurt enormously, despite the fact that he embodied a certain perfection.

"You're crazy," said Aunt Ida. "What, we should freeze food and send it to California, like they don't have food there? Kurt's always at the hospital anyway; he never eats. I was out there last month. I filled the freezer. I'll bet you anything it's still full."

"I'm so jealous," said Mrs. Reckler. "He's such a wonderful doctor. He's so dedicated."

"And what am I?" Joe protested. "Chopped liver?"

"You wish," said Mrs. Reckler. "You should have gone to medical school, not that you should be a doctor, God forbid."

"Thank you," said Joe. "Aunt Ida, isn't this touching? A mother's faith?"

"You be quiet," Aunt Ida told her sister. "Joe is a wonderful boy; he went to Yale, it's enough."

Joe's Yale degree had satisfied his entire family. Aunt Ida had no clear picture of what Joe did for a living; she told friends he was an artist. When they asked what particular kind of artist, Aunt Ida would reply, "How should I know? He's an artist; he's very good. He makes Art."

"I wish Kurt was more like Joe," said Aunt Ida. "More relaxed."

"Listen," said Mrs. Reckler. "If Joe were any more relaxed he'd be dead. I'm sorry, *bubbelah*," Mrs. Reckler told her son. "I'm very proud of you, even if you don't save lives. Here, I can't eat this—have half my roll."

"Mother, you know you're just going to take another roll and break it in half and eat half. It will add up to two halves. Why not eat just one whole roll and stop putting those little half rolls, those little roll corpses, back in the basket?"

"Wiseguy," said Mrs. Reckler. "Ida, he doesn't understand."

"Of course not," said Aunt Ida.

"If you only eat half," Mrs. Reckler explained, "no matter how many halves you eat, God doesn't count them."

The group proceeded into Aunt Ida's living room. Aunt Ida's home was furnished in a clean, modern style, with a dense overlay of *tchotchkes*. *Tchotchke* was a Yiddish word; Joe's mother had told him it meant "little things" or "junk." A *tchotchke* could be anything: a hammered Indonesian brass plate set on a bamboo easel, a seated family of black-glazed pre-Columbian figurines, a glass swan filled with liquid that changed color to indicate humidity, an octagonal raffia box holding matchbooks, a heavy green Venetian glass ashtray, a primitive Mexican papier-mâché donkey daubed in fiesta colors.

All three Esker sisters had a fatal weakness for *tchotchkes*, a lifetime *tchotchke* habit. Furnishing an Esker home was serious business. Joe's mother had once taken over two years to purchase just the right pair of lamps for the living room. Armchairs and couches were ample and solid, built to last, and upholstered in durable velvets which were, after a few years, slipcovered in cotton. All-wool, low-pile wall-to-wall carpeting had to complement the velvets; end tables were an investment. Serious furniture was exhausting, even grim, but *tchotchkes* were effervescent, lyric, dabs of personality strewn across sensible rooms.

The *tchotchkes* in the Reckler home tended toward either the Navaho or the Victorian. Joe had been raised among hand-thrown wide-mouthed clay bowls and a collection of wrought-iron banks depicting things like the Flatiron Building or an eager cocker spaniel. Aunt Ida's *tchotchkes* were primarily Mexican, reflecting many vacations south of the border. Bark shards painted with dancing figures were mounted on the wall. A woven "God's Eye" icon stared from a Japanese black lacquer sideboard. There was a shiny tin mirror with a nail-hole pattern. A multicolored hand-woven fringed serape was thrown across a square velvet love seat.

Tchotchkes were often handmade; the Esker sisters were partial to any sort of creative work. *Tchotchkes* were little things that sparked a room, "accents," emblems of lives spent scouting Thai bazaars and turnpike gift shoppes and Soho sale bins. Joe had been thoroughly indoctrinated with *tchotchke* fever. His own apartment was a bower of spooky marble hands and ruby glass vases and archaic brass paper-weights shaped like noses. Joe hated stark, minimalist, all-white rooms, *tchotchke*less Saharas; these rooms lacked humanity, imagination, shopping opportunities. Once fur-nished with a single Bauhaus tubular sofa and a severe hal-ogen lighting fixture, these rooms were done, sealed, dead. *Tchotchkes* were life, a shopping pulse, the harvest of busy hands and restless eyes.

There was a danger to career *tchotchke*-hunting. Mrs. Reckler had a dear friend, Susan Weidman. Susan had man-aged to overload a fourteen-room house. Her home had be-come so inundated with *tchotchkes* that she was unable to open the doors of several rooms. Visitors would huddle in corners, fearful of elbowing one of the eight candy dishes crowded on each of the six glass-topped coffee tables. While Susan was considered perhaps a touch overzealous, her haul was still much admired by the Esker sisters.

"So sit," said Aunt Ida, motioning to the two apple-green velvet sofas.

"This is beautiful," said Mrs. Reckler, handling a Mex-ican papier-mâché donkey painted in riotous shades.

"Guadalajara," said Aunt Ida, as Mrs. Reckler turned the donkey over, checking for a price tag.

"I am *not* looking for the price," Mrs. Reckler said. "I'm looking at the donkey's stomach; it's so nicely done. How much?"

"Who knows—it was in pesos," said Aunt Ida. "Fourteen dollars; I got it down to ten."

"Well, it's lovely," said Mrs. Reckler. "At any price." Although, of course, the donkey was just that intriguing bit lovelier at almost a third off.

"These are great," said Joe, holding a throw pillow stitched from a remnant of Mexican rug. "How much?"

"Oh shut up," said Aunt Ida.

"He likes to do that," said Mrs. Reckler. "He thinks he's making fun of us. He thinks that's all we care about. He's such a delightful child; let's kill him."

"Sit," Aunt Ida repeated, although she remained standing with her arms crossed, hugging her elbows. "Do you want more to eat? Should I bring something in?"

"Ida, we're fine," said Mrs. Reckler, reluctantly sitting on the couch. Her eyes scoured the room with Poirot-like precision, checking if there was anything she had missed, anything freshly purchased to be admired and fondled.

"Aunt Ida, sit down," said Joe, plopping himself into a fat velvet armchair. He put his feet up on the equally tubby velvet ottoman.

"Get your feet off there," Mrs. Reckler told her son.

"It's an ottoman, it's for feet," Aunt Ida told Joe. "Don't move."

"Excuse me," Joe told his mother.

"Ida, if you don't sit down," Mrs. Reckler warned, "I'm going to shoot you, and then you'll fall down."

"I don't like to sit," said Aunt Ida, perching on almost an inch of couch. "I'm restless. But I'll make you happy. Or at least I'll shut you up."

Joe adored his Aunt Ida; she had an irresistibly sharp tongue. At Passover, at the Seder, Joe had always made certain he sat beside Aunt Ida. All the men in the family would bunch at the far end of the table and conduct the Seder, reading aloud from the Haggadah, the text that recounted the epic of the Jews' flight from bondage in Egypt.

The men, led by Aunt Ida's husband, Uncle Boris, took their task to heart; all secret rabbinical urges burst forth. Uncle Boris had a booming, sonorous voice. He chanted, in both Hebrew and English translation. "And so Moses said unto the Jews," Uncle Boris would intone. "Gather your possessions and let us begin our journey to the Promised Land. *Yushua lachlala shooshownum.*"

"That Moses," Aunt Ida would whisper to her sisters and Joe. "What a kidder."

"Ida." Uncle Boris would scowl. "You're interrupting."

"Pardon me," Aunt Ida would say. "When do we eat?"

Uncle Boris had died a year earlier, after a horrific, prolonged struggle with cancer. Boris Fleischer had been a professor of economics at Queens College. He had been a warm yet precise man, someone with a specific methodology for life, a timetable. Ida and Boris had been very much in love, and they had complemented each other. Boris would set a rigid program for the day, and Aunt Ida would make him laugh until he forgot all about it.

Aunt Ida cast a humorous, skeptical eye on life. Joe found this practically an ideal perspective. Aunt Ida had only one fault: she was constitutionally unable to do anything nice for herself. Aunt Ida devoted her life to helping others, to making sure everyone was fed and comfortable and had an umbrella.

As far as Joe could tell, Aunt Ida had never sat fully on the seat of a chair, partaken of a meal sitting down at the table with her guests, or passed a store without slipping in and buying something to give away. For Aunt Ida, shopping was sinful, a selfish indulgence. She repented by shopping only for others and distributing the booty.

"Here," said Aunt Ida, returning from her bedroom with two plastic shopping bags. She gave one bag to Joe and the other to his mother.

"Ida, what is this?" said Mrs. Reckler, not opening her bag. "Are you crazy?"

"I was out, I picked up a few things, I though you would like them," Aunt Ida reasoned. "If you don't like them, I'll give them to someone else."

"Ida, we can't take these," Mrs. Reckler insisted. "Whatever they are."

"Yes we can," said Joe, burrowing into his shopping bag.

"See, he has the right attitude," said Aunt Ida.

"Uch," said Mrs. Reckler, reluctantly opening her own bag. "Oh," she said, impressed. "Aren't these lovely?"

Mrs. Reckler withdrew a pair of unglazed terra-cotta candleholders. "Ida, I love these, but you should keep them."

"What do I need them for?" said Aunt Ida. "They're junk."

"Aunt Ida, thank you," said Joe, holding four blank videotape cassettes. "I need these."

"You have a VCR?" said Aunt Ida. "I thought maybe you did and you could use tapes. They were on sale."

Aunt Ida shopped exclusively at an insider's warren of discount outlets on Long Island. Joe had once accompanied Aunt Ida on her diligent rounds. He had never seen such stores. They were basically warehouses, drafty, fly-by-night storefronts jammed with folding, cafeteria-style tables placed end to end in makeshift aisles. The merchandise was dumped out or piled high. Each island of goods was spiked with a hand-lettered cardboard sign reading 6 FOR 59¢ or SUPER SPECIAL—ONE DAY ONLY! or HERE TODAY, GONE TOMORROW! These stores sold just about anything—children's sneakers, shearling bicycle seat covers, but primarily *tchotchkes*. Joe thought of these stores as clandestine Mafia strongholds, where the mob fenced its colonial spice racks and quilted ironing board pads and brass plant misters.

These stores had names like Larry's Bargain Barn, Kitchens 'N' Things, and—Joe's favorite—Girl Meets Buy. Some of the merchandise had literally fallen off the backs of trucks and was sold slightly damaged, waterlogged or dented, "As Is." Other lots were closeouts, batches of plastic shoe trees or wire album racks that regular stores had been unable to palm off. There was something primitive about these stores, something stripped down and tribal. Discount outlets were the shopping equivalent of a gin mill or a needle park.

Aunt Ida haunted these stores, where the merchandise changed almost daily. Occasionally she unearthed real treasure, but more often she would drag home sacks of inexplicable Made in Taiwan curios. Over the years Joe had received, among other artifacts, fifty rainbow notepads, a magic wand with a stuffed Lurex star at one end, a rotating plastic stand that held poker chips, and a device called a "Lazy Debbie," which allowed one to balance a telephone receiver on one's shoulder.

Joe always welcomed Aunt Ida's gifts, even if the majority disintegrated within a few months. Joe understood that Aunt Ida had a deep, primal need to shop. By accepting her *tchotchkes*, he was allowing her to shop again.

"Ida, I can't stand it," said Mrs. Reckler. "You're always buying everyone things, but you won't spend a nickel on yourself. Pola said you saw a coat at Abraham and Straus. It was perfect, it was on sale, but you wouldn't buy it."

"I have a coat," Aunt Ida scoffed. "What do I need, two coats?"

Aunt Ida was asking the wrong people. Mrs. Reckler and Joe both felt that coats were an infinite need, a wardrobe's black hole.

"All right," said Aunt Ida, standing again. "What would anyone like to eat?"

Aunt Pola arrived at seven that evening. She lived in a garden apartment in Kew Gardens, a half hour's drive from Aunt Ida's. A friend dropped Aunt Pola off.

"Look who's here!" said Aunt Ida, going to the screen door.

"Look who's here!" said Aunt Pola.

"Look who's here!" said Mrs. Reckler.

"Look who's here!" said Joe.

"Stop making fun," said Mrs. Reckler, swatting her son.

"Listen to your mother," said Aunt Pola, presenting her cheek to be kissed.

"Hi, Aunt Pola," said Joe, kissing his aunt. "Let me take that."

"I'll take it," said Aunt Ida, wrestling Aunt Pola's suit-case away from Joe.

"Ida," said Mrs. Reckler. "He'll take it. Let him be good for something."

"You take it," decreed Aunt Pola, handing the suitcase to Joe.

"Fine," said Aunt Ida, throwing up her hands. "Pola, come in. Why are we standing in the hall?"

"I'm coming, I'm coming," said Aunt Pola. First she stood still and gave Mrs. Reckler a rigorous once-over, from head to toe. "Hedy, you look wonderful," Aunt Pola concluded. "Is that a new dress?"

"This rag? I've had it for ages. I'm ashamed to be seen in it. Bamberger's. On sale."

Aunt Pola nodded approvingly. "That's a pretty brace-let," she said, grabbing Mrs. Reckler's wrist. She held the wrist and the bracelet up to the light. "This is gorgeous. I bought gold like this, in Florence. That's Italy, Joe. Where is this from?"

"Bloomingdale's," said Joe. "That's America. On sale."

"How much?" asked Aunt Pola.

"It doesn't matter," said Mrs. Reckler, retrieving her wrist. "Please. I'll leave it to you in my will, then you'll know. It was $59.00."

"$59.00?" clucked Aunt Pola. "You paid that?"

"Reduced from $275," said Mrs. Reckler. Even Joe was floored at his mother's imaginary bargain.

"Let me see that," said Aunt Ida, seizing Mrs. Reckler's wrist. "Very nice."

"Did they have any more?" asked Aunt Pola. "I'll pick one up."

"No," said Mrs. Reckler. "There were no more. Sorry."

"Ipsy-pipsy," said Aunt Pola. "She buys a bracelet, all of a sudden she's royalty."

"Girls," said Aunt Ida, "and boy, could we please move out of the hallway? You're blocking traffic. Pola, come in. Eat something."

"That's a gorgeous sweater," said Aunt Pola, studying Joe's back as he headed into the living room. "Let me look at that."

Joe stood still while Aunt Pola tugged a handful of his sweater, scrutinizing it as if through a diamond-cutter's loupe.

"It's Italian," boasted Mrs. Reckler. "Missoni."

"Missoni," said Aunt Pola. "I've heard of it. It's a beautiful thing. How much?"

"I'm not telling," said Joe, who had removed the price tag.

"Uch, he's not telling," said Aunt Pola. "How much?"

"None of your business," said Joe, grinning. Joe liked to frustrate Aunt Pola. It was fun to tease her, to test her resourcefulness.

"You're right," said Aunt Pola. "He's right. It's none of my business."

Mrs. Reckler and Aunt Ida exchanged a glance; they were stunned, both by Joe's refusal to quote a price and by Aunt Pola's gracious acceptance of this heresy.

"Go ahead, tell her," said Aunt Ida, worried. Aunt Ida was the middle sister, so she tended to be the peacemaker.

"No; if he doesn't want to tell, he shouldn't tell," said Aunt Pola, settling on a couch in the living room. "This is the United States, people have rights, he's a citizen. How much?"

"Aunt Pola," said Joe, parking his aunt's suitcase in a corner. "I'm not going to tell you."

"Fine, that's fine," said Aunt Pola evenly. "Hedy, it's fine, really. Joe, come here."

Joe sat beside Aunt Pola.

"You don't have to tell me, I don't need to know. It's a gorgeous sweater. The Italians knitted it, that's enough. But tell me, let me ask you something—how much for a sweater *like* this?''

Aunt Pola was, in a word, awesome. She was fearless, the most robustly straightforward person Joe had ever met. There are people in the world with doubts, people who waver, people who question. Aunt Pola was not one of these people.

Aunt Pola was a vibrant seventy-seven years old and, as she would be the first to inform a total stranger, still going strong. She was compact, just over five feet tall, but sturdy. Aunt Pola reminded Joe of a keen-eyed Indian squaw, a fierce Chippewa priestess bartering with the gods of rainfall and fire, and winning. She also resembled Helena Rubinstein, the self-made cosmetics tycoon, and other diminutive Jewish titans, women who ruled empires but brought their lunches to the office in brown paper bags.

Aunt Pola's brow was strong and unlined. Her hair was only lightly streaked with silver and pulled back in a no-nonsense bun like her sisters'. Aunt Pola's glance was flinty. She managed to look both noble and crafty, like Golda Meir addressing the United Nations Security Council. Nothing got past Aunt Pola; she was someone to be reckoned with.

Growing up, Joe had occasionally found Aunt Pola intimidating. Joe had not been alone in this; his mother and Aunt Ida still deferred to their older sister. When Joe was five, his parents had taken him to the outdoor sculpture garden of the Museum of Modern Art, on East Fifty-third Street. There was a stunning bronze in the sculpture garden, Rodin's towering figure of Balzac, a cloaked monolith. Joe had been convinced that the statue was actually a rendering of his Aunt Pola.

As he grew older, Joe had come to find his Aunt Pola both effervescent and heroic. Aunt Pola was always fair. She listened and then made judgments. These judgments tended to be transferred to granite tablets. Aunt Pola trusted herself, without reservation. She had the calm and the magnetism of the conqueror.

"For a sweater *like* this?" Joe told his Aunt Pola. "You would pay a similar price to what I paid."

"He's not going to tell me," Aunt Pola announced, shaking her head. "He's *meshugge*."

"He's a rotten kid," agreed Mrs. Reckler.

"Oooh, you're very brave," Aunt Ida whispered to Joe.

"Ida, what did you tell him?" asked Aunt Pola.

"Nothing," said Aunt Ida. "I told him he should tell you. Let's eat."

Everyone retired to the kitchen, where Aunt Ida peeled the Saran and aluminum foil from the many platters. Aunt Ida and Mrs. Reckler nibbled. Aunt Pola heaped a plate with food, sat at the kitchen table, and enjoyed a meal.

Everyone then proceeded to the living room, and Aunt Pola unzipped her suitcase and disinterred several bundles swaddled in brown paper. Aunt Pola had returned only a week earlier from her most recent sojourn in Israel.

"It was glorious," Aunt Pola said. "I had such a good time. I went everywhere, to a kibbutz, to an archaeological dig. They even let me dig a little. I thought I found something, a piece of metal. They said it was just a nail, I said enough digging. I was with a group, very nice people. We only lost one, Mrs. Hoffman. She had a stroke."

"Oh no," said Mrs. Reckler.

"How terrible," said Aunt Ida.

"Listen, she was eighty-eight years old, she was at the pool," said Aunt Pola. "It was very quick. It was a terrible tragedy. I won't speak ill of the dead, but to tell you the truth, she was a nudge."

Joe laughed; his mother glared at him.

"She was a nudge?" Mrs. Reckler asked, now suppressing her own laughter. "Pola, I'm not laughing, my son is laughing, he's very sick."

"Don't laugh," chided Aunt Ida, swallowing a giggle.

"She was a lovely woman," Aunt Pola continued. "Three grandchildren, the son-in-law's a psychiatrist. May she rest in peace, but she always wanted me to take her shopping. She always tried to sit next to me, so I'd take her. Word gets out."

Aunt Pola was the most unstoppably powerful shopper of

the three Esker sisters, no small achievement. Joe was always astonished at his Aunt Pola's prowess, at her daring, at the sheer sweep of her transactions. Aunt Pola haggled in Bloomingdale's—and triumphed. The sales help of all Aunt Pola's favorite shops knew her on sight. They allowed her to leave their stores with armloads of clothing, none of it paid for or recorded. Aunt Pola shopped for her daughter and grandchildren as well as for herself. She would choose things, take them home, and her family would obediently troop over for a trying-on session. Aunt Pola would then return the rejects and pay for what was kept.

Joe understood completely why the stores succumbed to Aunt Pola: utter reverence. Aunt Pola was an obvious champion, and tribute was paid. Also, she bought in bulk. She would name a price, the salesclerks would offer token objections, and Aunt Pola would get her way. Aunt Pola did not really shop; she campaigned. She laid siege to a store. Had Aunt Pola been in government, conventional warfare would have become obsolete. If a nation acted up, Aunt Pola would buy it.

Aunt Pola dearly loved Israel. She saw Israel as a place where Jews could be safe and respected, free from the savagery of the past. Aunt Pola made it a point to visit Israel at least once a year; she also browsed the globe, with passport, MasterCard, and comfortable shoes, ransacking Rome, Paris, Geneva. Aunt Pola had a feisty curiosity about the world, a healthy international nosiness. She liked to see how people everywhere lived and handled their problems.

Aunt Pola was an indefatigable traveler, uncomplaining and up for anything. She still scrambled up Peruvian mountainsides and hiked to Nepalese jungle ruins, but her most inexhaustible energies were always reserved for the marketplace.

Within days of Aunt Pola's return from an expedition, the sisters would gather. Aunt Pola had always amassed gifts for everyone. First she would pass around her latest snapshots. In these photos Aunt Pola was usually pointing, so that the viewer, while impressed by Aunt Pola's new straw sun hat, would not miss the Matterhorn in the background, or Mount

Fuji, or the bus parked at a rest stop outside Tel Aviv. Following a proper appreciation of these snapshots, gift distribution would commence. This event always made Joe feel like a raw recruit stationed in Lapland, during mail call, when the sergeant would heave packages from the States to the assembled G.I.'s.

Wherever she traveled, Aunt Pola would always obtain a cheap extra cardboard suitcase while en route. This suitcase was necessary to truck the gifts back to the U.S.A. Aunt Pola's personality was most useful during her confrontations with Kennedy Airport's customs officials, uniformed troubleshooters thirsting to exact what Aunt Pola considered unnecessary duties on foreign goods. "I didn't buy a thing," Aunt Pola would always confide to these inspectors, having snipped any contradictory tags or labels from her purchases. "I went for the sheer pleasure."

"Ida, this is for you. I hope you like it," Aunt Pola said, handing her sister a wrapped brown paper bundle. "I think it will go with everything, and if you don't like it just tell me, and I'll keep it."

"Please, I love it," Aunt Ida insisted, her gift still unwrapped. "Give me a chance."

Aunt Ida unwrapped her bundle. Inside was a heavy necklace made of many pieces of polished carved black stone knotted together.

"Oooh," warbled Mrs. Reckler, lauding the gift.

"Oooh," said Aunt Ida, holding up the necklace.

"That's beautiful," said Joe.

"If you don't like it," repeated Aunt Pola, "just tell me."

"I like it, I like it," said Aunt Ida, undoing the clasp. "Pola, you shouldn't have. I shouldn't wear this."

"Why not?" said Mrs. Reckler. "You have a neck."

"I got it in Haifa," said Aunt Pola. "This little store, a woman I used to work with had told me about it. It's on this little side street. They have jewelry and pillows and some scarves, which weren't very nice. I saw this necklace and I fell in love. I said, That's for Ida. You can't believe what the man wanted for it, if I tell you, you'll keel over, you'll stop breathing. It came to something like seventy-five dollars in

American. I love every human being in Israel, but they're all highway robbers, every last one of them. I said, No dice, buster, I've been to Israel before. Boom, it was fifty dollars. I said, Very nice, but who are you kidding, goodbye, Charlie. I walk out the door, just like that, I'm going, I'm gone. I get out in the street, then I hear him calling, Mrs. Berman, oh Mrs. Berman. I'd told him my name. So I go back in, I say, Yes, what is it, what's all the hollering? He says, for me, because I'm so good to Israel, because I have such a kind face, for me it's forty dollars. Big deal. So I thank him and I turn right around. I ain't buying, thanks but no thanks. This time I don't even get out the doorway. Mrs. Berman, Mrs. Berman, yoo-hoo. I won't tell you what I paid, but I'll say this: that shopkeeper, he was glad when I left the country.''

"You're crazy," marveled Aunt Ida. "I could never do that, I'd be too scared. But I'm glad you did."

"Well, it looks beautiful on you," Aunt Pola said. "It suits you. Here, Hedy, this is for you."

Mrs. Reckler unwrapped her package, which contained a necklace identical to Aunt Ida's. Aunt Pola always bought in multiples, so no one would be jealous.

"Ooooh," said Aunt Ida, admiring Mrs. Reckler's necklace. "That's gorgeous. I have one just like it."

"Pola," said Mrs. Reckler, "you shouldn't have done this. But I'm glad you did, because I was going to steal Ida's."

Mrs. Reckler tried on her necklace. Aunt Pola unwrapped a third bundle; inside was a third identical necklace. "I loved it so much," Aunt Pola said, "I bought one for me. I thought, We'll call each other up, so we don't all wear them at the same time."

Aunt Pola donned her necklace. The three women now resembled Incan divinities, in full ceremonial gear. Joe suddenly saw himself before a grave tribunal, marking him for human sacrifice, or graduate school. The three women looked sensational, with the barbaric grandeur of the enigmatic granite heads on Easter Island.

"And this is for you," said Aunt Pola, tossing Joe an inch-square white cardboard box. Much as Joe loved Aunt Pola, he had to admit that her taste in gifts for nephews was not without flaw. Over the years, Joe and his brother had received some eminently unwearable mustard-and-aqua-striped ski sweaters, some luxurious yarmulkes, and Greek peasant belts too wide for any known belt loops.

Joe opened his gift. Inside the box was a key chain, a triangle of olive wood embossed with a gold electroplated menorah emblem.

"Ooooh," said Aunt Ida. "For your keys."

"That's beautiful," said Mrs. Reckler. "Say thank you."

"Thank you," said Joe. Joe would have said thank you without his mother's prompting, but she was awfully quick.

"I don't know what boys like," Aunt Pola admitted. "But I thought maybe you have loose keys. And here's another one. Give it to your brother."

"Thank you," Joe repeated. "And thank you for my brother."

Joe stared at his new, incongruous key chain. Joe vowed to use it; its very absurdity pleased him. Aunt Pola's gifts were not meant to impress or dazzle. They were wholly well intended, a means of sharing her safaris with her relatives. In Joe's family, shopping was love. The Esker sisters were in no way crass. They valued one another, and art, and education, far above any material goods. But the Esker sisters lived to shop, at home and abroad. They shopped as if shopping were a sixth sense, a genetic gift. They shopped effortlessly, singly and in formation. Shopping was their shared language, their sisterly song.

Joe pitied families that did not shop. He assumed that in some clans, like the Kennedys, familial bouts of touch football were the equivalent of shopping. But shopping was better; you knew you were loved, because you got a key chain. You were worth bargaining for.

10

Everyone went up to bed. Joe was to spend the night in his cousin Kurt's boyhood bedroom. Joe put on his Yale track shorts and a plain white T-shirt. Kurt's room was alien territory, painted an indestructible brown and stocked with finely detailed model cars, a worn catcher's mitt, and a sagging shelf of Kurt's fraying textbooks from college and medical school. When Joe was twelve, he had once lined his entire room with aluminum foil, while under the sway of a *Time* magazine article on Andy Warhol.

When Joe was fourteen, his mother had decided to redecorate his room in a more acceptable mode. Joe's father had hammered Joe a worktable constructed from a plywood door mounted on legs. Mr. Reckler had nailed a swath of pegboard rising from the back of the worktable. He had used a jigsaw to hew the pegboard into a silhouette of the Manhattan skyline. Joe and his mother had sought out wallpaper and shag carpeting together, in eye-blasting yellows and oranges. Mr. Reckler had also carpentered Joe an intricate, superbly mitered wall unit of shelves and drawers. Joe and Mrs. Reckler had cased the local hardware store and stolen the coordinated porcelain drawer pulls Joe had lusted for.

The Recklers were properly doting parents who indulged Joe endlessly. Joe, in return, had always advised his parents on issues of taste. He had chosen windbreakers and neckties for his father and earrings and place mats for his mother. Even now, with Joe living many miles away, the Recklers requested their son's guidance in every purchase. They were afraid that if they dared to acquire a wicker hamper or Portuguese wall hanging without Joe's approval, Joe would eventually visit and stare at the new arrival, shooting hazardous lasers of Manhattan disdain.

Joe felt hungry. He pulled on his terry-cloth robe and cotton athletic socks and tiptoed downstairs. When he crept into the kitchen he discovered his mother sitting at the kitchen table in a pool of yellow light, polishing off the coffee cake and thumbing through the previous week's *New York* magazine. Mrs. Reckler had taken a shower and washed her hair; her hair was now concealed beneath a fluffy pink towel turban.

"I'm not eating," Mrs. Reckler announced, as Joe entered the kitchen.

"Me neither," said Joe, breaking off a hunk of coffee cake.

"Do you want some milk?" Mrs. Reckler asked.

"No, thank you," said Joe. Mrs. Reckler poured Joe a tumbler of milk anyway; she was always concerned about Joe's calcium intake. Balanced nutrition was not Joe's strong suit; Mrs. Reckler felt that milk redeemed any snack.

"Should I make you an English muffin?" Mrs. Reckler asked.

"No," said Joe, picking up the magazine and turning to the movie reviews.

Mrs. Reckler had soon fixed a paper plate of two well-buttered English muffins and a bowl of cornflakes for Joe.

"Mother, I told you I didn't want anything," Joe said. "Just coffee cake."

"I didn't make this for you," Mrs. Reckler insisted. "It's for anyone who wants it."

"Excuse me," said Joe. "Is there someone in this room I'm not aware of?"

"I'll just have a half of a half," said Mrs. Reckler, splitting a half of an English muffin in two. "Mmmmm," she said. "I'm not saying you should have any, far be it from me, but this is delicious."

"You think I'm brain-damaged," said Joe, as he took the other half of the English muffin. Mrs. Reckler was wise enough not to comment on Joe's action. She was victorious, and she knew it.

"You know," said Mrs. Reckler, "the other night I stayed up thinking all about you. I tried to remember everything that happened when you were little, even when you were a baby. I tried to remember what strange thing I did to you, what I did to make you turn out the way you did."

"Well," said Joe, "you took me shoplifting."

"No, I mean something stranger, like dropping you on your head. Something that made you only like candy and sleeping late. You're a wonderful boy and I love you very much, but you're very weird. And I wanted to remember what I did, and tell you about it, so you'd know."

"And?" said Joe eagerly. "What did you remember?" Joe longed to harbor a deeply suppressed memory of some sort. He liked to think that something supremely dreadful had happened to him as a child, something so staggeringly heinous and warping that he had blanked it out entirely. In the movies, people were always visiting dedicated psychiatrists who hypnotized them, usually with a swinging pocket watch. While in a trance, the people would twitch and remember some superbly traumatic childhood incident that would explain everything—why they were a paranoid schizophrenic or a chronic sleepwalker or afraid of birds.

Though Joe was quite pleased with his life and habits, he envied the melodrama of a rigidly denied memory. He was dying to be an enigma, a renowned case study, an Oscar-winning role.

"What did you remember?" Joe asked his mother, imagining, hoping that as a tot he had committed a thrill slaying or been fiendishly kidnapped by chanting cultists.

"Well, I thought and I thought," Mrs. Reckler said. "And I couldn't remember a thing. I read Dr. Spock. I did everything just like the other mothers. You had a perfectly normal childhood."

"So, in other words," Joe said, bitterly disappointed, "if I'm weird, it's my fault."

"Exactly," said Mrs. Reckler. "I'm sorry I couldn't remember anything. I thought it would be handy if you ever decided to see someone."

By "see someone" Mrs. Reckler meant going to a psychiatrist. When Joe was eight years old, his parents had arranged an appointment with a child psychiatrist. The psychiatrist's office had been cunningly littered with a carpetful of toys. While Joe played with the toys, the psychiatrist had subtly questioned him. The psychiatrist had believed that the plush dinosaurs and tinny Fisher-Price xylophone would occupy Joe, freeing his subconscious and allowing him to be caught off guard and reveal things. Joe had realized just what was afoot. He had plundered the toys and said as little as possible. Even as a toddler Joe had not suffered fools gladly.

Eventually the child psychiatrist had informed the Recklers that Joe was perfectly well adjusted and that they shouldn't worry or blame themselves. If Joe only wanted to eat candy and read magazines, he should be allowed to do so. "And we paid good money to hear this," Mrs. Reckler had commented at the time.

"Mother, I'm not going to a psychiatrist," Joe said, in Aunt Ida's kitchen. "You think that if I go to a shrink, I'll eat both English muffins."

In her heart, Mrs. Reckler knew that her son was extraordinarily healthy. He didn't snort cocaine, and he had not pierced his nose, shaved his head, and joined an ashram that peddled roses at the airport. He had not been institutionalized, like so many of her friends' children. Joe was only a benign felon and wasn't healthy in the ordinary way, he didn't correspond to the dictates of *Family Circle* magazine. This preyed on Mrs. Reckler.

"I just want you to be happy," Mrs. Reckler said. "Isn't it hard for you? Don't people think you're strange? I love you just the way you are, but I've always worried that you'd have a hard time in the world."

"The only person who thinks I'm strange," said Joe, "is you."

"Very funny," said Mrs. Reckler. "So tell me the truth, am I a terrible mother? Did I ruin your life?"

Mrs. Reckler would willingly sacrifice her own life for Joe's; she never wanted Joe to experience any sadness or difficulty or insult. She was a mother.

"So did I ruin your life?" Mrs. Reckler asked, her chin quivering.

"Yes," said Joe. "Of course."

"You are so rotten," said Mrs. Reckler, shaking her head. "And if you don't want to eat the second English muffin because it's cold now, I'll make you another one."

Mrs. Reckler unwrapped her towel turban and draped the towel over her shoulders. Her hair was almost dry. Instead of being tidily concealed in a neat bun, Mrs. Reckler's thick, dark-brown hair now flowed almost to her waist. Her hair was permanently crimped from decades of diligent braiding and coiling. She brandished her hairbrush, which had a hard wooden back and handle and harsh steel bristles, like spikes. She proceeded to brush her hair with vigorous strokes, enjoying the fierce pull on her scalp. Mrs. Reckler's hair was her enduring vanity. She loved feeling the lush, heavy mane on her neck.

Mrs. Reckler had been taught early in life that vanity was a sin, an unnecessary, somehow *goyische* distraction. She had never stepped into a beauty shop, a trip she considered a worthless, tacky expense. She had not trimmed her hair since the age of twenty-one. Every morning she plaited her hair into three equal strands and artfully braided the strands together. Then the single fat braid was wound into a tight knot at the base of her neck and secured with many ferocious-looking, wavy steel hairpins. Mrs. Reckler would always give her bun a tug, to make certain it was secure and her pride well hidden.

When Mrs. Reckler saw women with time-consuming hairdos, flips or lacquered, precarious beehives, she never envied them. They had to "do something" with their hair; they were flighty, insecure, helpless pawns of fashion. Mrs. Reckler knew that her hair was coarse and strong; she had no need to fuss with it. Only *shiksas* needed hairdos; they had limp, baby-fine, pale-blond hair, trivial peach fuzz. Mrs. Reckler knew that her hair was a gift; she had no need to show the world.

Joe peeked over the top of his magazine, watching his mother brush her hair. Her immodesty pleased him. When brushing her hair, Mrs. Reckler seemed less like Joe's mother. She became a woman, the beautiful, almost swaggering girl of her black-and-white wedding photos. Mrs. Reckler had been married during the early days of the war. She had worn a sleek and flattering pearl-gray georgette dress with rhinestone buttons, and a cocktail veil on a velvet band. She had looked devastating, like Rosalind Russell as a sinuous businesswoman. Mr. Reckler had worn a broad-shouldered gray gabardine suit, double-breasted; the Recklers had made an extremely handsome couple.

When Joe studied his parents' wedding pictures, preserved in creamy cardboard photographer's frames, he was very proud. His parents had been so serenely cool, so far superior to those goony, stiff-necked couples in overdone tulle and rented tuxedos. Joe's parents had looked bright-eyed and adventurous; they still did. Mrs. Reckler occasionally fretted that her family did not correspond to some bland, American ideal, to the chipper, pious folks on *Father Knows Best* or *Leave It to Beaver*. Joe was profoundly grateful that his family bore no resemblance to those televised dullards, those sponsor-pleasing oafs. His family was original, quirky, helplessly itself.

"About L. L. Bean," Joe said, eyeing the cornflakes but refusing to give his mother the satisfaction just yet.

"What about L. L. Bean?" said Mrs. Reckler. "We'll get the money, it's no big deal. It happens every day. I was watching the news; there's a kissing bandit out West. He robs banks and kisses the lady bank tellers. It was cute."

"Are you going to kiss the people at L. L. Bean?" Joe asked.

"Of course not; don't be disgusting," Mrs. Reckler replied.

"What's disgusting?" asked Aunt Ida, entering the

kitchen. Aunt Ida was wearing a floor-length beige chenille robe, which she had owned for years and kept meticulously laundered. Her hair was also down, a full sheaf swept over one shoulder.

"Nothing's disgusting," said Mrs. Reckler. "Why aren't you asleep?"

"I couldn't sleep," said Aunt Ida. "I was going to come down and make sandwiches for tomorrow."

"Don't you dare," said Mrs. Reckler. "We'll go to a restaurant on the road."

"Hoo boy," said Aunt Ida, sitting in a kitchen chair. Aunt Ida occasionally allowed herself to sit in the kitchen, since the kitchen was not a real room, a room for company. "Let me tell you something," Aunt Ida continued. "Pola doesn't eat in restaurants. Maybe McDonald's."

"Why not?" Joe asked. "Why doesn't she eat in restaurants?"

"It's a long story," said Aunt Ida.

"Don't tell him," advised Mrs. Reckler. "He'll think it's funny."

"Why not?" Joe demanded.

"Your Aunt Pola doesn't like to eat in restaurants"—Aunt Ida sighed—"because she doesn't like to leave a tip."

"Why should I leave a tip?" Aunt Pola asked, padding into the kitchen in her quilted lime-green housecoat, which resembled a large oven mitt. "When I cook a meal at home, I don't get a tip. These waitresses, why should they live better than I do?"

Aunt Pola's hair was loose too, streaming down her back. She sat at the table.

"Is this mine?" she asked, pointing to the remaining English muffin.

"Be my guest," said Mrs. Reckler, getting up to toast another muffin for Joe.

"I don't want one," Joe warned his mother.

"Sit," Aunt Ida told her sister. "Joe, what can I make for you?"

"Quiche Lorraine," said Joe.

"Very funny," said Mrs. Reckler.

"Mister ha-ha," said Aunt Pola.

"I do have a recipe," admitted Aunt Ida, going to her little tin index card file.

"He was *joking*," said Mrs. Reckler. "Ida, sit down."

"Ida, where did you get that robe?" asked Aunt Pola.

"Who remembers," said Aunt Ida. "B. Altman, it must have been forty years ago."

"It looks it," said Mrs. Reckler. "Ida, buy yourself a new robe."

"What for?" said Aunt Ida. "It's a robe. Who's going to see me? The Pope?"

The Esker sisters settled in for an advanced forum on where to purchase decent robes. Aunt Pola volunteered to bring Ida three robes, so she could choose. Joe watched his mother and aunts talking, their gestures free and similar. They were more than sisters, they were an Esker conspiracy, a squawking, cooing Long Island Philharmonic. Joe felt as if he were attended by his graceful muses, by the obliging goddesses of the marketplace. With their hair loose and full, the Esker sisters appeared almost Victorian, like wild seeresses in a woodcut or bold pioneers in modern dance. They were European-featured, uncompromising women with scant use for guile or mascara. Joe imagined that the Joint Chiefs of Staff would look frail and wimpish beside his mother and aunts. The Esker sisters would certainly do a better job of running the country.

Mrs. Reckler tapped lightly on Joe's bedroom door at nine-thirty the next morning. "Wake up!" she trilled, amused at disrupting her son's slumber. A half hour went by. Joe had still not emerged. Mrs. Reckler, now dressed, knocked again. "Get moving," she said, in a more martial tone.

"Ummph," Joe murmured, turning over in bed and tugging the covers firmly about himself.

"Are you up?" Mrs. Reckler called through the door.

"Ummmph," Joe repeated. Joe hated waking up, but even more, he loathed being forcibly roused. Being wrenched from bed by a knock or command made him feel as if he were in the Marine Corps, at a sadistic 5:00 a.m. bugler's beck and call. Joe imagined that he could endure nerve gas, battlefield gangrene, flying shrapnel, anything but early-morning coherency.

Mrs. Reckler cracked the door open a few inches. "Are you up?" she asked the shrouded lump huddled on the bed.

"No," Joe replied. "Go away."

"Is he up?" asked Aunt Ida, joining Mrs. Reckler at the door. "Let him sleep."

"He's *been* sleeping," said Mrs. Reckler. "If you let him, he's going to move in here."

"That's fine," said Aunt Ida, always willing to accommodate guests.

"Is he up?" asked Aunt Pola, adding herself to the crowd at the door. "What's his problem?"

"What's your problem?" Mrs. Reckler dutifully asked her shiftless son.

Joe poked his head up, without moving his body. "There are three Jewish women at my door," he said. "That's my problem."

"So amusing," said Mrs. Reckler. "All right, *bubbelah*. You asked for it. I'm sending your Aunt Pola in."

Aunt Pola swung open the door, like a gunslinger striding into a Klondike saloon. She was happy to be used as a threat, a motivator. She marched over to the bed and grabbed Joe's head in her hands. "Wake up," she commanded. "See," she told her sisters, shaking Joe's head as if she were mixing a Tom Collins. "Now he's up."

"Pola, stop it," said Aunt Ida, coming into the bedroom. She couldn't quite bring herself to wrest Joe's head from Aunt Pola; Aunt Pola was too assured. Aunt Ida contented herself with smoothing the blanket over Joe's feet.

Mrs. Reckler entered and sat on the bed. "Had enough?" she asked her son.

"Go away," Joe admonished his mother and aunts. "Go watch the leaves change."

Aunt Pola gave Joe's head a little swat and dropped it back on the pillow, like a rejected melon. "Are we going to have this problem every morning?" she inquired. "On the whole trip?"

"If he wants to sleep, we'll let him sleep," insisted Aunt Ida.

Joe opened his eyes. He watched the three women scattered on his bed, cheerful magpies discussing him and what was to be done. They were like blasé vivisectionists with a hapless lab animal. Joe decided to pull himself together before they began introducing electrodes or truth serum.

"I'm up," Joe said, rising on his elbows.

"Big deal," said Mrs. Reckler.

* * *

Joe eventually got dressed and joined his relatives in the kitchen, where everyone struggled to make a dent in Aunt Ida's breakfast buffet. Then Aunt Ida attempted to single-handedly haul everyone's luggage out to the Reckler Oldsmobile. Aunt Pola insisted that Aunt Ida surrender the luggage and allow her to carry the many pebbly, pastel Samsonite suitcases, plaid vinyl garment bags, and Joe's knapsack. Mrs. Reckler arbitrated the dispute by decreeing that Joe would handle everything.

"But I have a bad back," Joe improvised. Jewish men traditionally have bad backs; Joe anticipated torrential sympathy.

"Since when?" asked Mrs. Reckler. "Since when do you have a bad back?"

"Since you asked me to carry the luggage," Joe replied.

"Maybe he does have a bad back," Aunt Ida fretted, while Joe transported the luggage and layered everyone's belongings into the trunk of the car.

"From what?" Aunt Pola asked. "Too much sleeping?"

"I heard that," Joe called out.

"He has a bad back but good ears," Aunt Pola commented, as the sisters umpired Joe's efforts from the front stoop. "And how's Saul?"

"Saul is fine," Mrs. Reckler replied. "He has a new hearing aid, it works beautifully. But he hears what he wants to hear. If I say, Saul, I'm going to be working late tonight, fix your own dinner, he doesn't hear."

"You don't fix Saul's dinner?" Aunt Pola asked. Aunt Pola, who had worked her entire life, was still strict about a wife's eternal responsibilities.

"What am I, the cook?" Mrs. Reckler asked. "When I work till eight at night, I should run home to make him dinner? I leave a half a chicken in the freezer, he can heat it up."

"Saul heats things?" Aunt Ida marveled. "That's very good."

"He has a master's degree in physics," Mrs. Reckler said. "He should be able to do something."

"Very modern," murmured Aunt Pola, whose murmurs reverberated throughout the tristate area.

Joe slammed the trunk of the car, feeling highly accomplished, as if he'd engineered the launch of a space shuttle. "All ready," he declared. "Is that everything?"

"Come on, everybody," Mrs. Reckler called. "Do we have everything? Get in the car."

"I really shouldn't go," Aunt Ida decided. "What do I need to see the leaves change?"

"Ida," said Mrs. Reckler, "you're coming: you're going to have a nice vacation. You work very hard. Don't argue. Get in the car."

"I feel guilty," said Aunt Ida. "Leaving the house."

"What?" said Mrs. Reckler. "The house gets lonely? You can call the house. We'll send a postcard. We'll buy it something."

"I don't know," said Aunt Ida. "I should call Kurt and Danielle. Tell them I'm going."

"They know you're going," said Mrs. Reckler. "You talked to them this morning, twice already. They're aware. They've been notified."

"Pola, should I go?" Aunt Ida asked.

"It's your life," reasoned Aunt Pola. "Stay home, come with us—it's your decision. If you want to sit home in an empty house and do nothing, when you could be having fun with your sisters, that's for you to say. Don't ask me—what do I know? But just for my own curiosity, just for the record, Ida, when did you lose your mind?"

"All right," concluded Aunt Ida. "I'm coming. But only because you're forcing me. It's not my idea. Not one little smidgen."

"Fine," said Mrs. Reckler. "If the police stop us, you're a hostage."

"Ladies?" said Joe, who had opened all the car doors enticingly.

"I'll be right out. I just have to make a few calls," said Aunt Ida, scurrying back inside.

* * *

Half an hour later, Joe had coaxed his aunts and mother into the vehicle. Mrs. Reckler sat in the driver's seat, with Joe beside her. Aunt Ida sat behind Mrs. Reckler, and Aunt Pola behind Joe. The car doors were closed, but Mrs. Reckler had not started the ignition.

"Are we ready?" asked Aunt Pola. "Does anyone have to go?"

"Not me," said Aunt Ida. "What about the front seat?"

"I'm fine," said Mrs. Reckler.

"I refuse to answer," said Joe.

"Ipsy-pipsy," said Aunt Ida.

"He'll be sorry," Aunt Pola predicted. "When we're on the road."

"Do I need a sweater?" wondered Aunt Ida.

"Aunt Ida, you're wearing a sweater," said Joe. "Under your coat."

"Let me see," said Aunt Pola, opening Aunt Ida's coat and reviewing her sweater. "This is a very nice sweater. Did you make this?"

"Of course," said Aunt Ida. "What do you think, I'm going to buy a sweater? From strangers? It's a Simplicity pattern, the big needles."

"It's very good," said Aunt Pola. "I like the cables. I should make one for Alicia, but maybe in a different color, maybe a beige or an off-white." Alicia was Aunt Pola's grown daughter, who sold real estate and lived with her husband and four children in a New Jersey suburb. Mrs. Reckler gritted her teeth; discussions of knitting always vexed her. Mrs. Reckler's mother had rarely been glimpsed without flying needles. Ida and Pola were knitting fiends, a knitwear assembly line. They churned out sweaters not only for their own offspring but occasionally for Mrs. Reckler's as well.

Mrs. Reckler had tried to knit, she had made a token effort. She had mastered the basics, the beginner's stitches, but her heart wasn't in it. Knitting had always seemed so grindingly dull, a maternal burden along the lines of baking fresh cracked-wheat bread or exulting over a no-wax floor. Mrs. Reckler knew that there was more to life than domestic orgasm; still, she always grew shamefaced at her knitting disability. She would tell herself that knitting was therapeutic, relaxing, and a budget-stretcher. She would conjure herself before a homey fire, in a skirted, slipcovered wing chair, knitting and purling madly, with an appreciative golden retriever spread across her feet.

Mrs. Reckler had once knitted her husband a hip-length gray mohair cardigan; the process had taken her just over eleven years, and the end result had weighed almost fifteen pounds. She had knitted lumpish scarves for both her sons; these were five-year debacles. She would complete a few woolen rows and then dump the yarn in a squat Navaho basket and shunt the basket into a high closet behind louvered doors. A year later, her handicrafts guilt would have gained gale force, and the basket would be retrieved. Mrs. Reckler was currently tackling a second sweater for her husband, a cast-iron V-neck pullover, a torment she'd initiated a scant two years earlier. The ropy, medieval-brown yarn was stowed in a shopping bag in the car trunk. A trip to folksy New England felt appropriate for knitting, and she might be able to convince one of her sisters to complete some of the more intricate stitches.

Joe had always found his mother's attempts at knitwear rather hilarious. She clearly loathed every infernal click of the needles, and yet for twenty minutes or so every decade, she gritted her teeth, sat herself down, and grew determined to be demure and productive, to mutate into the sort of woman who might put up preserves, refinish furniture, and decoupage lampshades. Mrs. Reckler had also hooked several area rugs from mail-order kits. She would hunch over a few yards of buckram mesh, stuffing yarn through the holes with a special hook. The finished products were unfortunate, but Joe thought his mother was uncommonly noble. Even as a child, he had realized that living in the suburbs can do strange things to women.

"Hedy, are you knitting anything?" Aunt Pola asked, from the back seat.

"Yes," Mrs. Reckler replied. "I'm making a sweater for Saul."

"The same one?" asked Aunt Ida. "The brown, from two years ago?"

"Yes, Ida," admitted Mrs. Reckler.

"Don't worry," comforted Aunt Ida. "I'll do the sleeves. Remind me."

"Mama always said," Aunt Pola recalled, "Ida can knit like the wind, Pola's the same, but Hedy, she knits like she's wearing boxing gloves. On the wrong hands."

"Is that what Mama said?" Mrs. Reckler asked. "You know, I knew there was something I didn't like about Mama."

"Oh hush!" said Aunt Ida, terrified of the mockery.

"She'll hear you, up in heaven," Aunt Pola warned.

"Let her," said Mrs. Reckler, gunning the ignition. "Let her come down and do the sleeves."

"Are we going?" asked Aunt Ida, hearing the ignition turn over.

"Last call," said Mrs. Reckler.

"I'm fine," said Aunt Pola.

"I'm sure I left something on, I'm sure the gas is on and my house will explode," said Aunt Ida, who had already checked the gas twice before leaving her house, along with all the faucets, radiators, and windows.

"So you'll get a new house," said Mrs. Reckler, releasing the emergency brake.

"I wish I had your money," said Aunt Ida. "Goodbye, house!"

"Move 'em out," said Joe. "Blast off."

Mrs. Reckler looked both ways and guided the car into the street.

"Hoo, we're moving!" exclaimed Aunt Ida, as if she'd never been in an automobile.

"Hedy, let me drive," suggested Aunt Pola.

"Too late!" said Mrs. Reckler, driving merrily down the street.

"I'm so glad we're going," said Aunt Ida, after they'd been driving for five minutes. "It's going to be so nice, seeing the leaves."

"I love seeing the leaves change," said Aunt Pola. "That's the one thing they don't have in Israel. Leaves, and maple sugar candy."

"So Joe, are you excited that you're going to see the leaves change?" asked Aunt Ida, a bit maliciously.

"I'm delirious," said Joe. "It's always been my dream."

"Don't encourage him," said Mrs. Reckler. "Don't give him ideas."

"I love New England," said Aunt Pola, settling in. "It's really very beautiful this time of year. Nat and I always used to take a trip right around now, a long car trip." Nat had been Aunt Pola's husband. He had died five years earlier, from a heart attack on the ninth hole of a golf course in Tampa Bay, Florida. His death had been immediate and without pain. Nat had perished at play, doing what he loved best.

"Nat was crazy about New England," Aunt Pola recalled. "He'd play tennis every day, like a maniac."

"Well, I can't wait," said Aunt Ida. "I want some scenery."

"Keep your pants on," said Mrs. Reckler.

"Ida, is that your Loehmann's?" asked Aunt Pola, spotting a sign beside the road.

The significance of Loehmann's in the lives of the Esker sisters could not be overestimated. Loehmann's had been perhaps the first discount clothing outlet in America.

Loehmann's had been the first store to combine quality goods with unheard-of savings; this was a formula verging on alchemy. Frieda Loehmann had opened her flagship location early in the century, in deepest Brooklyn. She had dressed entirely in vampire black and, so legend had it, interred bulging rolls of cash in the waistband of her bloomers. She had policed her store, stalking and hovering, trusting no one. She had been an American pioneer, the shopping equivalent of Ford or Bell.

Joe considered Mrs. Loehmann to be a folk hero, a mystical presence in a league with Paul Bunyan and Johnny Appleseed. She had championed the cause of Jewish women, rising from the shtetl to seek name brands at 60 percent off. The Esker sisters saw their mother in Mrs. Loehmann. They recognized her pluck, her insight, and her fierceness. Mrs. Loehmann had been eccentric, tightfisted, and paranoid, but all in the visionary service of her ladies. Frieda Loehmann had gotten the job done.

Loehmann's was now a national chain, with branches throughout the East and Midwest. Joe liked to picture the first Loehmann's in Cheyenne, Waxahachie, or Boise. He imagined covered wagons of bonneted Jewish bargain-hunters, courageously expanding the frontiers of wholesale-and-below, befriending the Apache over racks of juniors' activewear. The chain was overseen by the Loehmann family, following the matriarch's demise. The stores were identical and never to be resisted. Bypassing a Loehmann's was insanity, a refusal of Lourdes. Mrs. Reckler sensibly steered the car into the Loehmann's parking lot.

"This is still the best Loehmann's," said Aunt Pola. "You know, Hedy, the last time I visited you in Jersey, we went to your Loehmann's, out on Route 18. But frankly, I was disappointed."

"You have to go on the right day," Mrs. Reckler said, defending her home turf. "Last time I went they had beautiful coats."

"I almost never go here," said Aunt Ida. "I mean, I was here last week, but I was looking for things for Danielle. I got her two scarves and a belt. All Perry Ellis."

"He's good," said Aunt Pola approvingly. "Him I like."

The store was one story and plain red brick, with a flat roof. A Loehmann's is always a vast square blockhouse, a no-frills shrine. The sign is illuminated blue plastic script; any further gesture at landscaping, any shrub or column, is justly regarded as frivolous and unnecessary. Loehmann's is for the hardened postgraduate shopper, the lethal black belt, the lifetime bargain addict beyond redemption. No one needs to be lured into Loehmann's.

Joe and his relatives flung open the plain plate-glass doors, like a grizzled posse. The store's interior was stripped down, basic: four walls and racks. The ceiling held sizzling fluorescent fixtures, and a Formica cashiers' island floated at the rear of the store. There were no up-to-the-minute mannequins, no tasteful signs balanced on brass easels, no coaxing displays. Loehmann's was a mine to be quarried, a mother lode.

Loehmann's does not offer menswear, so Joe did what all men do upon arrival: he sat down. At the front of the store there was a scattering of rickety metal folding chairs, for patient sons and husbands. Joe took a seat beside a paunchy, sixtyish gent in a jaunty straw hat with a batik headband. The man was chewing a cigar and perusing the sports pages of the *Daily News*. The man acknowledged Joe with a jovial nod. They were both intruders, witnesses, vestigial beings whose primary function was to hold pocketbooks, allowing their industrious womenfolk to have both hands free.

Mrs. Reckler, Aunt Ida, and Aunt Pola all heaped their pocketbooks in Joe's lap. "Hold these," Mrs. Reckler commanded. "Don't drop anything. You're in charge."

"Can I sell them?" Joe asked.

"Mr. Funny," said Mrs. Reckler.

"If you can get a good price," said Aunt Pola. Joe was not entirely convinced that Aunt Pola was joking. Aunt Pola always considered all possible angles of a situation.

"Come on," said Aunt Pola, leading her sisters. The three women headed into the churning sea of wobbly chrome racks. For some reason, Joe thought of the monument of the valiant enlisted men raising the flag at Iwo Jima.

The spindly racks were bulging with garments of exceedingly variable quality. Much was dross, polyester unwearables, topstitched Day-Glo pantsuits and blindingly floral sundresses. The Esker sisters split up, locating the aisle with the appropriate size and getting to work. They briefly appraised each item before frowning and passing on to the next contestant. They were nimble-fingered, intuitive. Joe could glimpse only the women's bobbing heads and shoulders, as they moved slowly but productively through the mounds of fabric. It was like watching tireless fieldhands decimating a cotton patch under a fluorescent sun. Joe waited for someone to cue an uplifting spiritual; then he realized that absorbed shoppers would never waste time singing.

Occasionally the women called out to each other across the furrows, waving a possibility.

"You think?" Aunt Pola asked, brandishing a brushed-denim jumper.

"It's those sisters—Polly and Esther," Aunt Ida commented, shaking her head in the negative.

"Maybe?" asked Mrs. Reckler, dangling a polished-cotton raincoat.

"Oh yes," said Aunt Ida. "That's for you."

"Try it on," Aunt Pola cautioned. "We'll see. You never know."

"For Danielle?" Aunt Ida inquired, contemplating a slinky charmeuse evening blouse. Mrs. Reckler joined her. "She'd love it," decreed Mrs. Reckler. "It's stunning."

"What's wrong?" asked Aunt Pola, striding over. "Aren't you feeling well?" Aunt Pola was staggering beneath an armload of at least ten pieces of sportswear. Mrs. Reckler and Aunt Ida had amassed only a paltry few things each. Aunt Pola took their lackluster showing as a sign of either shocking laziness or ill health.

"Hold on," said Mrs. Reckler. "Hoo boy, you work fast."

"I found some lovely things," said Aunt Pola. "Some dresses for me and a terrific bathing suit for Alicia."

"You would buy your daughter a bathing suit?" asked Mrs. Reckler. "You know her that well? Her taste?"

"Taste, get away," said Aunt Pola. "I'm her mother."

"Are you doing all right?" Mrs. Reckler asked Joe, pausing en route to the fitting room.

"I'm fine," said Joe. Joe felt privileged to watch his mother and aunts at Loehmann's. He felt like the timekeeper at some Olympic final, a ballboy at Wimbledon.

"Stay here," said Mrs. Reckler. "We're almost done."

Mrs. Reckler and her sisters vanished into the fitting room, as if heading to the Ganges with their village's laundry. To Joe, the Loehmann's fitting room possessed the deliriously scented mystery of a pasha's harem. It was a forbidden sanctum, a female holy of holies, into which no man dared venture.

Loehmann's did not provide separate changing cubicles, as in a department store. Privacy was considered a scandalous waste of floor space. The fitting room was a single tent-like, near-circular area, an open corral lined with floor-length mirrors and low, well-worn wooden benches. Hooks were available for hangers. The floor was carpeted and strewn with tags, straight pins, and rosettes of crumpled tissue paper. The Loehmann's fitting room was an arena, an equalizer. There were no secrets in the Loehmann's fitting room.

Mrs. Reckler and her sisters hung their choices on the hooks. They each loosely tied the sleeves of a rear garment over the entire bundle, to prevent poaching, a common precaution known as The Loehmann's Knot. Mrs. Reckler retrieved a dress from her preserve. She slipped on her reading glasses to inspect the label at the neck. The label had been sliced out with a razor blade by the management; only furtive threads remained. World-class designers shipped their collections to Loehmann's for a mélange of reasons. These designers did not wish it widely known that their goods were in residence at a discount house; thus the labels were shredded, assuring an anonymous profit.

The obliteration of labels was a minor obstacle to the Esker sisters, scarcely a deterrent. Usually they could recognize a designer's output on sight: "I saw that exact same coat in Bloomingdale's for $700." If the maker was not immediately identifiable, the remnants of the label were swiftly deciphered.

Aunt Ida and Aunt Pola dug out their own reading glasses, and they hovered over the label with their sister. All three sisters wore related eyeglass frames, an outsize style of pinkish plastic; the sidepieces twisted and jackknifed. The three women looked like stylish owls, poring over the label; they brought a KGB-like intensity to their task.

"It's a black label with a little silver," said Aunt Pola, eyeballing the shreds in the dress Mrs. Reckler was holding. "That means Halston. Very nice. You did well."

"Halston," said Aunt Ida, impressed. "Ipsy-pipsy. The Jet Set."

"We'll see," said Mrs. Reckler, unbuttoning the dress she was wearing. Soon all the sisters were clad in only their underwear, as were the ten or so other women tugging and unzipping and chattering in the dressing room. The women were of all ages, contours, and incomes. Aunt Pola regarded a frisky teenage girl disapprovingly; the girl wore only wisps of shimmery bra and panties.

"Look what they're wearing nowadays," Aunt Pola remarked to her sisters. "It's indecent."

"Pola, she's not on the street," Mrs. Reckler said. "She's

in the dressing room. If I had her body, I wouldn't wear any underwear."

"Yes you would," Aunt Ida said, worried.

"Some people," said Aunt Pola, now glancing at a buxom, wide-bottomed woman straining the seams of an untidy, stained slip. Aunt Pola had no qualms about staring at strangers; the world was there to be seen. The Esker sisters wore by far the nicest undergarments in the dressing room. They lived in abject terror of suffering a fatal car accident and having their clothing removed at the morgue to reveal less than spotless underwear. And if they didn't die, their fate would be far more apocalyptic: at the hospital, the staff would see their shame, their tattered slips or their panty hose with holes in the toes. The lives of the Esker sisters were ruled by the scathing opinions of unknown doctors, nurses, and morticians.

Mrs. Reckler often warned Joe of the peril of straying from one's home wearing unclean or frayed underwear. "What if you're in an accident," she would chide.

"Mom, if I'm in an accident," Joe would parry, "then the doctor will be looking at my broken leg or missing arm. He won't be checking out my underwear. Do you really think that if I was wearing dirty underwear, the doctor would say, 'Look at this slob. The elastic in his underpants is almost shot. Let him die.' "

"You never know," Mrs. Reckler would reply.

"I know what you're really afraid of," Joe would decide. "You're afraid that the doctor will say, 'Oh my, this accident victim has holes in his T-shirt. What kind of mother does he have? Bring her here.' "

"Don't bother me," Mrs. Reckler would answer. "Just go, wear dirty underwear, get in a car crash, then tell me what happens."

"This is beautiful," said Aunt Pola, admiring Mrs. Reckler's slip in the dressing room. "Where did you get this?"

Aunt Pola took a few inches of the slip between her thumb and forefinger, judging the fabric for heft and fiber content. She shopped indiscriminately. Even if someone else was wearing a garment, Aunt Pola still considered it for sale.

"I got it in New Jersey," said Mrs. Reckler. "Bamberger's. Do you want one? I'll pick one up for you."

"I'll think about it," Aunt Pola said, with regard to Mrs. Reckler's slip. "I'll see." Aunt Pola was very specific about her underwear. She preferred a particular brand of cotton, a caressing lisle available only from a certain shop in London. Whenever one of the sisters went abroad, she obligingly lugged back twenty pairs of lisle panties for Pola. On an Esker map, the planet was divided not into nations or even continents but into sizes and departments.

"So?" said Mrs. Reckler, facing herself in the mirrored wall in her Halston.

"It's beautiful," said Aunt Ida. "I'm crazy for it."

"Turn around," said Aunt Pola, who had a more critical eye. "Let's check the back."

"I like it," said the Loehmann's saleslady. This woman was not really a clerk so much as a free-floating opinion, a majordomo who wafted about, offering unsolicited advice. She became an honorary Esker sister for the duration of the fitting.

"You really like it?" Mrs. Reckler asked the woman, who was in her fifties, with an immobile helmet of aggressively streaked blond hair. The woman also wore oversize pinkish eyeglass frames, and she had a strawberry-shaped pincushion on an elastic strap around her wrist.

"I wouldn't say I liked it if I didn't like it," the woman replied.

"It's a good color," said Aunt Ida.

"Does it have all the buttons?" asked Aunt Pola. Aunt Pola hoped that at least one button would be missing. Then she could convince the saleslady to lower the price of what would become a "damaged, as-is" item.

"It's got all the buttons," said Mrs. Reckler, after a quick count.

"The belt loops?" asked Aunt Pola.

"They're fine," said Mrs. Reckler.

"And the hem is perfect," said the saleslady, taunting Aunt Pola. "So don't try anything."

The saleslady knew her clientele. Some diabolical women

infiltrated Loehmann's armed with manicure scissors. They would snip off a button or make a microscopic slash, and haughtily demand a reduction in price. An inventive shopper might hide a dress's matching belt in the depths of her purse and claim the belt was missing.

"Excuse me," said Aunt Pola, in a justly icy tone. She swept past the saleslady and murmured to Mrs. Reckler, "Don't pay attention to her. What does she know?"

"I'll ask Joe," Mrs. Reckler decided, heading out of the dressing room.

"So what do you think?" asked Mrs. Reckler, standing in front of her son out in the store. "Tell the truth."

"It looks great," said Joe. "It really does. It's wonderful. Buy it."

Joe believed in almost universal encouragement. He felt that buying things was always a good idea; not buying things was a form of denial and could only lead to regret, tension headaches, and a withered spirit. If the dress had been ugly or inappropriate, Joe might have made a puckered face and demanded to see another outfit. But Mrs. Reckler had very good taste, and the dress was terrific.

"What do you really think?" said Mrs. Reckler. "Don't lie to me; it's a lot of money."

"I'm not lying," said Joe. "It's a wonderful dress, you need a new dress, you can wear it in Vermont, you should buy it."

"Really? You really think so?"

Mrs. Reckler, as usual, was at war with herself. She was dying to be talked into the dress, to be forced to purchase it at gunpoint. On the other hand, she worried. She worried about the ungodly phone bill, the ever-looming mortgage on the Reckler home, the Blue Cross payments, Mr. Reckler's health, her children's lunacy, the vision of the entire family stashed in some mythical poorhouse. All of these worries, both accurate and imagined, conspired to deny Mrs. Reckler a new dress. Ultimately, she felt that world peace could be achieved only by her not buying the dress. Buying the dress tempted Armageddon.

"I shouldn't buy this," Mrs. Reckler said. She looked

down at herself. She stood as if the portions of her body covered by the dress belonged to someone else, some lucky stranger. "It is nice, though."

"It is very nice," said Joe. "How much?"

Mrs. Reckler pulled the computerized price tag from the sleeve of the dress.

"Too much," said Mrs. Reckler.

"How much?"

"Do you want us to end up in the poorhouse?" Mrs. Reckler asked.

"Where is this poorhouse?" Joe asked. "You know, I have never been able to locate it. Maybe it's really very nice. Maybe there's maid service."

"Oh, you think so."

"Mother, I don't know how to tell you this, but we are not living in the London of Charles Dickens. Buy the dress."

Joe's total conviction convinced Mrs. Reckler.

"No," Mrs. Reckler announced. "It's a beautiful dress, and it looks very nice on me, but I can't afford it. I want to see the leaves change, not buy dresses. Besides, I may want to get some things in Vermont; I'll need the money. No, not today."

"*Mother.*"

"Don't you 'Mother' me. I'm not buying the dress. So there."

"I don't understand something," Joe said. "Why is the phrase 'Christian martyr'? I'm sure a nice Protestant woman would buy the dress."

"I wish I had your money. Don't be anti-Semitic."

Mrs. Reckler returned to the dressing room and related her decision.

"Didn't Joe like it?" asked Aunt Ida.

"Joe," said Mrs. Reckler. "What does he know?"

"So you'll get something else," said Aunt Pola. "You'll keep going."

"Over your heads, ladies," crowed the brass-lunged Loehmann's saleslady. "Over your heads." Mrs. Reckler began obediently tugging the Halston off over her head. Stepping out of the dress might soil the hem.

"Oh my," said Aunt Ida, watching someone across the dressing room. The woman was struggling into a boned, strapless evening gown, an overdone confection of hot-pink lamé and rustling chiffon net. "Get a load of her."

An hour later, the group left Loehmann's. Aunt Ida had bought the charmeuse blouse for her daughter, "for evening, for when she goes out." Aunt Pola had acquired a poplin coat and two madras wrap skirts for herself, a bathing suit for her daughter, and a sweatshirt for her five-year-old granddaughter, an item with an appliquéd, sequined ice-cream cone, which everyone had declared "adorable." Mrs. Reckler had not purchased anything, but there was a coat she was "thinking about." Leaving Loehmann's empty-handed was a melancholy experience; "thinking about" something indicated a germ of hope for the future, like a wistful chorus of "I'll Be Seeing You."

"Mom, you didn't buy anything," Joe said, as everyone crossed the parking lot.

"I didn't need anything," said Mrs. Reckler stoically.

"So?" said Aunt Pola. "I didn't need anything, and I spent two hundred dollars." Statements like this reminded Joe of why he adored Aunt Pola: she embraced the irrational, with gusto.

The group got under way again, pulling out of the Loehmann's parking lot. "No more shopping," Mrs. Reckler announced. "Just leaves."

"Who wants to shop?" said Aunt Ida.

"Loehmann's isn't shopping," protested Aunt Pola. "It's an investment. The more I buy at Loehmann's, the more I save. It only makes sense."

"Look at the map," Mrs. Reckler said to Joe. "It's in the glove compartment."

Joe clicked open the glove compartment and found a pile of folded gas-station maps, along with a single glove and a fossilized pack of Wrigley's Spearmint Gum.

"Which map?" Joe asked.

"Paris, France," Mrs. Reckler replied. "The New England map. We spend thousands of dollars to send him to Yale, and he can't figure out which map."

"Maybe he didn't go to class," Aunt Pola speculated. "Maybe he slept."

"No," said Mrs. Reckler. "He worked it out; he told me once. He never took any classes before noon. Can you believe that?"

Joe's Yale career had been sublimely eccentric. Joe had believed that college was primarily a social experience, a four-year plan to mold one's budding persona. Joe's persona had not allowed for the study of calculus, biochemistry, or obscure foreign languages, such as French. He had enrolled in a series of special-interest seminars. These seminars had included such titles as "American Film Comedy of the 1930s: The Screwball Decade," "The Educated Woman in Modern America," and "The Golden Age of American Musical Comedy: Kern to Porter." Many of these seminars had offered celebrity guest lecturers, Broadway luminaries, and Oscar-winning film directors, all feeling rather spiffy about speaking at Yale. Joe had fond memories of his spell in New Haven. Attending Yale had been like leafing through a particularly juicy magazine, all candid interviews, intriguing ads, and bubbly cartoons.

"I don't like maps," Joe said, wrestling with the New England map. "The pioneers didn't have maps."

"The pioneers woke up before noon," Aunt Pola said.

"Listen to her," instructed Aunt Ida. "She knew the pioneers. If anyone gets bored, I've got plenty of books."

Aunt Ida reached into her canvas tote bag and withdrew a stack of children's books. Aunt Ida had been a grade-school librarian for over forty years; she had worked in gangrenous inner-city locations and in more placid, suburban surroundings. Aunt Ida believed that reading could nourish children, even save them. Aunt Ida was devoted to children, and yet she never seemed sappy or naive. She dealt with kids on a commonsense level. She encouraged them, she pushed them to discover the endless joy of books.

Unlike many of her colleagues, Aunt Ida had not grown cynical over her years in the public education system. Every working day, she encountered kids who hated to read, kids who couldn't read, kids who would never read; she refused to acknowledge defeat. Aunt Ida would try anything, any marionette or video game or licorice bribe, anything to get kids into what they referred to as the "liberry."

"I've got *Donny the Dinosaur*," Aunt Ida said, shuffling her selections. "And the sequel, *Donny the Dinosaur and the Big Lake*. I've also got an astronaut thing, and this new pop-up book, it's called *The Human Body*. See, you open each page and something pops up."

"Let me see that," said Aunt Pola, taking the book and opening it. "She's right. Look at that—it pops up. The appendix pops up, and the spleen. It's cute."

Aunt Ida always carried the latest children's books with her. She liked to read them before putting them on the shelves. At every family gathering, Aunt Ida would pass around the new releases for ages six to eleven. Joe occasionally found this unnerving, as the entire clan discussed Babar the elephant's latest shenanigans, or Fluffy the duckling's perilous encounter with a neighborhood cocker spaniel.

"Joe, what would you like?" Aunt Ida asked. "Dinosaurs or astronauts?"

"Don't bother him, he's busy," cautioned Mrs. Reckler.

Joe had by now unpleated the map of New England. This map was five square feet of toothpaste-green regions, plain white areas, and blue waterways. Spidery red, yellow, and black lines crisscrossed the states, and infinitesimal numerals were scattered like lint. The creased paper filled Joe's lap, crumpling against the dashboard.

"What am I looking for?" Joe asked.

"The exit for the parkway," Mrs. Reckler said.

"Which parkway?" Joe asked.

"The Hutchinson River," said Mrs. Reckler. "It's probably a big red line."

"Can't you just aim north?" Joe asked.

"Do you see it?" asked Mrs. Reckler. "I don't want to miss the exit."

"I can't find it," said Joe. "It's not on the map. This is a map of Paraguay."

"Of course it's on the map," said Mrs. Reckler. "You're hopeless."

"Mother," said Joe. "I don't drive. One of the reasons I don't drive is so that I will never have to read gas-station road maps. If I want to get somewhere, I have two options. I either tell the cabdriver where I want to go, or I tell Daddy, and they take me."

"You still don't drive?" said Aunt Pola.

"Don't ask," said Mrs. Reckler.

"Why not?" said Aunt Pola. "You're a big boy; you should drive."

"If he doesn't want to drive, he shouldn't have to drive," said Aunt Ida. "It's no crime. But, Joe, why don't you drive?"

"It's not my fault," Joe explained. "I took the driving test."

"And?" said Aunt Ida.

"And I passed the written test. I got one hundred percent," Joe said.

"Of course," said Aunt Pola. "And?"

"So I had some trouble with the road test. I failed it."

"So you'll take it again," said Aunt Pola. "And you'll pass."

"I failed it six times," said Joe, pleased with himself. If he was going to fail, he liked to fail big.

"Six times?" said Aunt Ida. "What did you do? Have a collision?"

"No," said Joe. "But I'm convinced it's not my fault. The people who give the tests are extremely petty. The last time I took the test I was doing just fine, until the end, when I had to parallel park. They set up these rubber cones along the side of the road, and I had to park in between the cones. And so I tipped one over. I just sort of nudged it. And the guy giving me the test turned to me and said, 'You just killed a child.' And I said, 'No I didn't; I just killed a rubber cone.' And he said, 'Get out of the car.' And he flunked me. I think he was anti-Semitic."

"I think you had a fresh mouth," said Mrs. Reckler ruefully. "Six times—can you believe that? It may be a world's record."

"So you'll take it again," said Aunt Ida sympathetically. "With new cones."

"Ones that jump out of the way," suggested Mrs. Reckler.

"After you fail it six times," Joe said, "they don't let you take it again for a few years."

"They're not so dumb," said Aunt Pola.

"Someday you'll drive," Mrs. Reckler predicted. "When you're ready."

"Mother, do you really want me on the road?" Joe asked. "Would you really like to drive behind someone who failed his driving test six times?"

"You have a point," said Mrs. Reckler. "Clark drives enough for both of you."

Clark was Joe's older brother. Clark owned, at last count, six motorcycles in various increments of disrepair, a van, and a truly miraculous 1963 Dodge Dart.

"So how's Clark?" Aunt Ida asked. "And the motorcycles?"

"We're not discussing it," said Mrs. Reckler firmly.

"Ipsy-pipsy," said Aunt Ida.

"Hedy, let me drive," said Aunt Pola. "I need the practice."

"Did you hear?" Mrs. Reckler asked Joe. "About Aunt Pola's car?"

"No," said Joe. "What? What happened?"

"Nothing," said Aunt Pola. "It was stolen by a den of thieves, that's all that happened."

"That's awful," said Joe. "When did they steal it?"

"Just last week," said Aunt Pola. "I was coming home from the supermarket, from D'Agostino's, and I parked where I always park, on the street, a block away from my building. I've been parking there for years. When Nat was alive, that's where he parked. So I leave the car, I lock it, and the next morning, when I come down to drive out to see Alicia and the kids in Jersey, my car is gone. It's disappeared."

"The white car?" Joe asked. Aunt Pola drove a blindingly white Buick, a roomy vehicle drenched in ornamental chromework. The car was a thundering gas-guzzler, but Joe had always found it entrancing. He liked the fact that his Aunt Pola drove what most people thought of as a pimpmobile.

"The white car," Aunt Pola confirmed. "They took my big Buick, just like that. Boom and vamoose. So I march down to the police station, and I go up to the front desk. And

I say, 'I would like to report a very expensive stolen vehicle. And I would like it returned.' And the man there, the police sergeant, he just yawns, like he couldn't be bothered. He gives me some forms and he says, 'Don't count on it, honey.' "

"He didn't care," said Aunt Ida. "It wasn't his car."

"So I say, 'Officer, I want my Buick back, so I can get out to Jersey.' And he says, 'Lady, it's not going to happen.' And he explains to me, he says that when people steal cars, they don't just go sell them somewhere, or drive them around. They take them to these special garages, these hideouts, and the garages strip the cars down and sell the parts. It's a whole system; it's very organized; it's like a big business. These people, these terrible thieves, they steal thousands of cars every year, and no one ever sees their Buick again."

"It's disgusting," said Mrs. Reckler.

"You're telling me," said Aunt Pola. "So I fill out the forms, and I call my insurance people. And even though my old car was practically brand-new, to them it's used and it's not worth so much. So if I'm lucky, they'll send me maybe a couple of bucks. And meanwhile I have to wait until they process my claim, and then I can finally buy another car, for no money, so the terrible thieves can steal it again. Believe me, I'd like to get my hands on those thieves, every last one of them. I'd give them a piece of my mind, I'd knock a few heads together. I'd say, 'So what are you stealing cars for, from nice old ladies? Go work for a living! Get a job! Take the bus! It won't kill you!' Can you imagine? What sort of person steals? I can't imagine it."

Mrs. Reckler glanced sharply at Joe. He looked back, wounded. After all, he hadn't heisted his Aunt Pola's beloved Buick. He wouldn't dream of stealing a car. In order to steal a car, he would probably have to drive it.

Mrs. Reckler had never stolen a car either. Whenever the Reckler family had required a new vehicle, Mrs. Reckler had let her husband do all the choosing and registering and comparison shopping. If I was going to steal a car, Mrs. Reckler thought to herself, I would have Saul do it.

Joe and his mother both shivered. They had both suddenly

pictured themselves under arrest for some imaginary grand auto theft. They would not be remanded into police custody, nor would they be shipped up the river to some forbidding federal penitentiary. Their punishment would be far more terrifying: the police would hand them over to Aunt Pola.

"It's a terrible thing," Mrs. Reckler said, taking a deep breath. "Car thieves. Go figure. I don't know what's going on in the world."

The group made what Aunt Pola referred to as "good time." By noon they had passed out of both New York State and Connecticut and were well into Massachusetts. While the leaves in these areas were indeed changing, the group had not yet entered Vermont, the threshold of changing-leaf country. "This is pretty," Mrs. Reckler said, eyeing the Massachusetts countryside. "But it's not Vermont."

"So I don't have to look yet?" Joe inquired.

"Not yet," agreed Aunt Ida. "Rest your eyes."

"So how was Connecticut?" Aunt Pola asked. "I slept."

"We had terrible problems with the Comanches around Westport," Joe said. "But the cavalry saved us."

"Don't be fresh," said Mrs. Reckler.

"Jews never have trouble with Indians," Aunt Pola said. "Joe, do you know why?"

"Why?" asked Joe, genuinely intrigued.

"Because," said Aunt Pola, "we buy their things. The blankets, the pottery, it's all very nice. We have an understanding. I've been out West, they loved me."

As usual, Joe wasn't sure to what degree his Aunt Pola was kidding. Aunt Pola never condescended to minority groups; she judged everyone with equal skepticism. Aunt Pola's only criteria involved the treatment of the Jews; a friend of the Jews was a friend of Aunt Pola's. An enemy of the Jews was an Arab; in Aunt Pola's estimation, the entire Republican Party counted as Arabs.

Joe's brother lived on the outskirts of a barely existent town called Farley, Massachusetts. Clark had invited his relatives to stop by for lunch on their autumnal odyssey through New England.

"I'm so excited," said Aunt Ida. "We're going to see Clark. I've never been to his house. What is it, like a farmhouse?"

"It's very nice," said Mrs. Reckler, a bit grimly. "There, see, I said it was very nice," Mrs. Reckler said to Joe.

"It is very nice," said Joe. "It's filthy, but it's very nice."

"It's filthy?" said Aunt Pola. "Hedy, why is it filthy?"

"Don't ask me," said Mrs. Reckler. "I don't live there. I live in New Jersey."

"Pola," said Aunt Ida, "if the house is filthy, it's not Hedy's fault. She keeps a clean house."

"You think so," said Joe gleefully.

"What?" said Mrs. Reckler, outraged. "Our house is spotless."

"I don't know . . ." said Joe.

"It isn't spotless?" asked Aunt Pola.

"Sometimes . . ." said Joe.

"Oh shut up," said Mrs. Reckler. "He's teasing me. He loves to do this. You see, my son thinks I'm a Jewish Mother."

"Imagine," said Aunt Ida.

"So you're a Jewish mother," said Aunt Pola. "So what's so bad?"

Mrs. Reckler hated the popular caricature of the Jewish

Mother. In this broadside, the Jewish Mother is vilified as chronically guilt-inducing, emotionally smothering, and maniacally obsessed with cleanliness, higher education, and nourishing food. The Jewish Mother demanded that her sons become kidney specialists and her daughters the wives of kidney specialists. The Jewish Mother was monstrous, a castrating ogress bearing waxed fruit, blintzes, and mutation mink. Mrs. Reckler justly found this caricature offensive. She disliked being pigeonholed, reduced, labeled.

"Whenever I hear someone talking about Jewish Mothers," Mrs. Reckler told her sisters, "my blood boils. It's racist; it's like calling someone a Mammy. Joe thinks I wish he was a doctor, living in Scarsdale, with a Cadillac."

"I do not," said Joe.

"Would that be so bad?" asked Aunt Pola. "He could do worse."

"I know what Hedy means," said Aunt Ida. "If I freeze a cutlet for Danielle, I'm being a Jewish Mother. If I clean my house, I'm a Jewish Mother. Why can't I just be a person?"

"Exactly," Joe agreed. "A neurotic, obsessively clean, self-sacrificing person."

"You see?" said Mrs. Reckler. "He's making jokes. He thinks it's hilarious. He tells his friends all about me; he makes jokes."

"I do not," Joe insisted. "I tell my friends that my mother is a chilly Swedish woman in a lab coat."

"You see?" said Mrs. Reckler.

"You know who's responsible?" said Aunt Pola. "That Philip Roth. I could kill him."

"He's very talented," said Mrs. Reckler, trying to be fair.

"Talent—get away," said Aunt Pola. "For what he did, he should be very sorry. The books he writes, they don't do the Jews any good. We don't need that. If everything were fine, if there were no Arabs, if the people in Mississippi didn't still wear white hoods, I'd feel otherwise. I'd say go ahead, write your disgusting books. You know who I feel sorry for?"

"Who?" asked Joe.

"His mother," said Aunt Pola. "Mrs. Roth. Imagine what she must go through. She probably can't leave the house. That poor woman—I hope he sends her money."

"She's probably very proud," said Aunt Ida timidly.

"Of what?" asked Aunt Pola. "That her son made her a laughingstock? That her child hurts the Jews? I'm sure she's very proud. Just busting her buttons."

"You know what's sad?" said Mrs. Reckler. "I know that at my funeral everyone will say, 'She was a Jewish Mother.' They won't say what kind of person I was or what I did with my life, they'll just make jokes."

"Mother, that's not true," said Joe. "I don't think of you as a Jewish Mother."

"So what is she, Irish Catholic?" asked Aunt Ida.

"Have I ever told you what to do with your life?" Mrs. Reckler asked Joe.

"No," Joe admitted.

"Have I ever said I'll kill myself if you don't become a dermatologist?"

"No," said Joe.

"Have I ever criticized you for not buying me a mink or for leading a ridiculous life?"

"No," said Joe.

"Well, then I'm not a Jewish Mother," Mrs. Reckler concluded.

"What if I hadn't gone to Yale?" asked Joe.

"You'd be dead," said Mrs. Reckler, giving Joe's cheek a sharp pinch.

Clark Reckler lived in a decrepit farmhouse in an isolated rural zone. There were no other homes nearby, just abandoned fields and islands of raw forest and telephone poles. The house was covered with splintering, weather-beaten clapboard and listed dangerously to one side. The front yard was mostly packed dirt marked by deep tire tracks, and clumps of dusty weeds. A truck tire swung from a fraying rope knotted to the limb of an ancient, barkless oak. Nuzzling one side of the house was the carcass of an unpainted Volkswagen Beetle, a steel shell lacking doors, window glass, and an engine. Three motorcycles, surrounded by motorcycle innards, were stationed on tarpaulins around the yard.

Mrs. Reckler drove into the dirt driveway, parking behind Clark's corroding yellow van.

"This is where he lives?" said Aunt Pola.

"It's beautiful," said Aunt Ida. "It's . . . rustic."

"If you say so," said Aunt Pola.

"It's not my house," said Mrs. Reckler. "Don't ask me."

"It's fine," said Joe. "It's very . . . Clark."

"Well, hey," said Clark, trotting out of the house. He was followed by an adoring dog, a hopeful, scruffy beast with a red bandanna tied loosely around its neck.

"So hello," said Mrs. Reckler, kissing her elder son.

"So hello," said Aunt Pola, kissing Clark. "So this is where you live."

"We love your house," said Aunt Ida, kissing Clark.

"It's very Tobacco Road," said Joe, shaking his brother's hand.

"Well, come on in," said Clark, waving everyone into the house. Clark was tall and wiry; he loped. He was wearing ripped, grease-soiled jeans and a plaid flannel shirt with half a sleeve missing, chewed off during engine surgery. Clark's thick, coarse hair was parted in the middle and billowed to his waist. A full, biblical beard and straggly Fu Manchu mustache obscured much of his face. Clark was barefoot; he had the look of a roaring Hell's Angel turned peaceful Mennonite farmhand.

"So you haven't cut your hair," said Aunt Pola, following her nephew into the house. Clark had not cut his hair since he was fourteen; he was now twenty-eight. Every time Aunt Pola saw Clark, she brought up the advisability of a haircut. She did not give up easily.

"Of course he hasn't cut his hair," said Mrs. Reckler, tugging on her son's mane.

"I'll cut my hair when you cut yours," said Clark to Aunt Pola.

"Very good," said Aunt Ida, admiring Clark's quick thinking.

Clark led everyone across a creaking porch supported by

cinder blocks, and into the front parlor of his farmhouse. Two of the walls had been spray-painted a startling Day-Glo orange; a third was a mystic grapey purple. The fourth wall was completely hidden beneath a curtain of empty Coke and Budweiser cans, intricately stacked to the ceiling. The Budweiser cans had been used to form a circular peace sign and Clark's name, within the field of Coke cans.

"Look at that," said Aunt Ida, standing before the glinting wall of cans, as if at a gallery. "You must drink a lot."

"Are they all empty?" asked Aunt Pola.

"Yup," said Clark. "Sometimes there's a little bit of Coke or beer left in the cans, but the rats take care of it."

"I'm leaving," said Mrs. Reckler.

"Sit," said Joe.

"Are there really rats?" asked Aunt Ida.

"Nah, just at night," said Clark jovially.

"So we're safe," said Joe.

"Everybody sit down," said Clark. "Don't make me nervous."

The sisters bunched in the center of the room, debating their seating options. Lumped against one wall was a couch, a sunken expanse of grimy cushions shrouded by thin dime-store Indian print bedspreads. There was a Naugahyde recliner, patched with black electrical tape, and there was the front seat of a car, a blue vinyl bench, stationed on the floor. Mrs. Reckler went for the couch, Aunt Pola perched on the recliner, and Joe and Aunt Ida shared the car seat.

"I feel like we're still driving," said Aunt Ida. "Is this from a real car?"

"Yup," said Clark. "I got it at the dump. It's a '57 Chevy. I got the hubcaps too." Clark gestured proudly to these hubcaps, pocked chrome bubbles nailed to the wall over the couch, to either side of a bleached animal skull.

"Very nice," said Mrs. Reckler. "Like a Van Gogh."

"This is a nice chair," said Aunt Pola, yanking on the lever that made the recliner recline. Aunt Pola's feet rose with the adjustable footrest.

"That recliner was in Saul's study," said Mrs. Reckler.

"Remember?" Much of the Recklers' used furniture would arrive at Clark's home; he happily accepted donations.

"Really?" said Aunt Pola. "I never would have recognized it."

"So," said Clark. "Can I like get anyone anything to drink?"

"Certainly," said Mrs. Reckler. Mrs. Reckler approved of Clark's good manners, even amidst the rubble of his living room. "What have you got?"

"I've got beer," said Clark, "and orange juice, and some cheap wine, if we didn't drink it all last night. Patty and I had some folks over."

Patty was Clark's girlfriend. They had shared the farmhouse for the past two years.

"Where is Patty?" asked Mrs. Reckler. Mrs. Reckler liked Patty, particularly in contrast to some of Clark's earlier attachments. These girls had included an ex–heroin addict and an especially grumpy woman with two small children.

"Patty's out back," said Clark. "She'll be here in a minute. She's fixing her bike."

"He means motorcycle," Mrs. Reckler explained to her sisters.

"I'll have a beer," decided Aunt Pola.

"Me too," said Aunt Ida. "Why not?"

"I'll have OJ," said Joe. "In a glass." Clark tended to chug most beverages directly from the bottle or carton. He felt this was the natural thing to do.

"Picky, picky," said Clark.

"I'll have orange juice too," said Mrs. Reckler. "Thank you very much."

Clark left for the kitchen, with his hound at his heels.

"So," said Mrs. Reckler. "*House Beautiful*, you think?"

"It's very nice," said Aunt Ida. Aunt Ida would approve of, and cheerfully visit, the Black Hole of Calcutta if a nephew chose to reside there.

"It's a hellhole," said Aunt Pola. "How can he live here?"

"He likes it," said Joe. "He's very casual."

"Casual?" said Aunt Pola. "You know how I'd clean this place? With a match."

"Look," said Mrs. Reckler. "I agree it's not a palace. It's not my taste. In fact, it's a garbage dump. But if I say anything, I'm dead."

"Good thinking," Joe agreed.

Clark had left home when he was sixteen years old, and he had always settled in similarly demolished surroundings. Clark had never finished college; his consuming passions had always been the grittiest machinery and the more unfinished garages. Initially the family had conceived of Clark as a brooding, leather-jacketed rebel, bouncing off the Recklers' bourgeois values. It had soon become apparent that Clark did not have a revolutionary bone in his body, let alone the soul of a vengeful Marxist. Clark was simply different, an iconoclast. He was a natural grease monkey hatched into a nice Jewish home. It was as if he'd been switched by cackling gypsies at birth.

Clark was exceedingly sweet. He was a bright, boundlessly outgoing individual who saw no need for excessive ambition or what he deemed unnecessary sanitary habits. Like all the Recklers, Clark was bone stubborn. He did as he pleased. He did not take money from the family, and he would not wear a proper corduroy sports jacket and a knit tie to Seders or other family events. Clark was as idiosyncratic as Joe. They could not have been less alike, but they were devoted.

Mrs. Reckler and Clark were often at potentially explosive loggerheads. In her heart, Mrs. Reckler still believed that someday Clark would realize the error of his ways, smack his forehead, enroll in graduate school, and become a classics professor, with suede elbow patches and a briar pipe. Mrs. Reckler loved Clark deeply, but she had no idea who Clark's real mother might be. She could not comprehend how she could have given birth to a being who decorated his home with beer cans.

"Here you go," said Clark, returning. He had two cans of beer jammed under one arm; his free hand gripped a carton of orange juice and two paper cups. He distributed these beverages, and everyone sipped.

"So," said Clark. "How's your trip going?"

"Very nicely," said Aunt Pola. "Clark, let me make you a proposition. If you move into a nice clean apartment, I'll buy you some glassware."

"I hate apartments," Clark said. "I hate landlords. This place is fine. We've got five acres and a barn. We don't need glassware."

"Hi, folks," said Patty, entering from the kitchen. Patty wore grease-spotted, repeatedly patched overalls over a faded red union suit. Her waist-length light-brown hair was tied back with a strip of rawhide, and she wore sturdy hiking boots with steel toes. Patty had an open, round face, scrubbed and immediately friendly. She was sunny and direct, a woman without flirtation or neurosis.

"I'd shake your hands," said Patty, "but I'd get gunk on 'em."

"Patty, come in and sit down," said Mrs. Reckler. "Patty, you remember my sisters, Ida and Pola."

"Sure thing," said Patty, sitting Indian-style on the floor and wrestling with the dog. "You're going to see the leaves change, right? You're going up to Maine."

"So, Patty," said Aunt Ida, "do you have your own motorcycle?"

"Yup," said Patty. "It's a Triumph, and Clark helped me rebuild it. It's basically a dirt bike, but I use it to get to work too."

Patty worked as a receptionist at a nearby mental health center. Clark made his money by reviving other folks' motorcycles and pickup trucks. He would occasionally take a day job at a motorcycle dealership, but he would always quit after he had squirreled away some funds and grown weary of the hours. Patty and Clark were less interested in careers than in serenity, establishing a nest.

"Patty, when you drive your motorcycle," Aunt Pola asked, "do you wear a helmet?"

"Sure," said Patty, draping her arm over Clark's knee.

"Thank God," said Mrs. Reckler. "Clark never used to wear a helmet. I always told him, I don't care if you get in an accident and die. But if you get in an accident and become a vegetable, don't come crying to me."

"That's touching," said Joe.

"Isn't it?" agreed Clark.

"Look at me," said Mrs. Reckler. "I have one child who can't get a driver's license and another one who only drives a Harley-Davidson. Where did I go wrong?"

"Beats me," said Clark.

"If you had been a decent mother, we'd both be driving Toyotas," Joe said.

"Face it, you have terrible children," said Patty.

"See?" said Mrs. Reckler. "She knows." Mrs. Reckler and Patty exchanged a knowing smile; Patty was willing to admit that Clark was difficult to live with.

"You don't have terrible children," said Aunt Ida. "They're wonderful boys."

"We are," said Joe.

"I am," said Clark.

"They are wonderful boys," Mrs. Reckler decided. "And I love them dearly."

Mrs. Reckler gazed at her sons; when she wasn't worrying about her children, she was terribly pleased with them. Somehow, despite their many eccentricities, they seemed happy. Mrs. Reckler was proud of Joe and Clark, because they drove her crazy.

"What's not to love?" said Joe.

15

Everyone relocated to the kitchen for lunch. The kitchen wasn't so much untidy as antiquated and worn. Most of the appliances dated from the 1950s, and the cobblestone-patterned vinyl flooring peeled and curled at the seams. The bulbous Kelvinator refrigerator was covered with colorful decals, which Clark had applied. The decals were mostly trademark logos, and said things like "Kawasaki," "Bell Helmets," "A-1 Motor Oil," and "Valvoline."

Everyone sat around a heavy, thickly varnished pine kitchen table. The carpentry was impressively sturdy.

"Clark made this table," Mrs. Reckler announced.

"Oh really?" said Aunt Ida, running her hands over the glossy, planed tabletop. "It's beautiful. You made this? Really? With a hammer?"

"Yup," said Clark. "We needed a kitchen table, and we couldn't afford to buy one, and I found all this lumber out in the barn. It's pretty solid."

Aunt Pola knelt and poked at the table from underneath. "This is very nice," she said, knocking on a cross-brace. "You know, I used to build things."

"Boys, do you remember?" Mrs. Reckler asked her sons. "Do you remember your blocks?"

"Of course," said Joe, recalling a childhood oak wagon with fat wooden wheels, painted schoolhouse red and filled

97

with oak building blocks in various useful shapes. "They were great."

"It was during the Depression," said Aunt Pola. "There were no jobs, so Nat and I opened our school. It was a nursery school, in a basement, in Brooklyn. Hedy, you were barely born. Ida, do you remember?"

"Of course," said Aunt Ida. "You made me help out in the mornings. I was furious. Mrs. Berman's Academy for Wee Ones."

"Of course you helped," said Aunt Pola. "You loved it; it was a good experience. We had no money. I mean, I have no money now, but back then, believe me, we had *no* money. So Nat and I built everything. We made little chairs and tables, and we made blocks for the children to play with, to build little towns."

"What happened to the school?" asked Patty.

"It closed," said Aunt Pola. "We ran it for six years; we did all right. But Nat got an offer to teach at P.S. 90, and then I got my offer to be vice-principal, so we closed the school. But we kept one of the little wagons with the blocks in them. First Ida's kids had them, and then you boys."

"They were great blocks," said Clark. "Where are they now?"

"Who knows?" said Aunt Pola. "I wanted to give them to Alicia's kids, but they disappeared."

"Don't look at me," said Mrs. Reckler. "After the boys were teenagers, I gave them back, all the blocks. You said you would put them in the basement of your apartment building."

"I suppose I did," said Aunt Pola. "And now they're gone. It's a great mystery."

"Probably the same guys who took your car," suggested Aunt Ida. "Now they're stealing blocks."

The random disappearance of the blocks saddened Joe. Even more than the blocks, Joe liked the tale behind them. He tried to imagine Pola and Nat Berman concocting a school during the bleak climate of the Depression, hammering and sawing, transforming a Brooklyn basement with bright paint and hard work. Aunt Pola was a powerhouse now, in the

1980s, when women were almost permitted such unseemly behavior. In the '30s she must have been extraordinary, forging ahead, relying on no one. Of course, Joe also found the title Mrs. Berman's Academy for Wee Ones highly amusing. Joe could just picture his Aunt Pola keeping those wee ones in line.

"I liked those blocks," Clark lamented. Clark's tone was almost angry. He sounded cruelly betrayed. Clark had an extremely righteous sense of injustice, and his blocks, his beloved property, had been wrenched from him.

"Don't worry, *bubbe*," said Mrs. Reckler, pinching Clark's cheek. "I'll buy you new blocks."

Clark rolled his eyes at his mother's pinch. Eye rolling reached majestically balletic proportions in the Reckler family. Joe liked to see his mother and Clark teasing one another. It always took the pair a while to relax in each other's presence, to warm up, to allow pinching.

"Who wants salad?" asked Patty, approaching the table with a large Tupperware bowl brimming with greens.

Patty and Clark served a delicious lunch, complete with meat loaf, two different patterns of paper plates, home-grown tomatoes, and crusty homemade raisin bread, one of Clark's specialties.

"This bread is delicious," said Aunt Pola, polishing off a hefty wedge. "You really made this?"

"With a hammer," Joe said.

"Be quiet," Mrs. Reckler told Joe. "You wish you could bake bread like your brother. And your father."

"Saul bakes?" said Aunt Pola, somewhat suspiciously.

"He loves it," said Mrs. Reckler. "What, I should bake?"

"My father loves baking bread to the point of real pathology," Joe told his aunts. "He bought this bread cookbook a few years ago. And he baked from scratch, with kneading and yeast and letting the dough rise with a dish towel over it. And after he had baked his first two loaves, he was so proud that he took the loaves into the living room and he put them on the velvet ottoman. He posed them, and he got his camera and took pictures."

"It's true," said Mrs. Reckler, laughing. "He still does

it, when he bakes a particularly beautiful loaf. He drives me crazy; he keeps showing me the pictures. He said, Hedy, isn't this a beautiful loaf of bread? And I say, Yes, Saul, I remember that loaf; I ate it.''

All the sisters laughed. Mr. Reckler and Clark did enjoy a nearly unnatural fondness for baking bread. The unassailable logic of the ancient process appealed to them. They derived tremendous personal satisfaction from assembling ingredients, duplicating a recipe to the letter, and producing a flawless, highly appetizing finished product, a laboratory triumph. Prior to his retirement, Mr. Reckler had been a physicist and an editor of science textbooks. He saw baking bread as a marvelous equation, a matter of X and Y combining to form a tasty, pumpkin-flavored, walnut-studded Z. Clark found baking bread cozily similar to successfully repairing a transmission, a matter of correct parts and professional procedure. Both Clark and his father occasionally had to be forced to eat their fragrant, buttery creations. Devouring the breads seemed secondary, even savage, disloyal to the loaves.

"So, Joe, why don't you bake?" asked Aunt Pola. "What's your problem?"

"Please," said Joe scornfully. "I am my mother's son. And my mother bakes Duncan Hines cakes."

"Oh, you!" said Mrs. Reckler, swatting Joe. "I do not!"

"So you make cakes from a mix," said Aunt Ida. "It's nothing to be ashamed of. Not really."

"I never bake cakes from a mix," protested Mrs. Reckler. "My son is a liar."

"All right, I'm sorry," said Joe. "She doesn't bake cakes from a mix. She buys cakes."

Mrs. Reckler gasped and swatted Joe again.

"You buy cakes?" said Aunt Pola. "From the store?"

"I do not!" said Mrs. Reckler. "Occasionally, once in a very blue moon, once in a million years, I may make a cake from a mix, to save time. I *never* buy cakes. I'm going to kill you," Mrs. Reckler told Joe.

Aunt Pola and Aunt Ida baked cakes solely from scratch, the way their mother had taught them to, as a time-honored feminine skill required for landing a respectable spouse. The Esker sisters all remembered their mother in a flowered, tuniclike apron, relentlessly pummeling a slab of dough, her arms floured to the elbows, strands of hair stuck to her moist brow. Aunt Pola and Aunt Ida had even learned to bake challah, the traditional Jewish braided bread, from scratch. As a very young mother, Mrs. Reckler had once attempted a scratch cake. She had found the *Joy of Cooking* recipe barbaric and time-consuming, an insidious plot to imprison women in their kitchens for days on end, measuring vanilla and separating egg whites. Joe loved his mother because she knew there were far better things to do than perform ostentatious pioneer-gal chores in the kitchen. Joe actually far preferred the luxurious chemical tang of mix cakes and canned frosting; this was a natural by-product of his Quick 'n' Easy New Jersey heritage.

"Well, *I* bake mix cakes," said Patty. "They taste fine. As for Clark . . ."

Patty rummaged through a pile of back mail and tattered address books on a Formica countertop. She disinterred a batch of stiff Polaroid photographs and fanned them out on the table. Each Polaroid featured one of Clark's recent breads, blushing modestly in direct sunlight.

"Aren't they great?" Clark said. "See, this one was my first date-nut bread."

"How did it taste?" asked Aunt Ida, admiring the Polaroid.

"We still don't know," sighed Patty. "He won't let anyone near it. He froze it. It's still in the freezer, in Reynolds Wrap."

"Good boy," said Aunt Pola approvingly. "You see, he's thinking ahead." Clark may have had tresses to his waist, and he may have zipped over the back roads on his mufflerless Harley-Davidson, and he may not have finished his junior year, but his ancestry has been proved beyond a doubt: he froze things.

Aunt Ida finished her lunch in just under two minutes. No one had actually seen her eat, but her plate sparkled.

"Ida, you're done already?" said Mrs. Reckler.

"It was all delicious," said Aunt Ida, dabbing at her lips with a paper napkin. "Patty and Clark, you make a wonderful lunch. My compliments to the chef."

"Ida, why do you eat so fast?" asked Mrs. Reckler. "You always do this. You make me feel like a slob, because I'm still having salad and you've polished off dessert."

"Ida always eats fast," Aunt Pola said. "She's afraid if she doesn't eat her food the Cossacks will take it back."

"The Cossacks?" asked Patty. "In Massachusetts?"

"You never know," said Aunt Pola. All of the Esker sisters had been born in America, so they had never experienced any actual acquaintance with Cossacks. Early in the century, their parents had emigrated from Russia, via Ellis Island.

"Mama always used to say," Aunt Pola recalled, " 'Clean your plate, make it shine, or the Cossacks will.' "

"Mama never knew any Cossacks," said Mrs. Reckler.

"That's true," said Aunt Ida. "But I always believed her. I always believed she had Cossacks waiting in the next room, sitting on the sofa, ready to take my food. I was so confused, I thought the Cossacks worked for Mama."

Joe and Clark's grandparents had died while both boys were still infants. From photographs, Joe knew that his mother's mother had been a big-bosomed, somewhat stern-looking woman, who wore severe gray coats and wielded a handbag the size of a valise. She always gripped the strap of the handbag with both hands, as if she had dropped a brick inside the purse and was about to slam someone. Joe's grandfather had been a tall, white-haired fellow with a hazy, regal mien, the air of someone who was about to either pontificate or request more soup.

"You didn't know Grandma," said Aunt Pola, to Joe and Clark. "She was some tough cookie. Hoo boy."

"Was she ever," said Mrs. Reckler. "You know what she did once? I'll never forget it. One time, it was Ida's birthday, she was twelve. And Mama made cupcakes, from scratch, of course, with chocolate frosting. She made a whole lot of cupcakes, and she put a candle on one, and she brought them all out on a tray. And Ida blew out her candle, and we all ate the cupcakes.''

"Man oh man, I remember those cupcakes," said Aunt Ida, shaking her head.

"That sounds nice," said Patty.

"You think so," said Mrs. Reckler. "Well, remember the chocolate frosting? It was Ex-Lax. Mama had melted all of these laxatives in a pan and made frosting. And she didn't tell anybody."

"After we ate those cupcakes," said Aunt Ida, "boy, were we busy."

"That is the most horrible story I have ever heard," Joe said. He was suddenly not at all unhappy that he had never known his grandmother. "Why did she do that? With the Ex-Lax?"

"That was just Mama," said Aunt Pola philosophically. "She believed in regularity. Good digestion. The plumbing, she called it. A clean mind, a clean body. The Cossacks, they weren't so clean. Mama was a wonderful woman. A saint."

"She was," agreed Mrs. Reckler. "And a maniac. You see, Clark? You think I'm so bad? You're lucky. You waited a generation. I'm diluted."

"I don't know about that," said Clark.

"Exactly," Joe agreed.

"Oooh!" howled Mrs. Reckler. "I'll kill them!" Mrs. Reckler reached out to smack both her sons at once, but Joe and Clark, giggling like idiots, jumped up from the kitchen table.

16

After lunch, Clark took the group on a gentlemanly tour of his estate. The farmhouse sat amid untended meadow and low dirt hills, all fairly bedraggled, too exhausted to be thought of as scenery. There were also chunks of mangled concrete strewn about, half buried by weeds; these were the foundations of earlier, long-razed outbuildings.

"Don't look," Aunt Ida told Joe. "It's still not Vermont."

"Be careful in the barn," Clark instructed.

"Why?" asked Aunt Pola, swinging open the rotting barn door.

"We think it's going to fall down," Patty said cheerfully.

"The landlord says he's probably going to have it torn down," said Clark. "He's worried about the insurance and shit like that, in case the whole thing crashes on somebody."

"I think I'll just stay out here," said Joe.

Aunt Pola was already inside the barn, her hands on her hips, staring up at the sagging beams in the dim, dust-swirled light. The barn was empty except for a mound of moldering window frames and Clark's metal tool chests, anodized aluminum bureaus neatly stuffed with graduated lug wrenches and advanced power drills and handy coils of jumper cables.

"So what goes on out here?" Aunt Pola asked. "Is there a cow?"

"You have a cow?" asked Aunt Ida. "A moo cow?"

"Don't be ridiculous," said Mrs. Reckler. "What's he going to do with a cow? Fix the carburetor?"

"Actually, we were thinking about it," said Clark. "Getting some chickens or something. Livestock."

"But I said I wasn't taking care of them," said Patty. "And so we stopped talking about it."

"Good girl," said Mrs. Reckler. She and Patty swapped a supportive nod. They both knew that Clark was highly adept at pipedreams, at plotting elaborate projects that he was certain would require no capital and little effort.

"You know, this could be very nice," Mrs. Reckler said, squinting into the barn. She and Joe and Aunt Ida hovered in the doorway of the barn, taking precautions in case of bat activity or sudden cattle drives. Only Aunt Pola had been bold enough to enter.

"If you would fix it up, this could be very cozy," Mrs. Reckler continued. Mrs. Reckler's own urge toward fantasy now swung into high gear. In her mind, she renovated the unsalvageable barn into a picturesque country retreat out of *Better Homes and Gardens*, something thoroughly exterminated and quaintly refurbished. She invented whitewashed walls, ginghamy café curtains, gleaming plank floors, and earthenware jugs, or perhaps porcelain pitchers, arranged with dried wildflowers.

"Mother," said Clark pointedly. Clark always strenuously resisted his mother's attempts at remaking his tumbledown surroundings. He knew that if his mother were allowed free rein, the barn might soon boast shelf liner, framed antique lithographs, and Oriental bowls of potpourri.

"I'm only suggesting things," Mrs. Reckler huffed. "If you want to live in a barn that's going to fall down on your head, be my guest, by all means. I'm just saying it could be very nice. It's not a criminal offense."

"We don't live in the barn," Clark chided.

"I think it's a lovely barn," said Aunt Ida. "If I was a cow, I'd be very happy here."

"Not if you were a decent cow," said Aunt Pola, shaking her head.

The group trekked back to the main house. Joe was dispatched to the Oldsmobile to fetch the gifts Mrs. Reckler and her sisters had bought for Clark and Patty.

"This is for you," said Aunt Ida, handing Clark his own plastic shopping bag full of videocassettes. "But half of them are for Patty."

"Good deal," said Clark, admiring the tapes.

"Thank you," said Patty. "We need these; we tape everything."

"A barn and a VCR," commented Aunt Pola. "Country life."

"This is for you," said Joe, passing Clark his menorah key chain. "From Aunt Pola."

"And, Patty, this is for you," said Aunt Pola, providing Patty with a small brown paper bundle. Patty undid the bundle and found an abstract blotch of metal, a miniature boomerang of burnished copper daubed with teal-blue enamel and raised red speckles.

"Thank you," said Patty. "What is it?"

Joe was caught off guard by Patty's forthright question. Stumped as they might be by some of Aunt Pola's more enigmatic gifts, no one in the family had ever dared demand an immediate translation.

"It's lovely," said Aunt Ida, covering for Patty.

"It is," said Mrs. Reckler. "It's a lovely thing."

"It's a brooch," said Aunt Pola. "See, here's the clasp. I got it in Tel Aviv; it's an abstract Star of David. I know you're not Jewish; that's why I thought the abstract would be good."

"I like it," said Patty, pinning the brooch to the strap of her overalls. "I'm an honorary Jew."

"Don't wish it," said Aunt Pola. "People will come burn your house down."

"Who?" asked Patty, confused. "Who'll burn my house down?"

"Don't ask," said Aunt Pola. "But being a Jew, it's not easy. It's no ride in the park."

"But you'll be very bright," said Joe. For this remark, Joe received a pinch from his mother, on the elbow.

"Neat," said Clark, inspecting his key chain. "I can always use one of these."

"It's for keys," said Aunt Pola. "And it's got this little menorah. Up here, I bet you don't see too many menorahs."

"Not on key chains," Clark admitted.

"I have one too," said Joe, and he and Clark nodded at each other. This nod transmitted the message "Aunt Pola means well, and if we're not appreciative Mom will pinch our elbows, and at least it's not an embroidered yarmulke."

"Patty, this is for you," said Mrs. Reckler, handing Patty a tissue-wrapped package. "I hope you can do something with it."

Patty pulled back the tissue, revealing six precisely folded yards of beautiful fabric, a nubbly, pale-yellow linen. Mrs. Reckler could never resist pretty fabrics, especially remnants, odd lengths tossed out on sale tables. She was forever falling victim to end runs of vivid Indonesian batik or lush wide-wale loden-green corduroy or tiny French herbal prints. Mrs. Reckler responded to fabric on a primal level, as sensuous color and inviting texture. This was fortunate, as Mrs. Reckler hated to sew. As with knitting, she could perform simple stitches if forced to at saber point, but she considered actually owning a sewing machine, some computerized, humming behemoth, to be shudderingly close to a prison sentence. Sewing, a matter of threading microscopic needles, straining your back, and following a flimsy, indecipherable paper pattern, struck Mrs. Reckler as the reason God invented swearing.

"This is beautiful," said Patty, draping the linen over her arm and studying it. "I can make a skirt. Thank you so much."

"She sews?" said Aunt Ida approvingly. Aunt Ida and Aunt Pola, of course, could whip up five ruffled cocktail aprons and a fringed fitted chenille bedspread with coordinated pillow shams all in an afternoon, on their trusty, indispensable Singer zig-zags.

"Of course she sews," said Mrs. Reckler. "I'm the only one who can't sew, so I buy all of this fabric and give it away. Patty, do you really like it?"

"Of course," said Patty, somewhat perplexed by the question.

"Patty," said Joe, "in this family you have to *swear* that you *adore* something, otherwise we'll think you're just being polite. If you don't swear, my mother will give you a cash refund. My mother will now pinch my elbow because I told you this."

"I'm not pinching anybody," said Mrs. Reckler. "I just wish I had a gun. Only I don't know who I'd shoot, Joe or myself, for having such a terrible child."

"I *swear*," Patty dutifully told Mrs. Reckler. "I really do love it."

"I believe her," said Aunt Pola. "And, Patty, if you're lying, it's fine. Just mail the fabric to me; I'll make curtains."

"Here," said Mrs. Reckler, thrusting a shiny cardboard box at Clark. "You'll hate it."

"If I'm going to hate it," said Clark, "why are you giving it to me?"

"Oh, I don't know," said Mrs. Reckler. "Because I'm your mother. I'm sorry; maybe you'll like it. I hope so."

"Place your bets," said Joe.

"Be quiet," Aunt Pola told Joe. "Clark, open it. Let's see."

Clark opened the box, holding it away from his body, as if the pipe bomb within might detonate at any second. Inside the box, swathed in tissue, was a pale-blue, full-cut oxford-cloth shirt with a button-down collar.

"I was at Bamberger's, they were having a sale in menswear," said Mrs. Reckler, rushing to her own defense. "It's all cotton; you don't have to wear it with a tie. But I thought you might like a nice shirt, so you can take Patty to the movies or out to dinner."

"I can take Patty to Burger King and I can wear a T-shirt," Clark said, staring at the shirt with deep suspicion, as if the cotton were woven with strands of kryptonite or soaked in some invisible molecule poisonous to his species.

"I get to go to Burger King," said Patty. "Aren't I lucky?" Patty was wisely refraining from direct comment on the shirt.

"It's a beautiful shirt," said Aunt Pola, and then, to Mrs. Reckler, "Did they have any more?"

"I don't remember," said Mrs. Reckler. "Yes, but this was the last Medium."

"Mom," said Clark, "why did you buy this?"

"Because I'm a crazy person," said Mrs. Reckler. "Look, wear it or don't wear it. I could care less. Believe me, I'm not going to sit up nights wondering if you're wearing a decent shirt without holes in it."

"Yes you will," said Joe.

"You're gonna get smacked," Aunt Ida advised Joe.

"Mom, I'm not going to use this," said Clark. "You always do this."

Mrs. Reckler was committed to filling Clark's home with inappropriate gifts. For many years now she had been attempting to shop her son into submission. She believed that a dress shirt or a pressed pair of chinos could possess supernatural abilities. Mrs. Reckler was certain that if Clark would just try on a Harris tweed sports jacket with leather buttons, if he would just slip into it, the garment would realign Clark's metabolism and cause him to apply to Princeton, or at least to wash his socks.

On a rational level, Mrs. Reckler knew that Clark was happy, amid the spare gas tanks and stray spark plugs that accessorized his bedroom. On a spiritual plane, Mrs. Reckler refused to believe that anyone could be both happy and grimy. Happiness for Mrs. Reckler entailed a loaded dishwasher and an extra handkerchief, mildew-free grout between the bathroom tiles and something with a hood when the weather was wintry or wet. She could forgive Clark his affection for reckless, exhaust-spewing motorcycles and could accept his woodland retreat, but she would never comprehend his utter disinterest in a nice clean shirt.

Mrs. Reckler was a fan of appearances, and Clark hankered for ultimate comfort. Both mother and son occasionally allowed their convictions to balloon into manias, even into weapons. As a teenager, Clark would wheel his motorcycle into the Reckler living room while his parents were out for the evening. Angling the vehicle on the freshly vacuumed wall-to-wall carpeting, leaning it on its kickstand in front of the just-plumped velvet sofa, he would snap a Polaroid of his

anarchic motorcycle and then wheel it out of the house, returning it to its rightful quarters in the garage. Mrs. Reckler
would be unaware that a photo session had occurred, until
she came upon the Polaroid tossed artfully on Clark's desktop.

Mrs. Reckler's revenge always took the form of di-
abolically unwelcome presents. Over the years, Clark had
returned scores of hearty down-filled vests, designer bathrobes, and collegiate Shetland crewnecks. Mrs. Reckler
wanted Clark to look nice, so strangers wouldn't stare at him
and so her sisters wouldn't think she was an irresponsible
mother, the breed of mother who allowed her child to appear
before the public dressed in rags.

Clark and his mother shared a fierce pride. Neither would
submit to a cease-fire, or even treaty negotiations, in the
vigorous war of the nice shirts.

"Mom," said Clark, in his living room, "I'm not going
to wear this, so just take it back."

"You don't know you're not going to wear it," Mrs. Reckler countered. "You don't have magical powers, you can't
see into the future. Who knows, one day everything else you
own might be in the laundry bag, and you'll go to the drawer
and all you'll have is this shirt, and you'll have to wear it."

Mrs. Reckler's eyes glittered. She had masterminded a
fail-safe scenario.

"I'd walk around naked," Clark replied. "Or I'd take
something dirty out of the laundry bag and put it on."

"But what if everything was already in the washing machine?" said Mrs. Reckler.

"I'd take a Magic Marker and draw a shirt on my skin,"
Clark said.

"He wins," said Aunt Ida.

"Because he's crazy," said Aunt Pola. "He's a cuckoo
bird."

"Isn't this a mature discussion," said Joe.

"You know," said Patty, slinging her arm around Clark's
neck, "your mother only has one problem. She doesn't know
her son is a pig."

"That's right," said Clark proudly.

"He's not a pig," said Mrs. Reckler. "He just wants people to think he's a pig, to get back at me."

"That's right," said Joe. "Late at night, when no one's looking, Clark puts on white tie and tails."

"Patty," said Mrs. Reckler, "how do you put up with it? Don't you ever want Clark to look nice? Just for a change? Just for half a minute?"

"Of course," said Patty. "But I'd have to tie him up first."

"Exactly," said Clark, grinning.

"I give up," said Mrs. Reckler. "Do what you want. I could care less. Really."

"Let's go," said Aunt Ida. "Leave the shirt; maybe when we leave he'll try it on."

"Maybe when we leave he'll use it to polish his motorcycle," speculated Aunt Pola.

"Not a bad idea," said Clark, nodding.

"Clark, I tell you what," said Aunt Pola. "If you cut your hair, move out of this godforsaken dump, and go back to school, you can come and visit me in West Palm." Aunt Pola had retired in glory from the New York City school system five years earlier, after spending over four tireless decades rising from vice-principal to assistant superintendent of her district. She now lived six months of every year in a retirement community in West Palm Beach, Florida. The community was called Heritage Village. Aunt Pola owned a Heritage Village condominium, a spacious pastel one-bedroom apartment with a view of the pool and of the mahjongg fiends who surrounded it.

"I'll have to think about that one," said Clark, of Aunt Pola's offer.

"You'd have a good time," Aunt Pola predicted. "Patty, you can come too. Patty, I tell you what. Tonight, when Clark is asleep, you cut his hair and burn all his clothes, and then you can both get on a plane. And don't worry—it's West Palm, it's not Miami."

"What's the difference?" asked Patty.

"Well," said Aunt Pola, shocked, "it's a world of difference. Miami is very . . . ordinary. It's very nice, don't get me wrong, but it's nothing, absolutely zilch. West Palm is gorgeous; it has special features. It's not just a lot of old people in toreador pants, talking about their gallstones.''

"It's not?" said Aunt Ida. Aunt Pola shot her a look. "Oh, it's *not*," Aunt Ida assured Clark and Patty. "It's a wonderful place. When the queen of England goes to Florida, she stays in West Palm.''

"Really?" said Aunt Pola, impressed but not surprised. "Well, she's a smart woman, that's why she's queen. So, Clark and Patty, what do you say? Do we have a deal?''

Aunt Pola had always had a bedrock faith in bribes. Over the years, Joe and Clark had been offered crisp five-dollar bills, new Schwinn bicycles, even U.S. Savings Bonds, all in exchange for proper haircuts, acceptable table manners, and decent attire at weddings. Aunt Pola's bribes rarely worked, but she felt better, knowing she'd tried. Aunt Pola believed in morality, in doing things for the right reasons, but she also believed that a little nudge never hurt anyone, that the promise of a Batman comic book could get the ball rolling.

"I tell you what," Patty told Aunt Pola. "Clark can keep his hair and his clothes, and you can come stay here with us, instead of going to West Palm.''

"Oooh, she's very good," said Aunt Ida, appreciating Patty's counteroffer.

"No, thank you," said Aunt Pola. "This is no place for an old person.''

"What about an old person with a vacuum?" asked Joe.

"Be quiet," said Mrs. Reckler. "We're leaving.''

Mrs. Reckler kissed Clark. She gripped him by the shoulders and stared at him, shaking her head. "I love you very much," she told him, "whoever you are." Then Mrs. Reckler kissed Patty. "Patty, you're either a saint or a lunatic. I don't know how you stand it.''

"She's a lunatic," said Clark, hugging Patty.

"He's so sweet," said Patty, exchanging another sympathetic grimace with Mrs. Reckler.

"Goodbye," said Aunt Ida, kissing both Clark and Patty. "Don't listen to anyone. I think your house is lovely and you both look very nice.''

"But your son's a doctor," said Aunt Pola.

"His house is filthy too," Aunt Ida assured Clark.

"Goodbye and goodbye," said Aunt Pola, kissing Clark and Patty. "Remember, whenever you come to your senses, I'm waiting in West Palm with an empty guest room. And clean sheets. And a bar of soap."

"Keep waiting," said Clark.

"He's so fresh," said Aunt Pola, giving Clark's cheek a viscerally sharp pinch.

"We're going," said Mrs. Reckler, nearing the front door. "I would ask if anyone has to use the bathroom, but I don't want to even think about Clark's bathroom."

"Should we look?" asked Aunt Pola. "Just for a shock?"

"I'm sure it's very nice," said Aunt Ida.

"Do you have a brochure?" Joe asked his brother.

"Get out," Clark commanded his relatives.

Mrs. Reckler and her sisters picked their way through the front yard, avoiding the rusted coffee cans and brake drums, and out to the car. Joe lingered behind, for a word alone with his brother and Patty.

"What's wrong?" Joe asked. "Don't you want to go to West Palm?"

"Why don't *you* go to West Palm?" asked Clark. "And why don't you wear that shirt?"

"You could have pretended," Joe said. "You could have said you loved the shirt and then put it in the bottom drawer."

"That just would've encouraged her," said Clark. "Then she would give me another shirt. Where does she find them? I hate those shirts."

"Why does your mother do that?" Patty asked. "It's really strange. I mean, she's been around Clark for a long time. Why does she keep trying?"

"Oh, Patty," said Joe. "You are such a normal person."

"I am?" asked Patty. "As opposed to what?"

"A Jewish person," said Joe. "A relative of the Esker sisters. You see, my mother thinks that if Clark would just wear a nice shirt, he would become a Supreme Court Justice by the weekend."

"Exactly," said Clark.

"And my brother," said Joe, "thinks that if he puts on a

nice shirt, his skin will rot and fall off and the earth will leave its orbit and fly into the sun.''

"And we'd all fry," Clark agreed.

"So what do you think Clark should do?" Patty asked, with genuine curiosity. "What should he do when your mother gives him a shirt?"

"He should lie," said Joe. "It's very simple."

The fundamental difference between Joe and Clark was that Joe saw life less as a matter of truth and more as a question of style. Joe lived to steal and shop and nap; Clark liked to repair and build and swig beer. Clark knew nothing of his mother's or brother's larceny; Clark was not a shopper. He went for gaskets and fan belts and gearshifts. Neither Joe nor Mrs. Reckler would consider such items worth browsing for, let alone trying on.

Clark and his father both had ordered minds, calmly scientific outlooks. They liked to relax at home on the front steps, debating alternative methods of fixing the lint trap in the washer-dryer, or the Oldsmobile's fuel-injection system. Joe and his mother had sensibilities awash in luxury goods, in sinful dreams of rampant *tchotchkes* and thrilling Broadway overtures and back-to-school wardrobes. If something broke, Clark and Mr. Reckler patched it, and relished the challenge. Joe and Mrs. Reckler leapt to buy a new one, and maybe grab chocolate-chip ice-cream cones with sprinkles while they were out.

The Reckler family was a yin-yang proposition, a merry caldron of opposites. One team preferred to shop and pocket, to pursue happiness in the giddy temptations of the outside world. The other team was more sedentary and contented. If the Recklers had been a Cro-Magnon cave family, Joe and Mrs. Reckler would have been the hunters, venturing out in the moonlight to stalk dinner and furs. Clark and Mr. Reckler would have tended the fire and completed the cave paintings.

Joe and his brother got along famously, as each thought the other was insane. There was no jealousy. Clark loathed Manhattan, finding it gruesomely strident and overcrowded, and Joe didn't have a driver's license. The brothers marveled at each other, applauding the show. Both Clark and Joe found the fact that they were related pleasingly comic.

"You're actually traveling with them?" Clark asked. "In the same car?"

"Uh-huh," said Joe. "I'm building up good-child points. I figure after spending a week in that car and watching the leaves change, I won't have to do anything else nice for at least ten years. I could kill someone, and if they brought me to court I would just say, 'But, Your Honor, I spent a week in New England with my family.' And the judge would say, 'You may go free.' "

"I like your aunts," said Patty. "And your mother is nutty, but she's terrific."

"Yeah, 'cause she gave you some fabric," said Clark. "She just bought you off."

"Of course they're terrific," said Joe. "They're wonderful. But I'm still not flying down to West Palm."

Clark handed Joe a homemade banana-almond bread, crunched in foil and tied with a red ribbon. Joe found this very generous, although he secretly wished that Clark would make inroads in baking things with frosting.

Joe ran out to the car. Everyone else was already on board. Clark and Patty waved goodbye, and Cleo, the mongrel, barked helpfully.

"Are we ready?" asked Aunt Ida, from the back seat.

"Believe me, we're ready," said Mrs. Reckler, backing the car out of the dirt driveway.

"Bye-bye!" said Aunt Pola, waving to Clark and Patty. "Look at them. It's like *American Gothic*. Where's the pitchfork?"

"She's a lovely girl," said Aunt Ida. "Just lovely."

"I love Patty," said Mrs. Reckler, steering the car out onto the road. "What she's doing with him I'll never know."

"He's lovely," said Joe.

"Smack him," advised Aunt Pola.

"Your brother is a marvelous boy," said Mrs. Reckler to Joe. "But a girl would have to be loony to live in that house.

Patty is adorable. I always want to tell her, Patty, you can do better.''

"You're such a nice mother," said Joe. "Wholesome."

"I am a nice mother," said Mrs. Reckler. "I went, I visited, we didn't fight too much. I didn't burst into tears or burn the house down. I think I'm a total gem."

"Mom, they're very happy," said Joe. "I agree with you, I couldn't live that way either, but they like it."

"They like it because it drives me crazy," said Mrs. Reckler. "That's the appeal."

"That's not true," said Joe. "They just like living in filth. It's their taste. Early Filth."

"That's right," said Aunt Ida. "That's their thing."

"It's a thing, all right," said Aunt Pola, nestling in her coat.

Aunt Ida and Aunt Pola began a conversation centering on antacids. Mrs. Reckler lowered her voice, so only Joe could hear her.

"I love your brother very much," said Mrs. Reckler. "But after being in that house, I just decided something. When we do L. L. Bean, maybe we'll take $12,000. Just a little tad more."

"Why?" asked Joe. "What for?"

"The kitchen," said Mrs. Reckler.

17

The group rolled into Bennington, Vermont, a little before nine o'clock that night. Mrs. Reckler drove into the parking lot of the Grand Vermonter Motor Inn, where the Recklers had often checked in on past idylls through New England.

"We're here!" she called out, parking the car.

"We made good time," said Aunt Ida.

"I can't wait to get out and stretch my legs," said Aunt Pola. Leg-stretching was an integral component of any Reckler vacation. The practice entailed standing in a parking lot and moaning. Joe watched as his mother and aunt stepped out of the car and rubbed their lower backs and took tentative steps.

"Oh, it feels so good to get out," said Aunt Ida, rolling her shoulders.

"I can barely walk," said Aunt Pola. "Joe, can you walk?"

"I'll try," said Joe. Joe liked the fact that in his family, sitting in a car was considered an arduous activity, a marathon event.

"I'm coming," said Mrs. Reckler, who was applying fresh lipstick as she inspected herself in the mirror clamped to the eyeshade. Mrs. Reckler wanted to look nice, even for the motel desk clerk.

"All right," said Mrs. Reckler, stepping out of the car. "Oooh, I'm all knotted. We'll get the keys and we'll all take nice long hot baths and use the facilities."

As usual, Joe felt that his mother's remarks were directed primarily at him. He had just been accused of being both sooty and in dire need of a bathroom. Joe decided not to comment, as both accusations held merit.

The group filed into the Grand Vermonter's Manager's Office. The motor inn was appealingly designed as a cluster of freestanding buildings, modern but sheathed in planks of silvery, weathered birch. Each building was two stories high, and the enclave faced inward, onto a grassy courtyard with a built-in pool, from which mist rose. There were graceful, leafy maples sheltering the pool, and winding flagstone paths. The Grand Vermonter felt less like a motel and more like a superbly landscaped garden apartment complex, pale towers at a clearing. It was set back from the road, for a restful exclusivity, a cloistered mood. Mr. and Mrs. Reckler had happened on the Grand Vermonter fifteen years earlier; they had returned almost every autumn since.

Joe also appreciated the Grand Vermonter, as he did all motels and hotels. Joe was a great devotee of impersonal luxury. He reveled in crisp, freshly laundered sheets and those miniature soaps wrapped in shiny paper bearing a flattering "artist's rendering" of the premises. To Joe, the Grand Vermonter was a cooing nanny, a wayside cloud of pampering to nestle in, devoid of responsibility. Joe prized grand, expense-account Manhattan hotels, world-class dazzlers like the Plaza or the Pierre, and he felt equal ardor for the less bombastic charms of Holiday Inns and Ramadas, mass-market lodgings with clanking ice machines and gooey abstract assembly-line oil paintings of the Golden Gate Bridge. Joe loved any place that loved him back, stroking him with room service, folders of complimentary stationery and postcards, and cardboard triangles explaining the dialing for long-distance calls.

The Manager's Office was a glassed-in corner of one of the Grand Vermonter wings. Aunt Pola had insisted she make the reservations, since Mrs. Reckler had provided transportation.

"We have a reservation," Aunt Pola told the desk clerk, a pleasantly goony fellow with a wide polyester tie and a prominent tie tack. "It's under Berman."

"Berman," the desk clerk repeated, rummaging through his desktop computer. "Oh yes, here it comes. That will be room nineteen, in the rear. Here's your key; just sign here, if you would."

"Where's my key?" Mrs. Reckler asked her sister.

"I'll keep the key," said Aunt Pola. "In my bag."

"No, I mean where's the key to my room? And the key for Joe's room?"

"What are you talking about?" said Aunt Pola. "We're all in nineteen."

"What?" said Joe.

"Pola, what are you talking about?" asked Mrs. Reckler. "You only reserved one room?"

"Of course," said Aunt Pola. "With a double bed for me and Ida, another bed for you, and they're bringing in a cot for Joe."

"Excuse me," said Joe. "I don't understand. What are we, an Olympic team?"

"Pola, are you crazy?" said Mrs. Reckler. "One room?"

"What, there are only four of us," said Aunt Pola. "Why waste the space? What's the problem?"

"*Pola,*" said Mrs. Reckler, who then realized that the desk clerk was listening with avidity. Mrs. Reckler grabbed her sister's arm and dragged her to a far corner, beside a redwood planter eternally abloom with plastic rhododendron.

"Uh-oh," said Aunt Ida, to Joe. "Trouble in Dodge City."

"Aunt Ida," said Joe, "is she crazy?"

"Uch," sighed Aunt Ida. "No, she's not crazy. That would be better; we could commit her. She's just Pola. She's . . . what would you call it . . . ?"

"Thrifty?" said Joe.

"You're a nice boy," said Aunt Ida.

"Pola," Mrs. Reckler said to her sister, trying to keep her

voice down. "This is too much. It's my money, I want my own room, and so does Joe. Maybe Ida does too, she deserves it."

"Hedy, calm down," said Aunt Pola. "You're getting hysterical. Believe me, it's for the best. Why throw money away, down the drain? We'll have fun."

"Pola," said Mrs. Reckler, "the last time I lived with you and Ida was back in Queens, and believe me, it had its drawbacks. I'm an adult now; I like having my own room. Joe likes his privacy."

"His privacy?" Aunt Pola snorted. "What is he hiding?"

"Life is short," said Mrs. Reckler. "And I'm not spending my vacation in the girls' dorm."

Mrs. Reckler went to the desk to negotiate additional rooms. Aunt Pola joined Ida and Joe. "Your mother is a crazy one," Aunt Pola told Joe.

"Aunt Pola," Joe said, "we'll be too cramped in one room."

"Ida, you be the judge," Aunt Pola said, turning to her remaining sister. Ida flinched. "Ida, tell me: I trust your common sense. You've always been the sensible one, at least in the past. Should we all stay in one room, like a big happy family? Where we'll have a terrific time, where we'll be together like a family should be, and where we'll save Lord knows how much, from these highway bandits? Or should we all sit in different rooms, all alone, like animals at the zoo, like strangers at Alcatraz? I tell you what: why not, instead of staying in separate rooms, why don't we just take the money and burn it, have a big bonfire, like we could care less, like we don't need to buy food, and gasoline for the trip. You tell me, Ida, you settle it. I'll respect your wishes. Is that what we should do? Have a big bonfire?"

Aunt Ida's eyes darted from side to side, seeking escape. She pulled her coat closed. "You do what you want," Ida finally said, the eternal diplomat. "You're both my sister. I'm not taking sides."

"Ida, that's very touching," said Aunt Pola. "Yes, Hedy and I are both your sisters. Only, one of us is your smart sister, and the other—Joe, don't listen—and the other sister is cracked in the head.''

Mrs. Reckler returned to the fold at this moment.

''So,'' said Aunt Ida, grateful to be off the hot seat. ''What's new?''

''They're full up,'' said Mrs. Reckler, grimly. ''Until tomorrow night. So just for tonight, we'll share. We'll make the best of it. Let's get our things.''

Aunt Pola tried not to be smug. ''You see?'' she said. ''It's God's will. He knows. We'll have fun.''

''Whoopee,'' Aunt Ida said to Joe, nudging him with her elbow.

The room would have been more than pleasant had it been occupied by, at most, a relatively petite honeymooning couple. It was filled mostly by two double beds with quilted floral bedspreads and matching quilted headboards. There was also a blond Danish-modern desk, a woklike hanging brass lamp on a chain, and a cumbersome Zenith color TV bolted to a metal tripod. The room's one small window overlooked the parking lot.

''Pola,'' said Mrs. Reckler, ''at least you could have gotten a room on the courtyard, with a balcony.''

''Why do we need a balcony?'' asked Aunt Pola. ''We'll be outdoors all day. What's there to see? Some trees and a swimming pool. We've all seen those things. Joe, have you ever seen a swimming pool?''

''No,'' said Joe, just to cause trouble. ''And I was counting on it.''

''Don't be smart,'' said Aunt Pola. ''It's a lovely room. I'm crazy about it.''

''I don't know,'' said Joe. ''It's a little spacious. We'll get lost.''

''Hellooo!'' Aunt Ida called out, as if yodeling across a vast canyon. She and Joe were actually standing on either side of a double bed.

''I think it's a perfectly nice room,'' said Aunt Pola. ''Look, isn't this a nice lamp? See, it goes on and off. And here's a big desk, with drawers, and a color TV, with all these buttons to push. What more do you need? We've got all the modern comforts; it's like a paradise, like a suite at the Waldorf. But listen, if everyone's going to be upset, and mad at me, for saving us a fortune, I'll tell you what I'll do. Here's what I'll do—I'll feel bad. Because we're all staying here together, like a comfy-cozy happy family, and having fun in a beautiful room, I'll feel bad. That's my offer. Is it a deal?''

Mrs. Reckler, Joe, and Aunt Ida looked at one another. They pondered Aunt Pola's proposition. They nodded at one another, in complete accord.

''Sounds good,'' said Joe.

''Suits me,'' said Mrs. Reckler.

''They don't mean it,'' said Aunt Ida. ''Pola, don't feel bad.''

''Don't worry,'' said Aunt Pola.

The sisters fanned out, clicking open their Samsonite and mine-sweeping the premises for cleanliness.

''I don't really like wall-to-wall,'' said Mrs. Reckler, sitting on a bed and running the toe of her shoe over the blue-green ''Mediterranean'' shag carpeting. ''You can vacuum, but it never really feels clean.''

''The linens seem fine,'' said Aunt Pola, turning down one of the beds. ''They smell good. Of course, you never know. How could you?''

''It's spotless,'' called Aunt Ida, from the modern, white-tiled bathroom, which featured a minitub tucked beneath frosted sliding glass doors. Aunt Ida inspected the drinking glasses, which were swathed in crinkly paper bags, and the toilet seat, which was sealed with a paper band bearing the motto SANITIZED FOR YOUR APPROVAL.

''It's all very nice in there,'' Aunt Ida reported, emerging from her bathroom reconnaissance. ''Everything has paper on it.''

''But you know,'' Joe pointed out, ''they could just take dirty glasses and dump them in those little bags. I think you're all very naive.''

''Go ahead,'' said Mrs. Reckler. ''Make fun. Live in filth.

Although, girls, Joe has a cleaning person now, did you know that? At his apartment.''

"A cleaning person?" Aunt Pola asked. "A boy or a girl?"

"A boy," Joe replied. "He doesn't really clean all that well, but he has *joie de vivre*. He's an unemployed actor. He sits around and reads my magazines."

"And you pay him for this?" said Aunt Pola. "Listen, pay me and I'll come read your magazines. It's so hard to find someone who can really scrub, who gets down on their hands and knees with a bucket and takes some satisfaction. Personally, I wouldn't trust a boy. Boys aren't clean."

"Big news," said Mrs. Reckler. "Call the President."

"Could that be true?" Aunt Ida wondered. "What Joe said about the glassware?"

"Ida," said Mrs. Reckler, "are you crazy? You're listening to Joe?"

"Are you crazy?" said Joe.

"Besides," said Aunt Pola, "when you take the glass out of the paper, you rinse it out. Just to be sure. And I brought my can."

Aunt Pola brandished a spray can of Lysol disinfectant. "Whenever I go on a trip," she explained, "I bring the Lysol. So I never have to worry, if I'm at a gas station or even at someone's house who I don't know. And I also have my horseshoes, if anyone needs to borrow." Aunt Pola's horseshoes were a packet of tissue-paper toilet-seat liners in a curved horseshoe shape. These liners would be spread atop foreign toilet seats to avoid, Joe presumed, syphilis.

"We could paint the bathroom," Joe suggested. "Just to be sure."

"Hedy," said Aunt Pola, her hands on her hips. "Does he always talk like this? I'm beginning to see the advantages of the separate rooms."

One by one, each of the sisters headed for the bathroom, swinging her pebbly Avocado Green or Astral Blue Samsonite makeup case. These essential cases were the size of breadboxes, each with a handle on top. They were indestructible molded plastic bunkers lined with shirred rayon. The sisters overloaded their cases with cosmetics, blousy plastic shower caps, shampoos poured into smaller, travel-size plastic jars, hairbrushes, "personal-size" packets of Kleenex, and flowered satin "Protect-All" pouches that had been filled with earrings and bracelets and then rolled and tied.

Only women of a certain generation lugged these ponderous valises, women for whom the phrase "matched luggage" was gospel, women who had visited the General Electric Progressland at the 1964 World's Fair and never recovered. Joe found these cases somehow medical. He imagined that in an emergency, the Esker sisters could apply lipstick, Bufferin, and strands of onyx beads to entire busloads of needy women. Each Esker sister pillaged her makeup case and then left the bathroom in a robe and a nightgown, with her hair down, her teeth brushed, and her face shining. Joe took the last turn, slinging his green rubberized-canvas knapsack over one shoulder. Joe traveled light, although he was the only member of the group with a blow dryer and a jug of Salon Selectives Dry to Normal Hair Conditioner. Joe changed into his track shorts and T-shirt; over this he wore a short taxicab-yellow terry-cloth robe, a shaving coat.

"Don't you look nice," said Aunt Pola, when Joe emerged. "That's a very becoming robe. Hedy, where did you get that robe?"

"Aunt Pola, it's my robe," said Joe. "Why don't you ask me where I got it?"

"Yeah, yeah," said Aunt Pola, an old hand at robes. "Hedy, where's it from?"

"It's a Maineway," recalled Mrs. Reckler. "I bought it for him two years ago, when Saul and I took our last trip up here. At the outlet store."

"It's stunning," said Aunt Ida. "Come over here."

Aunt Ida handled the robe, as did Aunt Pola. Both insisted that Joe spin and model the garment.

"I love this robe," said Aunt Pola. "How much?"

"$900,000," said Joe. "Marked down from a million. Can my mother shop, or what?"

"Hedy?" said Aunt Pola, ignoring Joe entirely.

"You know, I don't really remember. Maybe $16.50.

When we get to Rockton, we'll go. It's the best store. Joe, do you think Clark needs a robe?''

"Clark needs a set of spark plugs," said Joe.

"I just sent Kurt a robe," said Aunt Ida. "But it was seersucker, from Wallach's, for the summer. When I was out there, in Monterey, I saw his old robe. It made me retch. It was hanging in threads. It was like something from a Frankenstein movie. I said, Kurt, how can you wear that awful thing? He said, What awful thing? I said, Your bathrobe. He said, This robe? It's brand-new.''

"And he's a doctor," Aunt Pola clucked. Joe marveled at this comment. He wondered if before signing a release permitting a surgeon to perform a heart transplant, Aunt Pola would demand to know the condition of his bathrobe.

"Joe, here's your bed," said Mrs. Reckler. "I made it up. I think it's fine.''

The bed was not actually a cot. It was a rollaway bed, a metal frame that had been folded in half and stashed in a closet. The frame was equipped with a thin mattress, which Mrs. Reckler had made up with sheets, blankets, and a pillow. Joe climbed into bed.

"And in the morning, if you don't wake up," Aunt Ida warned, "we'll just fold you up."

Aunt Pola and Aunt Ida were now sitting beneath the covers of one of the double beds. Mrs. Reckler sat up in the other bed. Aunt Pola was slathering her face with vigorous strokes of Revlon's Ultima II night cream.

"What is that stuff?" asked Aunt Ida, eyeing Pola's routine.

"Revlon, for your information," said Aunt Pola. "Ultima II.''

"Ultima II," mused Aunt Ida. "What happened to Ultima I?"

"Ipsy-pipsy," said Mrs. Reckler to Aunt Pola. "Look who's spending money."

"Roberta, this woman I used to work with, she buys it for me," said Aunt Pola. "Half price, from a duty-free shop in the Virgin Islands. Roberta's husband is a pilot for United, so he's there all the time. It's no trouble. I put in an order.''

"Gimme," said Mrs. Reckler, and Aunt Pola gave the jar to Aunt Ida, who passed it between the beds to Mrs. Reckler, who dabbed a bit of the cream on her face. "It's nice," said Mrs. Reckler. "Usually I don't like anything on my face at night. I always feel greasy."

"I like it," said Aunt Pola. "It's rejuvenating. Can you believe I'm seventy-seven?"

Aunt Pola was proud of her age. She viewed her years as something apart from herself, as a square-cut emerald ring or a pedigreed Pekinese, something she could display haughtily to others. Aunt Pola equated age with acquired wisdom and dignified clout. When she was a hundred, she would be unstoppable.

This attitude, Aunt Pola's emphasis on age, occasionally irked Mrs. Reckler, who would turn sixty in another month. Whenever Mrs. Reckler jetted down for a weekend in West Palm, Aunt Pola would recite a neighborhood litany, as various senior citizens strolled or wheeled or caned past: "Can you believe she's eighty-five?" "Can you believe she'll be ninety?" "Can you believe she's older than me?"

Mrs. Reckler found West Palm to be vaguely disturbing, an ominously sunny stockade for tanning oldsters. While it was obvious that the residents of Heritage Village were happy and well cared for, the prospect of such "golden years" made Mrs. Reckler shudder. She did not intend to retire in the foreseeable future. She viewed retirement as surrender, as the abandonment of an active life. She preferred her days to be overrun with new faces and fresh dilemmas and the sheer zest of tangling with the outside world. She yearned for weekends but not retirement, the lulling pasture. She had strenuously resisted Aunt Pola's promotions of neighboring Florida condos.

"You know what I hate?" said Mrs. Reckler. "About getting old?"

"Everything," said Aunt Ida. "Especially getting old knees that hurt when you climb the stairs."

"No," said Mrs. Reckler. "I mean, I hate aches and pains, and when you think something's a sprain and it turns out to be arthritis, but that I can live with. What I hate is when people treat me like I'm old, like I'm an official old person. These young girls in my office, sometimes they act as if I'm their mother or, God forbid, their granny."

"Nobody treats me like that," said Aunt Pola. "I'd smack 'em. Hedy, you should tell those kids a thing or two. Open your mouth."

"It's not always so easy," sighed Mrs. Reckler. "I'm a wimp. I want everybody to like me."

"So call Aunt Pola," Joe suggested. "She can come to your office and smack everyone."

"Can you believe she's seventy-seven?" Aunt Ida asked Joe, with regard to Pola. "She looks seventy-six."

"Very nice," said Aunt Pola, giving Ida and Joe a look. "The two of you."

"Hoo, why did I say that?" said Aunt Ida. "Pola, I'm sorry. Now she'll take all the covers."

"Well, here we are," said Mrs. Reckler, depositing the jar of cream on the night table between the two beds. "We're in Vermont. In one room."

"That again," said Aunt Pola. "She's like a dog with a bone."

"When you were all little," Joe asked, "did you ever fight?"

"Girls, did we fight?" Aunt Pola asked.

"Don't worry, Pola," said Aunt Ida. "You didn't fight. Joe, tell me, did my nose just grow?"

"Oooh!" said Aunt Pola, and she pinched Ida's elbow.

"She's pinching!" said Aunt Ida.

"I never fought," averred Mrs. Reckler. "Of course, I was the baby. When I was growing up, Pola was practically married already, to Uncle Nat."

"But I was in the house," Aunt Pola insisted. "I came back."

"Did she ever," said Aunt Ida, guarding her elbow.

"What did you fight about?" asked Joe.

"You know, we didn't really fight," said Mrs. Reckler. "I fought with Mama, about everything. But not with my sisters."

"Your mother," Aunt Pola informed Joe, "she was Mama's heartache."

"No she wasn't," said Aunt Ida. "*I* was Mama's heartache."

"We were all Mama's heartache," said Mrs. Reckler. "She always wanted to know where we were going, and with who, and what were we wearing. A real third degree."

"I'm terribly sorry," said Aunt Pola. "Mama and I got along very nicely, thank you. Just peachy."

"Do 'My Sister Has a Fella,' " Joe begged. Joe was almost glad that everyone was sharing a room, so he could watch his mother and aunts carry on, swatting and wisecracking; they were the most marvelous vaudeville troupe. Their devotion was complete, but there was always room for elbow-pinching, for the infectious syncopation of family squabbles. Joe could now picture the Esker sisters as children, sharing a cramped bedroom, in their plain cotton nightgowns, their hair tumbling over their shoulders, their feet bare.

" 'My Sister Has a Fella,' " Mrs. Reckler repeated. "He always asks for that."

"I don't even remember the words," said Aunt Ida.

"Yes you do," commanded Aunt Pola. "I'll start."

The sisters all sat up in their beds and took their cue from Pola, the maestro. They chanted a girlhood rhyme, illustrated with precise hand gestures performed in unison. They recited with great seriousness, exchanging supportive glances, as if the rhyme were fresh neighborhood gossip, or a secret pledge.

"My sister has a fella," the sisters said.

"She sees him every night.

"They go into the parlor. . . .

"Turn out the silver light!

"I peek in through the keyhole

"And hear my sister say,

" 'Stop, Charlie! Don't, Charlie!

" 'Keep your hands away!' "

When the sisters discussed the "silver light," they reached their hands up and mimed flicking off a light switch. When they berated poor Charlie, they made slapping sounds by briskly smacking the backs of their hands.

After the sisters finished the rhyme, they burst into giggles, rocking in their beds, gasping for air.

"You remembered!" said Aunt Pola.

"It's ridiculous." Aunt Ida giggled.

"Oh my," gasped Mrs. Reckler.

Joe beamed. He wouldn't have traded his relatives for the world.

Joe woke up the next morning at nine. His mother and aunts had been bustling for over an hour. Joe kept his head on the pillow and spied on the women's activities through slitted eyes. The women were all dressed and were industriously making their beds.

"So he's still asleep?" said Aunt Pola, in a rather loud whisper, as she straightened the sheets on her bed.

"So why shouldn't he be asleep?" whispered Aunt Ida, aligning the sheet from the opposite side of the bed. Ida and Pola were working as a team, reminding Joe of hyperefficient nurses.

"Are you asleep?" Mrs. Reckler called out to her son, as she plumped the pillows on her own bed.

"Why are you doing that?" Joe asked, fully awake, sitting up in bed.

"Doing what?" asked Aunt Ida, smoothing the blanket with a practiced stroke.

"Why are you making your beds?" Joe asked. "This is a motel. Someone comes in and does that. It's included."

"And they'll do a rotten job," said Aunt Pola, as she and Aunt Ida wrangled the quilted bedspread into creaseless perfection.

"But even if you make the bed," Joe continued, "the chambermaid will still take off the sheets and put on new ones. You're wasting your time. You're insane."

"Listen," said Aunt Pola. "The girl will come in here, she'll see how a bed should be made. She'll learn something. She'll thank us."

"Joe doesn't make beds," Mrs. Reckler said. "It's too exhausting."

"Maybe he never learned," Aunt Pola said, casting a critical eye on Mrs. Reckler's freshly pristine bedspread.

"That's right," said Joe. "I was never taught. I grew up in a home where no one made their beds, not ever. I wanted to make my bed. I begged to make my bed, but my mother always said, No, not in this house. It was horrible, it was like living in the woods."

"Oh shut up," said Mrs. Reckler.

The three women stood beside their exquisitely made beds. They did not dare sit down, for fear of denting their handiwork. At times the Esker sisters became prisoners of their own good manners.

"I'm sitting," Mrs. Reckler declared, boldly balancing on the very corner of her bed. "I don't care."

"Suit yourself," said Aunt Pola.

"Joe," said Mrs. Reckler, "your mother and your two lovely aunts are all bathed and dressed. It's a beautiful day outside, and we are in Vermont. Does this mean anything to you?"

Joe thought hard; he shook his head. "Not really," he said.

"Joe," said Mrs. Reckler evenly, "if you're not out of bed in two seconds, something terrible will happen."

"What?" Joe asked eagerly. "Will you all leave without me and go see the leaves change?"

"No," said Mrs. Reckler. "Not that terrible. But something terrible will happen, and it will involve your Aunt Pola."

"I'm up!" Joe all but howled, racing into the bathroom with his knapsack.

"He's so easy," said Aunt Pola. "He's a good boy."

Joe scrubbed his face and hands, shaved, combed his hair, and put on blue jeans, a denim shirt, and a sweater. His mother and aunts wore stylish dresses accessorized with colorful scarves and jewelry. Everyone was dressed to see the leaves change; they wanted to look nice, in case the leaves looked back.

"Don't you look nice," said Aunt Ida, as Joe left the bathroom.

"You do," said Mrs. Reckler, sounding surprised.

"What happened?" asked Aunt Pola.

"Thank you," said Joe. "I'm just going to stay in the room and watch TV."

The women all monitored themselves in the mirror one final time, checking their hair and lipstick.

"You all look very nice," Joe said. "What happened?"

"Don't be smart," said Mrs. Reckler. "Do we really look nice?"

"I look nice," said Aunt Pola. "You know, Hedy, I can get you this dress. I had it made."

Everyone studied Aunt Pola's dress, an implacable column of beige polyester with fuzzy brown ball fringe bobbing from the hem. The dress looked perfectly nice, if a trifle eccentric. The dress reminded Joe of a cheerful popsicle decked out for a fiesta.

"It's just a tube," said Aunt Pola. "It's Dacron. I bought a few yards at Newberry's and I took them to my dressmaker, this wonderful Puerto Rican woman near me, and she put in the sleeves and the neckline, and sewed on the trim. I liked it so much I went back to Newberry's and bought twenty more yards of the tube fabric. I bought it in an avocado green, a mustard, and a hot pink. I had her make me up three more dresses, only on each one she changed the trim. One has rickrack, another has some Aztec embroidery, and the other just has a nice double ruffle at the bottom. I live in these dresses, they're so comfortable. They're so easy to wash; I throw them in the machine. I had Mrs. Ortiz—she's the dressmaker—I had her make one up for Ida. She loves it. Ida, isn't it a wonderful dress?''

"Oh yes," Ida said quickly. "It's wonderful."

"So, Hedy, when I get back I'll call Mrs. Ortiz, she'll make you one; I have plenty of fabric. Which would you like, the ball fringe or the rickrack?"

Joe watched his mother with glee. Aunt Pola's tube dress was far from Mrs. Reckler's taste. Joe knew that his mother would not be caught dead in unbendable beige dacron with holiday fringe. Aunt Ida had clearly been coerced into her own tube dress, which she had neglected to pack for the trip. The peculiar dash of the tube dress suited only Aunt Pola. Her wardrobe depended on travel-ready practicality and her seasonless days in West Palm had supplied her with a fatal weakness for pastels.

"Oh Pola," Mrs. Reckler began, thinking fast. "You should keep the fabric. For yourself."

"It's no problem," insisted Aunt Pola. "I can get more, it's very cheap, $5.98 a yard. I can have Mrs. Ortiz make you two dresses, the rickrack and the fringe."

"Well, I'll think about it," said Mrs. Reckler tactfully. "But thank you."

"What's to think?" said Aunt Pola, shaking her head. "Believe me, you'll live in this dress. It's a godsend."

"You could all wear the same dress," Joe suggested maliciously. "Like the McGuire Sisters."

"Let's go," said Mrs. Reckler, guiding Joe emphatically out the door, by the small of his back.

"So," Joe said to his mother, as they lagged behind Aunt Pola and Aunt Ida on the stroll to the motel's coffee shop. "Don't you want a tube dress?"

"It's a very nice dress," Mrs. Reckler said loyally. "It's very practical."

"You can get two," said Joe.

"You're a hateful child," said Mrs. Reckler. "Your Aunt Pola is a wonderful person."

Joe giggled.

"You're gonna get it," his mother warned.

The coffee shop was attached to the motel's front office and overlooked the parking lot. There was counter service, a few tables and four upholstered booths; every surface was either easy-care aqua Formica, chrome, or orange Naugahyde. Joe preferred coffee shops. They were junk restaurants. Coffee shops were cozy, low-pressure, an approximation of eating in front of television. He was fond of the miniature individual boxes of cold cereal, and the laminated menus, and the aluminum paper-napkin dispensers. All of Joe's meals resembled dessert and breakfast, and coffee shops were ideally suited to this narrow culinary repertoire.

"Do we want a table or a booth?" asked Aunt Ida, as the group stood just inside the glass doors of the coffee shop.

"Is there a person here?" asked Aunt Pola, peering around for some form of maître d'.

"This isn't Lutèce," said Mrs. Reckler, citing a fashionable Manhattan restaurant. "Let's just sit down."

"Where?" said Aunt Ida. Aunt Ida didn't want to make the decision, she didn't want to risk the responsibility or Pola's criticism of her choice.

"The tables are nice," offered Aunt Pola. "Or we could take a booth."

"Why are you making such a production?" asked Mrs. Reckler. Joe sighed. When all three Esker sisters were involved, everything always became "a production." At moments like this, Joe always had a choice of two responses: he could run howling into the street, looking to be hit by a car, or he could be amused, on some demented anthropological level. He could pretend to be filming a penetrating *National Geographic* television documentary on "The Seating Habits of the Bickering Jews." Since he was in Vermont, light-years from civilization or a cab, he opted to be amused.

This was a wise and a calming decision. Heart attacks were not uncommon among the men in Joe's family. Joe wondered if these attacks could be traced to decades of witnessing the Esker sisters select a table in coffee shops.

"Let's take a booth," said Mrs. Reckler. "They look nice."

"If you say so," said Aunt Pola. "You know best."

"We could take a table," said Aunt Ida. "It's possible."

"Fine," said Mrs. Reckler. "A table."

"What's wrong with a booth?" asked Aunt Pola.

"Nothing!" said Aunt Ida.

"A booth is fine," said Mrs. Reckler. The sisters had still not moved.

"Let's go to the booth," said Aunt Pola. "Come on."

"Go ahead," said Aunt Ida.

"Ida, if you'd like to sit at a table, just say so," said Aunt Pola. "Don't be *meshugge.*"

"Joe," said Mrs. Reckler, "go sit down."

Joe was about to ask "Where?" but he snapped to his senses and marched over to a booth and sat down with the grim resolve, the hellbent leadership, of a MacArthur or even a Churchill.

"So we've decided," said Aunt Pola. "I see he wants the booth."

"Go," said Mrs. Reckler, shooing her sisters toward the booth.

"We're going," protested Aunt Ida. "We just didn't want to make a mistake."

"What mistake?" Joe asked, as the women settled in around him. "What could happen if you chose wrong? What if we were sitting at a table?"

"Joe," said Aunt Pola, "don't be fresh." Aunt Pola looked around the coffee shop from her newly seated vantage point. "This is very nice."

"Pola, it's a coffee shop," said Mrs. Reckler.

"What looks good?" said Aunt Ida, scanning her scalloped paper place mat. "You see, it's all printed here, on the mat. 'Wake-up Specials.' "

"Oh, that sounds nice," said Aunt Pola. "In West Palm,

I always have breakfast by nine a.m. There's an All-You-Can-Eat Early Bird. It's only $1.29, with a Bottomless Cup of Coffee.'' Joe suddenly envisioned his Aunt Pola decimating the coffee shop's larder, and perhaps bankrupting the motel, under an All-You-Can-Eat stratagem. Joe thanked God that the arrangement was not All-You-Can-Carry.

''Remember, we can always get a doggie bag,'' said Aunt Pola.

The group finished their breakfasts. Aunt Pola recalculated the addition on the check, which included everyone's meal. ''Well, that wasn't worth $7.98,'' she declared.

''Give me that,'' said Mrs. Reckler. ''It's my treat.''

''What, are you crazy?'' said Aunt Ida. ''I'll pay; I'll put it on my Visa card.''

''Ida, I'll take care of it,'' said Mrs. Reckler. ''Don't make a scene.''

''Don't offend me,'' insisted Aunt Ida. ''Don't be cuckoo.''

Any restaurant check became a moral battlefield in Joe's family. Both Mrs. Reckler and Aunt Ida were rampagingly generous. Joe, who would be considered a child until the day he died, was not eligible to foot any bill.

''I tell you what,'' said Aunt Pola. ''Why don't you two girls split it.''

''Fine,'' sighed Mrs. Reckler.

''All right,'' sighed Aunt Ida. ''But I'll pay for lunch.''

''Can you believe that—sixty-five cents for toast,'' Aunt Pola announced, in tones of shock and grief, as the group walked across the parking lot to the car.

''It was a double order,'' Joe mentioned.

''A double order,'' Aunt Pola brooded. ''Do you know what I could buy for sixty-five cents?''

''A second home,'' Joe suggested.

''Oooh,'' said Aunt Ida, pinching Joe's shoulder. ''You're gonna get it.''

''I could buy a lot of things,'' said Aunt Pola. ''Let me tell you, it's a crying shame, it truly is.''

"Forget the sixty-five cents," said Mrs. Reckler. "We're in Vermont, and it's a gorgeous day. We're going to see some beautiful scenery; let's all be grateful."

There were trees with colorful foliage bordering the parking lot. Joe glanced at these trees.

"Not yet," Aunt Ida advised her nephew. "These trees are nice, but they're not scenery."

"So I shouldn't look?" Joe asked.

"You can look," Aunt Ida decided. "But don't appreciate."

Joe and Aunt Ida laughed together, climbing into the car.

"What's so funny?" asked Aunt Pola. "What are those two laughing at?"

"Who knows?" said Mrs. Reckler, putting the key in the ignition. "I don't listen, so I don't worry."

Bennington was a graceful town, almost a musical-comedy backdrop of New England, a sprightly setting for *Good News* or any other demure June Allyson frolic. On the outskirts was Bennington College, a tasteful haven for wealthy students. Bennington College was famed for its "creative" undergraduates, fine-boned, aggressively wispy young dandelions in linty black leotards and hoop earrings, constructing performance-art pieces based on their attitudes toward Nicaraguan atrocities and cats and their unfeeling paramours at Dartmouth.

"Bennington is a good school," said Aunt Ida, as they drove past the campus, an undulant, near-Impressionist landscape of velvety lawns and handsome brick buildings in the austere Federal mode.

"It's a very good school," said Mrs. Reckler. "It's fancy."

"It's not Yale," said Aunt Pola.

"God bless you," said Joe to Aunt Pola.

"It's very . . . artistic," said Mrs. Reckler.

"Please," said Joe. "It's for mime majors. I think it has the highest tuition in the country. It's for rich people who want their kids to take cocaine near trees."

"You're such a snob," Mrs. Reckler told her son. Joe was indeed high-handed about such matters. Like any New Jer-

sey suburbanite who had clambered to Yale, Joe was posi-
tively regal when it came to higher education. Joe was not
an evil snob. He did not revere Yale for its blandly corrupt
Old Money contingent, for its shameful manufacture of dim-
bulb stockbrokers and banking honchos. To Joe, Yale was
Cole Porter. It was a swanky piano bar, pure papier-mâché,
a Deco emblem of giddy pleasure. Joe found Harvard offen-
sively self-impressed and humorless. Harvard students were
taught to rule the world. Yale had a more irresponsible mien,
a genial flair; Yale students were instructed to chain-smoke
and read sheet music and doze through the alarm.

Joe was staunchly proud of Yale, for being not quite serious.
Still, Joe was enough of a snob to always reply "Connecticut"
whenever anyone asked him where he had attended college.
Even "New Haven" was too painfully eager a response. If
you just mumbled "Connecticut," everyone knew you meant
Yale, but that you were truly blasé and charmingly modest.

"Bennington is pretty," Joe admitted, as the car glided
past leaf-strewn dells and formal poplar groves. "It's like a
rest home for teenagers."

Soon the town and the college fell past, and the car moved
along a back road, hemmed in by forest. The trees swayed
overhead, and sunlight dappled the car windshield. Everyone
in the car began to relax, without even trying to. The dense
walls of trees were eminently peaceful. Here was a place
where there was nothing to fear, nothing to watch out for.

Suddenly the trees parted. The car was now clinging to a
hillside, high above an open valley, a far-reaching vista. Mrs.
Reckler slowed the car, as everyone turned to look at the
valley and at all the wide blue sky in the world.

"Look at that," said Mrs. Reckler, excited by what she
saw.

"It's gorgeous," said Aunt Ida, leaning over Aunt Pola.

"Hedy, stop the car," ordered Aunt Pola, "or you'll have
an accident."

"Good idea," said Mrs. Reckler, pulling onto a dirt area
on the shoulder of the deserted road. She parked the car, and
everyone scrambled out. The group lined up, at attention,

facing the Vermont valley, inhaling greedy lungfuls of the crisp, chill October air.

"Look at that," Mrs. Reckler sighed, entranced. "Joe, are you looking?"

Joe decided not to make a wisecrack. He was glad his mother cared that he was looking. The valley was breathtaking. Joe was first a suburban boy and then a devoted Manhattanite. As a rule, Joe regarded nature as dull, suspiciously rugged, somehow Waspy, and likely to be crawling with many-legged bugs and slimy worms. Ordinarily, Joe felt that basking in nature was an insult to his beloved New York, a city that confined nature to Central Park, where it could be comfortably viewed from the back seat of a taxi, with the Chrysler Building spire looming reassuringly in the distance.

The Vermont valley caused Joe to surrender his prejudices. He let himself go and hoped that Manhattan wouldn't mind. The valley was a lap, cosseted by rounded hills, acres of color molded into the gentlest slopes, the most welcoming peaks. Trees, showing off, filled the hillsides. Oaks and elms and maples turned peacock. Their green leaves had gone luscious yellow and apple scarlet and brilliant flame orange; the colors were exultant, absurdly beautiful. Leaves, in the autumn, could merely go brown or gray and heap on the ground. These flamboyant shades seemed proof of a benevolent God, a God who could create pure beauty, to entertain his humans.

Aunt Ida was struck by the beauty of the leaves, but she ducked her head slightly. Aunt Ida felt a bit guilty. Pleasure frightened her. For Aunt Ida, happiness was always suspect. She kept her guard up. If she never went overboard, if she never allowed a total release, she would never be caught unawares by the tragedy that lurked just beyond all joy. Aunt Ida scolded herself. Go ahead, she instructed her eyes, have fun, but be careful.

Aunt Pola stood with her hands on her hips, giving the valley the once-over, as if she owned it. Aunt Pola was comfortable with beauty. She demanded beauty. Aunt Pola had traveled the world. She took a great satisfaction in discovering grandeur. "Those are leaves," she declared, as if complimenting God, as a co-worker.

"It's so beautiful," said Mrs. Reckler, almost crying. "I want to live here."

"In Vermont?" asked Aunt Ida skeptically.

"Yes," said Mrs. Reckler, without turning from the valley. "I want to live in one of those little houses down there and have an orchard. I just want to sit on my porch and see all of this, every day."

"You don't want an orchard," said Aunt Ida.

"It's a lot of work," Aunt Pola cautioned, considering the idea.

"I don't really want an orchard," said Mrs. Reckler, sighing. She slumped a bit, accepting a more complex reality. "And if I lived here I'd go crazy. It's probably very boring. But . . . wouldn't it be nice? Maybe if I was rich and lived here."

"Now you're talking," said Joe. Joe had shared his mother's pastoral fantasy, for a moment. He had wanted to run down and buy her one of the tiny white clapboard houses in the valley below and hand her the deed as a gift. He wanted to buy his mother anything she wanted.

"Wouldn't that be perfect?" Mrs. Reckler asked her son. "To have lots of money and a house in Bennington?"

"And houses in Rome and London and Paris too," Joe agreed.

"Yes," said Mrs. Reckler, and she hugged her son. "You're just like me. It's terrible."

Everyone gazed at the valley for a few more minutes. Their awe gradually shifted to appreciation, and then to mild fidgeting. Aunt Ida turned away first, for safety. If God caught her staring at the valley for too long a period, something awful would happen. Aunt Ida felt it was best to ration one's pleasures; she had no wish to tempt punishment.

"Leaves," said Aunt Ida, adjusting her coat. *"Kineahora poo poo poo."* When something nice happened, Aunt Ida would usually say *"Kineahora poo poo poo."* This Yiddish phrase, loosely translated, was invoked to thwart the evil eye.

The *"poo poo poo"* symbolized spitting on the ground, denying that anything of import had occurred.

Joe scratched his neck. He tried to continue to focus on the valley, but he could feel his soul wandering. He stared a moment longer, so his mother wouldn't be disappointed in him. Joe felt the way he did at the ballet or the opera. He would soar for about a minute, and then boredom would come crashing down. Joe suspected that his brief attention span was the mark of a shallow person. He squinted at the valley and at the little church spire. He tried to dredge up at least a few seconds' more rapture. But it was no use. The more ferociously he concentrated and knotted his forehead, the more his thoughts drifted toward new pullovers and Three Musketeers bars. After a minute, almost all aesthetic experiences somehow became algebra.

"Does your leg itch?" Mrs. Reckler asked Joe, noticing that her son was shifting his weight and rubbing the back of one shin with the other foot.

"No . . ." said Joe hesitantly. "Is this . . . it?"

"Uch," said Mrs. Reckler. "You have no appreciation. You were always like this, you and your brother. When you were little, and we drove cross-country, we had to force you to stop reading comic books and look out the window. Daddy would say, 'Look, boys, it's the Grand Canyon,' and you would say, 'In a minute, I have to finish the page.' "

Joe knew his mother was right. To this day, his memories of Richie Rich and Little Dot were far more vivid than his recollection of the Rockies or Yosemite.

"It's very pretty," said Aunt Pola, scanning the valley, "but let's go."

"Everybody wants to go," protested Mrs. Reckler, steadfastly holding her gaze on the scenery. "Everybody's in such a hurry. I think you're all terrible, you can't appreciate a little beauty in the world."

"Joe, get in the car," called Aunt Ida, from her stronghold in the back seat. "With the terrible people."

"It's very beautiful," Aunt Pola admitted. "Hedy, I tell you what I'll do. When we get back to town, I'll buy you a calendar. I guarantee you, you'll get the same picture."

Aunt Pola climbed into the car; Joe sat in the front seat. Only Mrs. Reckler still stood outside, shivering. Now she was sad, for the spell had dissolved. Even she could not sustain her wonder, her longing, indefinitely. Suddenly she was aware that her feet hurt, in her new navy pumps. She was also hungry, and she was beginning to plot the location of the nearest bathroom. Mrs. Reckler cursed herself. She wanted to be a figure out of Brontë, poised at the edge of a sheer drop as lightning flashed about her. She wanted to give herself over to nature, with the slashing rain and buffeting wind in her face. She wanted to think the great thoughts, whatever they might be. She wanted to declaim verse at angry waves. She wanted to live out of time, on a plane where Chevrolet station wagons and 7 Eleven supermarkets did not exist. She wanted the life of a brooding, searching woman of vast mystery and valiant woe, but these new shoes had not been broken in. She had packed her more comfortable, broken-in shoes, with a lower heel, but she had wanted her sisters to see her new I. Miller pumps.

"All right," said Mrs. Reckler, offering the valley a final gaze. She sighed heavily. "All right," she repeated, opening the car door. "I give up. My feet hurt. I'm as bad as the rest of you. If I was a decent person, I'd stand out there all day, just looking. But I think I'll turn on the heat. Joe, are you chilly?"

"I'm fine," said Joe.

"Turn on the heat," said Aunt Pola, who was bundled in a heavy wool coat with knitted trim. "My teeth are chattering. It's the Arctic back here."

"Don't listen to her," said Aunt Ida. "We're fine."

"Ida, don't be ridiculous," said Mrs. Reckler, starting the engine and flipping on the heater. "Have a little heat. On me."

"Hedy, don't be crazy," Aunt Ida insisted. "I don't need it."

"Fine," said Aunt Pola. "Hedy, I'll take hers. Send it back."

"Where shall we go?" Mrs. Reckler asked. "I looked at this magazine back at the room, *New England Life*. We can go to the folk-art museum, or we can go on a driving tour of covered bridges, or we can drive up the mountain for more leaves.''

''Or we can go to the pottery,'' said Aunt Ida.

''What, you want to go shopping?'' said Mrs. Reckler. ''So soon? Don't you want some more scenery, maybe look at a weather vane or a covered bridge?''

''That's all very nice,'' said Aunt Pola. ''Let's go to the pottery.''

''Joe, do you want to go to the pottery?'' asked Mrs. Reckler, seeking an ally.

''Oh no,'' said Joe. ''I'd much rather go see the exhibit of Amish quilt fragments.''

''Hopeless,'' said Mrs. Reckler, driving back onto the road and toward the famous Bennington Pottery. ''You're all hopeless.''

''Ipsy-pipsy,'' said Aunt Ida, who knew that no one really had to talk Mrs. Reckler into heading for the pottery.

The Bennington Pottery was situated near the center of town. Mrs. Reckler's first on-site visit had been ten years earlier. Whenever the Reckler family had traveled, their destinations had always included unusual shops that sold goods unavailable in New Jersey or even in Manhattan. Joe recalled family vacations by the specialty stores his mother had introduced him to: Wall Drug, a legendary souvenir outpost in

South Dakota; The House of Peanuts, a gourmet nut palace on the boardwalk in Atlantic City; L. L. Bean in Maine; Marks & Spencer for scratchy woolens in London; the Galeries Lafayette for hand-stitched gloves in Paris.

Among them, the Esker sisters navigated the globe, guided not by tides and constellations and compass points but by stores and exotic shopping forays. Joe had indisputably benefited from this map. Forty-five minutes touring the Tower of London had been edifying enough, but Joe had learned far more at Harrods and on Bond Street and during an afternoon ramble through the jumble stands of Portobello Road. Mrs. Reckler had taught Joe a reverence for literature by familiarizing him with the world's most fabled bookstores: Sylvia Beach's shop in Paris, with its contraband copies of Joyce, and the elite Gotham and the populist Strand in Manhattan. Shopping took the sting out of culture. Mrs. Reckler also regularly sent off for catalogues from faraway shops. She rarely purchased anything but merely dreamed and charted an itinerary, thumbing through the glossy pages of heathery Fair Isle cardigans and impeccable Swiss watches and French jewelers' smocks, finding the catalogues as inviting and inspirational as novels.

Mrs. Reckler, as a housewares aficionado, had made a long-range study of the world's foremost potteries. She disdained Wedgwood and Spode. Such fine china was both too pricey and somehow pretentious, tacky even, a commonplace fantasy. Mrs. Reckler favored more rough-hewn goods: hand-thrown jugs and thickly glazed plates, pieces that showed the mark of the potter. Mrs. Reckler liked her tableware to exhibit a robust personality, suiting her Esker spirit, her peasant oomph.

The Bennington Pottery, founded in 1948, consists of a good-sized wooden factory and a smaller, connected wooden outlet store, both set beside long-unused railroad tracks. The buildings are down-home and modest. The sign out front is hand-painted and low to the ground. Mrs. Reckler parked in a lot bounded by ancient, relocated railroad ties and strewn with unglazed clay pots of geraniums.

"Here we are," said Mrs. Reckler. "I hope you're all happy."

Mrs. Reckler tried to feign nonchalance, but her cheeks were flushed. She couldn't wait to attack the outlet. Everyone in the car shared this blood lust, this fevered eve-of-battle anticipation. Not only were they all about to shop, but they had reached a Brigadoon, a store that they could only visit at most once a year. There was an urgency to the occasion, a search-and-destroy tingle. Even Joe, who would buy nothing, couldn't wait to browse through a bursting cornucopia of products he had no interest in owning.

Everyone piled out of the car, trying not to run. When Joe and his relatives were near a store, there was always the risk of stampede. No one spoke; emotions ran too high for chatter.

The group crossed the open threshold of the outlet store, and everyone sniffed. The air was filtered with a rustic perfume, a log-cabin scent of sawdust and clay and bayberry (the store stocked a few shelves of stout candles in pottery holders). This was a weekday, so the shopping population was light. About ten other people, mostly middle-aged women and their dutiful husbands, milled about. With each couple, either one or both partners carried a wire basket dangling from a forearm. The baskets were for accumulating purchases, but the effect was somehow bucolic, as if all the customers were ambling about a henhouse, plucking up fresh eggs.

The Esker sisters each lifted a wire basket from a stack by the front door.

"Here," said Mrs. Reckler, handing Joe a basket. "You take one too, in case we need it."

Joe slung the basket over his arm. He pictured himself as some sort of colonial water boy, backing up his mom, Molly Pitcher, as they tended to the wounded on a Revolutionary battlefield. At the pottery, Joe would serve as his mother's second-in-command, a reliable lieutenant requisitioned to hold pocketbooks, coats, and possible treasures. He was her Sabu or Jeeves.

As Joe watched his relatives stalk the various aisles, he tried to condemn them. He tried to discover an evil in their passionate shopping, a callous materialism, a lurking psychosis. But he could not: with the Esker sisters, shopping was entirely sensual, a form of dreaming. If I buy this beautiful item, a sister would think, then my home will become more beautiful. If I charge this lovely blouse, I will feel more beautiful, more confident, happier.

The Esker sisters loved their families and their jobs. Their shopping was not misplaced affection. They simply relished the possibilities of the world, the beckoning romance that overflowed the shelves of every gargantuan mall and intimate boutique and bargain basement. The group liked to touch and hold and inhale, to intently consider every object, to lend each item a life, a persona, a power to enchant.

To Joe and his aunts, nothing was sadder than an empty room, a blank wall. When Joe read the newspaper, he would see photographs of ghetto tenements, crumbling hovels lacking heat or hot water, ragged single rooms occupied by entire families. Occasionally these rooms would have a dime-store gewgaw nailed to the wall, a plastic tulip or a matador portrait on velvet. Joe found these decor additions somehow stirring, an attempt at brightening a nightmare, a banner against despair. Without the gewgaw, the hovel was soulless and bereft. The gewgaw was hope itself. Someone was trying; someone had shopped.

The Esker sisters had been raised amid Depression poverty. Their father had been a sorely underpaid cutter in the garment district. Any immaculately laundered tablecloth, any reverently dusted knickknack, had represented a major expenditure. The sisters had been taught to appreciate not merely success, a good living, but beauty. Artists had been revered, particularly if they were Jewish, like Gershwin. Movie stars had been worshiped, because they were gorgeous and sexy and able to afford all sorts of things for their extravagant Hollywood lairs. In Japanese homes, youngsters are tutored in calligraphy, as self-expression and discipline. The Esker sisters were instructed in the art and the glory of the bargain, the considered purchase, the daily browse.

Materialism is crass only if you don't value what you buy, Joe decided. Watching his mother and aunts shop, Joe saw humor and obsession and skill but never carelessness, cold-hearted greed, or the mere amassing of goods.

Joe prowled around the pottery. Raw pine shelving reached

to the ceiling, forming culs-de-sac and coves. Every few steps brought fresh merchandise. Aunt Pola was churning her way slowly but deliberately through the store. She constantly added to her basket. Aunt Pola made quick decisions, an empress decreeing executions and bestowing honors.

"Joe, get busy," Aunt Pola said, glancing at Joe's empty basket. "What's your problem?"

Joe rambled past shelves of mugs and platters and glassware. Aunt Ida was contemplating a pair of salt and pepper shakers. The shakers were simple four-inch-high cylinders of thick, rippled ceramic, glazed with a matte golden finish. Aunt Ida owned a set of dishes in this favorite Bennington finish.

"Do you like these?" Aunt Ida asked Joe, holding up the shakers.

"Sure," said Joe. "They match your dishes."

"They do," admitted Aunt Ida. "But I don't need them."

Aunt Ida put the shakers back on the shelf. Her hands dropped to her sides and then reached out and grabbed the shakers, as if impelled by some force other than Aunt Ida's brain.

"No," said Aunt Ida, putting the shakers back. This time her hands did not leave the shakers. They continued clutching the items, which remained on the shelf. It was as if Aunt Ida had become mysteriously glued to the shakers.

"Should I?" Aunt Ida asked Joe.

"Aunt Ida," said Joe. "They're salt and pepper shakers. Buy them."

"I know what I'll do," said Aunt Ida. "I'll just buy one. The salt. That's it. Fine."

Aunt Ida put a single shaker in her basket, satisfied with the concept.

"Aunt Ida," said Joe, "if you just buy one shaker, what will you do for pepper?"

"So who needs pepper?" said Aunt Ida. "It makes people sneeze. I'll have the salt. I shouldn't even buy that. It's crazy. What am I going to do with salt and pepper shakers?"

"Use them for salt and pepper," Joe suggested.

"She's doing it again, isn't she?" said Aunt Pola, striding down the aisle. Aunt Pola yanked a pair of the shakers off the shelf and hurled them into Aunt Ida's basket. Then Aunt Pola acquired a pair for herself.

"Thank God I'm here," said Aunt Pola, as she moved farther down the aisle.

"Now I guess I have to buy them both, don't I?" said Aunt Ida to Joe. Aunt Ida sounded relieved and delighted, grateful to have the decision out of her hands.

"Of course," said Joe. "It was an order. From the top."

"If I don't buy them," Aunt Ida reasoned, "she'll kill me. Right?"

"Right," agreed Joe.

"She's so handy," said Aunt Ida, her attention now snared by a gravy boat.

Joe wandered through the store, initiating a familiar Reckler game: If I was forced to buy something here, what would I pick? Joe didn't want dishes, so he pretended that a stogie-chomping mobster had put a revolver to his head and commanded him to choose a pattern, a service for twelve, or else Joe would be sleeping with the fishes. Joe became happily preoccupied, plotting his imaginary, revolver-inspired table. He settled on some glossy black dishes, on which he would serve geometrically arranged groupings of red M&M's.

Even when Joe was merely leafing through magazines, he would indulge in daydream expenditures. In this manner, Joe had selected a maroon MG convertible with spoke wheels, a twelve-slice toaster, Adnan Khashoggi's latest yacht, and whole libraries of bonus selections from the Book-of-the-Month Club and the Literary Guild. Joe rarely tired of brain shopping. You never had to figure out where to put things.

Joe eventually came upon his mother, lost in thought before a shelf stacked high with white dishes.

"Look at these," said Mrs. Reckler. "Aren't they gorgeous?"

The dishes were heavy, curling an inch all around, and glazed in the glossy, rippled Bennington white. Each dish weighed almost a pound. Bennington pottery is known for its heft.

"I've always wanted white dishes," Mrs. Reckler said.

Mrs. Reckler had maintained a private yen for white everything: white furniture, rugs, clothing. She had never dared actually install anything white, because of her family. Her sons were far too sloppy and heedless for pristine surfaces. Mrs. Reckler had always sensibly settled for indestructible, dense brown carpeting. She had paper napkins at the dinner table, and the sturdy Bennington goldware.

"So buy white dishes," said Joe. "Go ahead, why not?"

"Oh, they're so impractical," said Mrs. Reckler. "But then again, you boys aren't around anymore. . . . These are beautiful dishes."

Mrs. Reckler cushioned a plate in both hands, admiring the disk as if it were about to yield up cosmic truths. White dishes represented glamour, the shimmering all-white Deco boudoirs of the Astaire-Rogers films for RKO. Only rich people could afford white, because of the necessary upkeep of white belongings. White also embodied an ultimate cleanliness. One glance at a white rug, or a white Formica countertop, and anyone could tell it was spotless. Mrs. Reckler did not believe in arctic sterility, but she believed in white. In her dreams, she envisioned herself in flowing Grecian white silk, wafting across a white, tendrilly Flokati rug, toward a glass table spread with lovingly ironed, luxuriantly weighty white damask, set with mirror-bright white china and glinting crystal. Even in her dreams, this whitescape smelled superbly of Fantastik spray cleaner and Windex.

"Oh, isn't that lovely," said Aunt Ida, complimenting the plate in Mrs. Reckler's hands. "White."

"Isn't it gorgeous?" Mrs. Reckler swooned. "Feel."

Mrs. Reckler passed the plate gently to her sister, who hefted it and made appreciative noises.

"And see, these are the bread-and-butter plates," Mrs. Reckler said, stroking a stack of smaller plates. "And these are the mugs and the bowls. And look at this tureen. I would die for this. Wouldn't this look marvelous on my sideboard in the living room?"

Joe pondered his mother's remarks. In Hemingway's oeuvre, men would perish for brutal honor and their homeland; men would fall on bayonets to prove they were men. Mrs. Reckler would die for a tureen. Joe found this choice of sacrifices infinitely preferable. After Mrs. Reckler's death, people could look at the tureen and say, "Oh well, of course. It's lovely."

"White dishes," said Aunt Pola disapprovingly. "What a nightmare."

"Oh, Pola, they are not," said Mrs. Reckler. "They're beautiful. I'd put them in the dishwasher. I've always wanted white dishes."

"And they'll show every scrape and stain," prophesied Aunt Pola. "I'm warning you, all you'll do is worry, day and night. I like something with a pattern. If it cracks, nobody can tell."

Joe recalled Aunt Pola's china, which she had invested in over twenty years earlier. She owned at least eighty pieces in a hearty fruit and floral motif. Each plate bore a broadly drawn amalgamation of fat-bottomed pears, balloon-like grapes, and monolithic peonies. When food was served on these plates, many diners became squeamish. The food somehow always took on a Mexican cast. Aunt Pola loved this china, which had proved invincible. Joe had once tarried at Aunt Pola's china cabinet, and he had been astonished at the aggregation of pitchers, footed cake plates, and washtub-capacity punch bowls, all in that frightening Happy Harvest pattern.

"White dishes," Aunt Pola observed. "Who are you, Princess Grace?"

"Maybe," said Mrs. Reckler, clutching a new white plate. "I like these dishes. I'm thinking about getting a set."

"Mom, these dishes are great," Joe agreed. "Get 'em."

"Of course, I don't really need new dishes," Mrs. Reckler said, beginning to feel a touch spendthrift. Her grip on the plate relaxed.

"Mother," said Joe, rolling his eyes.

"I could just buy two place settings," Mrs. Reckler negotiated. "Just for me and Saul. We'll see how we like it."

"That's a good idea," said Aunt Ida, in favor of all compromises.

"Suit yourself," said Aunt Pola. "But why don't you just buy more of the gold? You have the gold."

"Exactly," said Mrs. Reckler. "I'm sick of the gold. I

use it every day; it's depressing. I keep hoping the dishwasher will eat it.''

"That's charming," said Joe.

"I've had the gold for years; it's time for a change," said Mrs. Reckler.

"What will Saul say?" asked Aunt Ida.

"Saul," said Mrs. Reckler, rolling her eyes. "I love Saul dearly, but if I ask him about dishes, he'll say, 'But, honey, don't we have dishes?' He doesn't understand."

"Saul won't like white," Aunt Pola predicted. "Men don't like white."

"Look," said Mrs. Reckler. "It's my kitchen, I choose the dishes. Saul would be happy like the boys, eating off newsprint."

"Excuse me," said Joe.

"Now I'm confused," said Mrs. Reckler, irritated, mostly with herself. "I shouldn't have asked for anyone's opinion. I should have just bought the dishes."

"I tell you what," said Aunt Pola. "We'll go back to the motel, and you'll think about it."

"Think about it," Aunt Ida agreed, as if the group were debating an imminent, possibly life-threatening surgical procedure.

"Just buy 'em," said Joe impatiently.

"I'll think about it," said Mrs. Reckler, reluctantly placing the dish back on the stack. She appreciated Joe's support, but he had been outnumbered. Mrs. Reckler had spent her life listening to her sisters, or fleeing from their influence. Standing in a store, with her feet beginning to throb again, she couldn't muster the necessary independence.

"Goodbye, white dishes," Mrs. Reckler told the stacks of china fondly, as her sisters dragged her off toward a table groaning with factory seconds. These items had visible flaws—cracks or chips in the glaze, malformations that lowered their prices considerably.

"Believe me," Aunt Pola told Hedy. "Don't be a fool. You'll thank me."

Joe and his relatives spent the remainder of the day shopping, at the pottery and at nearby concerns peddling fussy calico lampshades, milk-glass bud vases, heart-shaped cast-iron trivets, fabric-covered diaries, and thousands of brands of tea bags, packed in decorative tins, from Nocturnal Oolong Mint to Yesteryear Bayleaf Tickle. Most overtly quaint, shrewd New England towns bunched their shops to keep tourists' surrounded. Over the years, Joe had accompanied his mother to many elaborately restored, old-timey shopping complexes, mazes of fetching clapboard cabins linked by cunningly pitted cobblestone walks and poles topped with electrified carriage lanterns.

The sales help at these insidious theme parks often favored period dress, their modern, peroxided shag haircuts and press-on plastic fingernails peeking out from ruffled mob caps and bustled gowns with leg-o'-mutton sleeves. The male clerks went for knee breeches, tricorns, and suede weskits, incongruously paired with comfy Reeboks and chunky high-school senior-class rings. These shopping villages, based on the lucrative Williamsburg model, were usually dubbed things like Turntable Junction or Coventry Lane Specialties or Crossroads Emporia, Ltd.

Eventually the group returned to the motel room, their retreat a combination of exhaustion and the fact that all the

stores had shuttered for the night. They collapsed onto their
beds without removing their coats. As one, the Esker sisters
kicked off their shoes and moaned.

"Oooh, I'm a cripple," wailed Aunt Ida.

"I hate these shoes," said Mrs. Reckler. "I never should
have bought them."

"Well, everyone," said Aunt Pola, vigorously kneading
her toes with her fingers. "I think we did very well."

In impromptu heaps of crumpled brown paper bags and
tissue-wrapped bundles, the day's haul lay on the beds and
atop the desk and bureau. Joe, stretched out on the foldaway
bed, felt like a weary camper stumbling home to his bunk
after a vicious hike up the local mountainside. He wanted to
sleep for days. Easing off his sneakers, he became, effortlessly, an older Jewish woman.

"Uch," Joe said sincerely. "My feet are swollen."

All of them sighed, sinking into their beds. There was a
communal release of air, a gentle, satisfying *"Mmmmmm,"*
followed by a contented silence. Joe lay on his back and
listened to the lulling, even breathing that filled the room.

"I can't move," said Mrs. Reckler. "I cannot move."

"So who's moving?" asked Aunt Ida rhetorically.

Everyone was quiet again, a safari making camp amid the
day's kill. They experienced a blend of letdown and eupho-
ria, regret over items not purchased, glee over the accumulated swag. Joe had bought a hardcover edition of a book
long out of print, a section of rococo plaster balustrade, and
a sack of peppermint sticks. Joe had shopped like his Aunt
Ida, who gathered tidbits in quantity. He felt sated, full, as
if he could never shop again.

"Come on, Joe," said Mrs. Reckler. "Let's call your father."

Mrs. Reckler felt weary, drowsy, but indulging in a nap
seemed wicked. She reached for the phone, to check in with
her husband, to make certain he was managing by himself
in Piscataway.

"So hello, stranger," Mrs. Reckler said into the phone.
"It's your wife and child. How are you, honey?"

"So how is he?" asked Aunt Ida immediately.

"He's fine," Mrs. Reckler told everyone in the motel room, and then, into the receiver, "We've seen some beautiful countryside. I'm in the room now, with Pola and Ida and Joe."

"The usual suspects," said Aunt Ida. "Tell Saul I say hello."

"Tell him I say hello too," said Aunt Pola. "And that my feet hurt."

"He says he's sorry your feet hurt," Mrs. Reckler reported. "Is it cold there?" she asked her husband. "Up here it's October."

"Is he wearing a sweater?" asked Aunt Ida.

"He's wearing the sweater I made him," said Mrs. Reckler. "He says he looks very handsome."

"The sweater she made him?" Aunt Pola said.

"Remember, it took her a hundred years," said Aunt Ida.

"Shut up," Mrs. Reckler told her sisters. "Not you," she told her husband. "Are you riding your bicycle?"

"His bicycle?" said Aunt Pola. "He rides a bike?"

"His exercise bicycle," Joe explained. "It stays in one place; it's in the den. His doctor told him to ride it for at least thirty minutes a day."

"I don't understand that kind of bicycle," Aunt Ida admitted. "You pedal and you pedal, but you don't get anywhere. It must be very frustrating. I would think it would *give* someone a heart attack. *Kineahora poo poo poo.*"

"My mother rides it too," said Joe. "For her diet. She puts Elizabeth Bishop on the handlebars and reads."

"Elizabeth Bishop?" said Aunt Pola. "She's on the handlebars?"

"The book," said Mrs. Reckler. "Her poetry. Saul, have you had dinner?"

"Tell him to look in the freezer," said Aunt Ida.

"There's a half a chicken; it's labeled," said Aunt Pola.

"Just pop it in the microwave," added Joe.

"Saul, did you get all that?" Mrs. Reckler asked her husband. "Saul, I hope you're eating. I don't want to get home and find a freezer full of food. What? What have I bought?

Saul, what do you think I've been doing? Wasting my time shopping?''

"Shopping?'' said Aunt Ida. "Who's been shopping?''

"We've looked at a few things,'' said Aunt Pola. "Is that shopping?''

"He wants to talk to you,'' said Mrs. Reckler, passing Joe the phone. "Don't make jokes.''

"Hi, Daddy,'' said Joe into the phone. "No one's been shopping. We spent the day looking at covered bridges and authentic butter churns.''

"I'm not listening,'' said Mrs. Reckler. "I don't care.''

"I'm fine,'' Joe told his father. "We're all staying in one room.''

"And we're having a marvelous time," Aunt Pola bellowed.

"That was Aunt Pola,'' Joe told his father. "Don't ask. Today we saw the leaves change.''

"Ask him if the new cleaning lady came,'' prompted Mrs. Reckler.

"Did Mrs. Mantizo come?'' Joe asked.

"You have a new woman?'' said Aunt Ida.

"Where did you find her?'' asked Aunt Pola. "Will she come to my house?''

"She came, and the house looks great,'' Joe told his mother. "A news crew came by, just to photograph the sink.''

"Give me the phone,'' Mrs. Reckler said, instantly realizing that catastrophe was afoot. "Saul,'' she said, grabbing the receiver. "She canceled, didn't she?''

"Uh-oh,'' said Aunt Ida.

"She'll come home to a pigsty,'' said Aunt Pola. "Like a hurricane victim.''

"Saul, my darling,'' Mrs. Reckler said, "I am not going to think about any of this. I am not going to worry about you or the house. I am going to watch the leaves change.''

"Pish pish,'' said Aunt Ida.

"Yes,'' Mrs. Reckler told her husband. "We did see Clark. He has now decorated his living room in early Budweiser. But it was fine; I'll tell you later. Now, are you all right, really? Do you need anything?''

Mrs. Reckler listened for a moment and blushed. ''He says he just needs me,'' she told her sisters and Joe.

''The lovebirds,'' said Aunt Ida.

''Sure,'' said Aunt Pola. ''He needs her to turn on the microwave.''

''Eat something,'' Mrs. Reckler told her husband lovingly. ''It won't kill you. I'll be back in a few days. And don't go outside; it's cold. I'll call you tomorrow night, from Maine. We'll be on the road all day. I love you.''

Mrs. Reckler made kissing noises and hung up. Saul Reckler drove his wife crazy, because he was somewhat absentminded. His retirement had made him even more serenely cloudlike. He never minded his wife's rigor, her obsession with the condition of his underwear. Mr. Reckler had always been attracted to his wife's brimming energy and her drive. He needed someone to push him, and Mrs. Reckler was happy to oblige. They were still very much in love. Mr. Reckler was a kite being tugged through the sky by a very determined little girl.

''So,'' said Aunt Pola over her shoulder, as she watched television. ''Did Saul eat?''

''Who knows?'' said Mrs. Reckler. ''What am I, his mother?''

''Did he ride his bicycle?'' asked Aunt Ida.

''Call him,'' said Mrs. Reckler. ''You ask him. Daddy sounded good, don't you think?'' she asked Joe.

''He sounded great,'' said Joe.

''I left him food, he has a crossword-puzzle book, he's having a very nice time,'' Mrs. Reckler said, comforting herself. Mrs. Reckler, in the more irrational hemisphere of her brain, truly believed that without her detailed supervision, her husband would forget to eat, bathe, change his clothes, let the cleaning woman in, exercise, answer the phone, sleep, and watch television. Left to his own devices, Mr. Reckler would indeed neglect some of these pursuits, but not to the extent that he would become a ''Believe It or Not'' entry in the local paper, as Mrs. Reckler feared.

"You know, I was thinking," Joe told his mother. "Since Daddy retired, you're the only one in the family with a regular job."

"I know," said Mrs. Reckler. "I'm the only one who gets out of bed in the morning. And I can't tell you how tickled I am by this fact."

"Come to your senses," said Joe. "Join the family."

"Good idea," said Mrs. Reckler. "Then we'd have no money coming in. I remember, when your brother was about six years old, I asked him what he wanted to be when he grew up. He said he wanted to be retired. Thank God for Daddy's pension and Social Security and Blue Cross. Lord knows my children won't help any. Other children support their aged parents. Did you know that?"

"Really?" said Joe innocently. Every so often, Mrs. Reckler came across a tabloid account of a country-western singer or a rock star. After achieving megastardom and banking millions, these personalities would buy their parents homes in Nashville or Beverly Hills, usually with guitar-shaped swimming pools. Mrs. Reckler would clip these articles, scrawl the word "When?" across them, and mail them to Joe.

"Hedy, hand me the phone," said Aunt Pola. "And my bag."

"Who are you calling?" asked Mrs. Reckler. She passed her sister the phone and her chocolate-brown kid handbag. Aunt Pola's handbags were always the size and sturdiness of steamer trunks. More manageable, fussier bags were for teenagers or timid women without lists or brochures or jugs of mineral water. Aunt Pola's handbags were a breed of feminine attaché case, a power accessory. They were rivaled, for sheer threat, only by those of the queen of England.

"I'm not calling," said Aunt Pola. "I'm ordering."

Aunt Pola anchored her reading glasses on the tip of her nose and dialed the phone. She had been watching a home shopping service on television. This program broadcast twenty-four hours a day, offering a ceaseless onslaught of merchandise. Goods were temptingly displayed atop Lucite pedestals or against glittery drapes. The absurdly inflated "manufacturer's retail price" was flashed on the screen, followed by the program's own "low, low, rockbottom price." The items were changed every few minutes.

Unctuous, honey-voiced offscreen "hosts" gushed over the virtues of every "countertop miracle" appliance or "truly elegant" cultured-pearl necklace. This program and its brethren appealed to the basest of all shopping compulsions, invading the viewers' living rooms and bedrooms, convincing the lonely hausfrau and the insomniac farmer that they desperately craved a set of fourteen "jade-like" green plastic coasters imprinted with "genuine Japanese-style pagodas" for "only $19.98! That's right, home shoppers, you heard it correctly!"

The motel room television screen was currently filled with an ungodly item. Joe stared at the screen, unable, at first glance, to tell just what this item was, or what it accomplished.

"Aunt Pola," Joe asked, "are you buying that? What is it?"

"It looks nice," said Aunt Ida, squinting at the screen. Aunt Ida also could not make head or tail of the item.

"Pola," said Mrs. Reckler, "are you crazy? You're ordering from the Home Shopping Caravan?"

Mrs. Reckler had occasionally glanced at the various shopping channels, while station-hopping at home. All the goods available on these shows seemed to belong only in mobile homes. The staples of such programs were gold electroplate chains, of a design worn primarily by dental receptionists, and obscenely gooey ceramics, insipid figurines of tearful clowns clutching masses of brightly colored ceramic balloons. Mrs. Reckler would never consider shopping via television. She found the entire concept trashy, demeaning to the very notion of shopping. The only thing Mrs. Reckler had ever purchased from her television was a Channel 13 canvas tote bag, included as a bonus with her tax-deductible contribution.

"I buy things from this channel all the time," said Aunt Pola. "You get very good prices, and some of their stuff is adorable. Look at that—isn't that cute? It's for the vacuum."

Joe stared harder; Aunt Pola was correct. The item being promoted was a frilly, petticoated red-and-white polka-dot dress with a ruffly lace collar and hem, the sort of garment that even Shirley Temple might have deemed too sugary. The dress was not intended for a child, however. It was designed to cover an upright vacuum cleaner.

"Ohhh," said Aunt Ida, drawing out the word as she realized the full import of the Vacu-Frock. "It's for your vacuum. In case it goes to a party."

"I think it's sweet," said Aunt Pola. "Who wants to look at a vacuum? Hello? Is this the Home Shopping Caravan?"

Aunt Pola proceeded to give the Home Shopping Caravan operator her charge-card number and the listing for the Vacu-Frock. Aunt Pola then put her hand over the receiver and turned to her sisters.

"I'm ordering it for the two of you as well. Joe, do you want one?"

"I don't know," said Joe. "Do they have anything for evening?"

"Ida," said Mrs. Reckler, outraged. "Do you really want one of those?"

"Of course she does," said Aunt Pola. "It's adorable."

"It's adorable," echoed Aunt Ida, shrugging her shoulders. She leaned over the bed and whispered to her sister. "Hedy, just let her order it. Don't argue. You'll put it in the closet."

"My vacuum does not need a wardrobe," Mrs. Reckler insisted. "Pola, thank you very much, but no thanks. Don't order that for me."

"Ida, what's your charge number?" asked Aunt Pola. "They need your number."

"Just a minute," said Aunt Ida, rising and retrieving her pocketbook from the dresser. "What do they take, MasterCard?"

"American Express," Aunt Pola said. "Hedy, are you sure? It also makes a lovely gift."

"For who?" Mrs. Reckler said, trying to imagine whom she knew who would appreciate a Vacu-Frock.

"My American Express is in my other bag," said Aunt

Ida, rummaging through the drawers of the bureau. "My navy bag—where is it?"

"It's in the desk drawer," said Mrs. Reckler hurriedly. "Ida, I rearranged some things; I put your navy bag in the desk."

"Hedy," said Aunt Ida, discovering the contents of the lowest, and deepest, bureau drawer. The drawer held the white soup tureen that Mrs. Reckler had yearned for at the pottery. "Hedy," said Aunt Ida, "I thought you were going to think about this."

21

"Ida, let me see that," said Aunt Pola, returning the receiver to the cradle, her order completed.

"Pola, it's nothing," insisted Mrs. Reckler.

"It's beautiful, but I thought you hadn't decided," said Aunt Ida, hoisting the tureen out of the drawer and settling it atop the bureau. The tureen was about eighteen inches high and shaped like an egg. The upper half lifted off to allow access to the lower bowl. The egg sat on its own matching, molded plate. There was a notch in the rim of the lower half of the egg, where the curved handle of a ladle protruded. The tureen was classically formed, and decidedly odd. Mrs. Reckler had fallen in love with both the tureen's graceful design and its strangeness.

"When did you get this?" Aunt Pola asked. "I didn't see this at the checkout."

"You were going to think," said Aunt Ida. "It was very expensive. And white."

"You went behind our backs?" Aunt Pola said. "Is that what happened?"

"You should have told us," said Aunt Ida. "We could've helped you carry it."

"Or we could have talked you out of it," said Aunt Pola.

Mrs. Reckler stared at her sisters and then, rising, she stood beside the tureen, tracing its contour with her hand. She decided not to think and she decided to return to the valley, to stand atop a cliff, to shout poetry at the thunder. She decided not to be a good girl, or a nice girl, or a good mother, or a good wife. Mrs. Reckler lived much of her life in fear of public opinion. She loved her sisters, but she did not want to be talked out of anything.

"I stole it," said Mrs. Reckler simply, with a lilt, with the blithe defiance of a child.

"What?" said Aunt Pola. "Don't joke. Look, you bought it, the thing is done. It's very nice. It's not my taste, you'll regret it, but be happy. Make soup."

"I stole it," Mrs. Reckler repeated evenly. If she was going to forsake all respectability, if she was going to court infamy, she wanted her outlaw's decision recognized. She wanted to be believed. She even wanted to shock.

"What, you stole it?" said Aunt Ida hurriedly. "What, like a cat burglar?"

"Yes," said Mrs. Reckler, with aplomb. "While you were both in the basket shop, looking at wicker, I went back to the pottery. I stole the tureen, and I drove it back here, and I put it in the drawer."

"Hedy," said Aunt Pola, "are you all right? You look tired."

"I'm not tired," Mrs. Reckler insisted. "All right, I am tired, but I stole the tureen."

Joe was staring at his mother, nodding his head, the corners of his mouth turned down in deep respect. He wasn't sure just what she was up to, but he had an inkling. Most people thought of Mrs. Reckler as rock solid, a pillar of dependability and good humor. All this was accurate, but there was more to Mrs. Reckler. Joe knew, perhaps better than anyone, the depth of his mother's restlessness and the reality of her dissatisfaction with ordinary life in Piscataway, New Jersey.

"Hedy," Aunt Pola said, with a hand gesture. "You didn't steal anything, but just to humor you, just to humor a crazy woman, tell us why. Why did you steal the tureen?"

"Because," said Mrs. Reckler, her chin thrust forward. "Because I am almost sixty years old. Because it is a very beautiful thing. Because the price was ridiculous, and they never put things like this on sale, and even if they did, who knows if I would be around to pick one up. And I stole it because I didn't want to think about it, and not buy it, and regret not buying it all the way back to New Jersey. I stole it because I need to lose twenty pounds, and because my children are crazy and my husband can't defrost things. I stole it because I'm a terrible person, and because life is short, and I stole it because I wanted to."

Everyone was silent. Aunt Ida tried to think of something soothing to say, something to eradicate Mrs. Reckler's confession, but she couldn't invent an appropriate sentence. Finally, without moving, Aunt Pola spoke.

"So Joe, what do you think of your mother? And her tureen?"

"I think they're great," said Joe.

"Very nice," said Aunt Pola bitterly, shaking her head, acknowledging the common dementia of the mother and son.

"Hedy, you can take it back," said Aunt Ida, pouncing on this solution. "You can say you accidentally walked out with it, by mistake."

"She accidentally walked out with a tureen?" said Aunt Pola, turning to stare at Ida. "It slipped her mind? You're as crazy as she is."

"I'm not taking it back," said Mrs. Reckler. "I like it. It's going to look very nice in my living room; I have just the spot. Now, where shall we have dinner? Should I look in the paper?"

Mrs. Reckler's tone was brisk and matter-of-fact. The subject of her criminal behavior was closed. Mrs. Reckler wasn't even sure just how she felt about her confession; she decided to postpone thinking about such matters.

"That place down the road looked very nice," said Aunt Ida gamely, relieved at the return to acceptable topics. "That diner."

"What about the coffee shop?" asked Aunt Pola. Aunt Pola wanted to discuss the theft further, but she wanted to make sure the coffee shop was being considered.

"I'm not having dinner in a coffee shop," said Mrs. Reckler. "Or a diner. Get your coats. We're going someplace nice."

Mrs. Reckler was feeling a bit triumphant and a bit wild, in her liberation from decency. She drove the group to a local restaurant listed in one of her guidebooks, an elegantly historic establishment overlooking a placid lake. The restaurant was called the 1720 House, commemorating the building's construction date. The building had been superbly restored. The interior was an exactly preserved colonial tavern, down to the dark, split beams and gleaming, uneven, pegged plank floors. A warming blaze was set in a wide, crude stone fireplace with a heavy, unvarnished oak mantel. Atop the mantel sat a collection of antique pewter tankards. Diners sat in Windsor chairs at round tables sparkling with fine crystal arrayed atop white linen, beneath brass chandeliers which glinted from the firelight. The 1720 House had been awarded the maximum four stars in Mrs. Reckler's guidebook. She had dined there once before, on a romantic trip with her husband. Their meal was the gracious dividend of an unexpected tax refund.

"I'm having a steak," said Mrs. Reckler boldly. "With all the trimmings."

"What, did you get a second mortgage?" said Aunt Pola, studying the parchment menu through her reading glasses. "These prices. What do they serve here—platinum food?"

"It's all delicious," said Mrs. Reckler. "And I don't want to hear another word about the prices."

Aunt Ida's eyes grew round, staring over the menu at her sisters, anticipating a brawl.

"I'm not saying a word," said Aunt Pola, shaking her head at the extravagance of the menu. "Who eats here—Arabs?"

"Joe, what are you having?" asked Aunt Ida, trying to realign the conversation.

"I'm not sure," said Joe, who looked at the menu with utter disinterest. He knew the hand-lettered, Declaration of Independence–style calligraphy described no real food, no Milky Ways or Kellogg's Frosted Flakes.

"There's a dessert cart," said Mrs. Reckler. She wanted Joe to eat something, even if the something was mostly sugar. Tonight Mrs. Reckler almost approved of her son's diet. She was close to recognizing its grandeur.

Joe excused himself and went to investigate the cart, a brass contraption with a glass top. Joe eyed his choices suspiciously: everything seemed to have been soaked in almond liqueur or smothered in fresh strawberries or dusted with chalky cocoa powder. These were not true desserts; true desserts came in cellophane, often with a T-shirt offer imprinted on the wrapper. Joe settled on a torte. He decided he could pick off the frosting.

Mrs. Reckler called Joe's name, and Joe sauntered back to the table. He had clearly been under discussion.

"Joe, your Aunt Pola is worried," said Mrs. Reckler. "She wants to know if I'm a bad influence on you."

"Of course," said Joe. "I should hope so."

"Joe, be serious," said Aunt Ida.

"Try," said Aunt Pola.

"My mother is a wonderful influence," Joe said, taking his seat and reclaiming his napkin. "I could not have a better mother. Period."

Mrs. Reckler smiled at her son. "He's right," said Mrs. Reckler. "What can I say?"

"But this . . . this activity with the soup tureen," said Aunt Pola. "Doesn't it make you worry about your mother?"

"No," said Joe. "It's a beautiful thing."

"Sure, sure," said Aunt Pola. "That's not what I'm talking about. Doesn't it worry you that your mother is—well, there's no other word for it—a criminal?''

"Pola, she's not a criminal," said Aunt Ida. "She took something, it wasn't hers, that's not being a crook. It's just . . . forgetting to pay."

"And doesn't this bother you?" asked Aunt Pola, interrogating Joe with the relentlessness of a warden.

"Aunt Pola," said Joe, merely for information, "I'm a pickpocket."

There was a pause, broken by Aunt Ida's rapping hurriedly on the table.

"*Kineahora,*" said Aunt Ida. "Oh boy, *kineahora.*"

"You're a pickpocket?" said Aunt Pola, staring at Joe warily, as if he had just upped the stakes in a poker game.

"But, Joe," said Aunt Ida, "I thought you were an artist. I thought you painted. When you were little, you did wonderful paintings. I remember them, your mother put them on the refrigerator, with magnets."

"I was six years old," Joe explained. "Those were finger paintings. Now I'm a pickpocket."

"Thank you very much," said Mrs. Reckler to her son, rolling her eyes.

"Mother," said Joe, "monkey see, monkey do."

Aunt Pola looked at her sister Hedy, and then at her nephew Joe. She considered matters, weighed the situation, and decided what was best.

"I think I'll have the chicken," Aunt Pola decided. "Ida, have the chicken."

22

The recent confessions of Joe and Mrs. Reckler were ignored for the rest of the evening. Aunt Ida was particularly gratified by this conversational blackout. Mrs. Reckler went to sleep with an unexpected feeling of satisfaction, a sweet impudence. Joe slept as soundly as ever. Aunt Pola was outraged at her sister's calm. She toyed with marching over to Hedy's bed and giving her a good pinch. Aunt Ida slept for a total of fourteen minutes. The remainder of the night she spent wide-eyed, listening for police sirens.

The next morning everyone packed. Mrs. Reckler put the hotel bill on her charge card, at Aunt Pola's urging. "We'll divide it up later," Aunt Pola said, "remind me."

Everyone climbed into the car, and Mrs. Reckler set a course for Maine. For the first hour of driving, everyone munched on powdered doughnuts and looked out the windows, rating the leaves. Driving through a mountainous, heavily wooded area, the group passed a chaletlike structure landscaped onto an overlook. The building had a peaked, shingled roof dripping with curlicued gingerbread trim. Window boxes were lush with nodding morning glories and trailing ivy. The balcony railings and shutters were folksily hand carved with heart shapes and other scrollwork. With its cuckoo-clock charm, the place came off as festively Bavarian, consciously fairy tale–ish. It was as if a world's fair pavilion had been plunked atop an isolated Vermont crag.

"You see that building?" said Mrs. Reckler. "Joe, do you remember?"

"No," said Joe.

"Joe, it's the Trapp Family Lodge."

"Really?" said Aunt Ida, now craning her neck to look back at the incongruous building as it receded in the distance. "That's where they lived?"

"Some of them," said Mrs. Reckler. "I read about it in a magazine. Pola, you remember the Von Trapps, right, from *The Sound of Music*?"

"Of course," said Aunt Pola. "With that Julie Andrews. She was adorable. A little chilly but a very good singer. What a voice."

"I'm not talking about Julie Andrews," said Mrs. Reckler. "I'm talking about the real Maria Von Trapp, and her family, all the little Trapps. They were in Austria, and the Nazis were chasing them, and so they escaped to America."

"And they sang," said Aunt Ida. "They wouldn't shut up."

"Right," said Mrs. Reckler. "Well, after they came to America, they opened the Trapp Family Lodge. That was it back there."

"They opened a motel?" said Aunt Pola. "Julie Andrews ran a motel?"

"Maria Von Trapp opened the motel," said Mrs. Reckler. "Or the hotel; it's expensive. It's a lodge."

"You know what was weird about that movie?" said Joe. "It was about the Nazis, right? But the Von Trapps weren't Jewish; they were all little towheads. That movie was about the Nazi threat to the Lennon Sisters."

"Don't make jokes," Aunt Pola said sternly.

"So they came to America," marveled Aunt Ida. "To run a motel. I wonder why that wasn't in the movie."

"It would be inspirational," Aunt Pola agreed.

"If only Brecht had opened a Holiday Inn," Joe imagined.

"You're disgusting," Mrs. Reckler told her son.

"Have you ever stayed there?" asked Aunt Pola. "Is it a nice place? Clean?"

"I'm sure it's very nice," said Mrs. Reckler. "But not cheap." Mrs. Reckler found the background of the Trapp Family Lodge interesting in a historical sense, but she had never really wanted to check in at the lodge, and not only because of the expense. The lodge felt *goyische*, like a tinkly attraction at Disneyland. "Julie Andrews doesn't need my money," Mrs. Reckler commented.

"It's probably very noisy," agreed Aunt Ida. "All that singing—what a racket."

"Hedy," said Aunt Pola, "I know why you stole that tureen."

"Oh?" said Mrs. Reckler, not surprised at the abrupt change of subject. The roundtable on the Von Trapps had merely been a warm-up. Now Pola was ready to talk.

"You stole that tureen," declared Aunt Pola, "to punish Mama."

"Pola," said Mrs. Reckler, "I don't want to upset you, but Mama is dead. She's been dead for over twenty years now."

"Look at that tree," trilled Aunt Ida, in a vain attempt at avoiding further dissection of the tureen, Mama, or their ostensible relationship. "It's all red and yellow."

"I know Mama is dead, may she rest in peace," said Aunt Pola. "But she's watching, every minute. She sees you. And you said, Look, Mama, look what I'm doing. You always liked to upset Mama, always."

"I didn't *like* to upset Mama," said Mrs. Reckler. "I didn't *try* to upset her. It was just that everything I did seemed to have that effect."

"Really?" said Joe. Joe had known that his mother's dealings with his grandmother had been rocky, but he had never explored the extent of the conflict. Mrs. Reckler had dropped hints, but she had usually refused to speak against her mother.

"My mother, your grandmother, was a saint," Mrs. Reckler told her son. "But she could be a real pain in the neck."

"Are you listening, Mama?" Aunt Pola asked the quilted vinyl ceiling of the Oldsmobile. "Mama, did you hear that?"

"Of course she was a pain," said Joe. "She was a mother."

"Would you like to get out and walk?" inquired Mrs. Reckler. "I shouldn't be saying these things; I shouldn't talk about Mama, not in front of Joe. It'll give him ideas. He'll think he's allowed to talk that way about me."

"Never," Joe promised. "I swear." Joe was eager to hear more of his mother's past. He tried to appear minuscule and contrite, no barrier to revelation. Joe was a seasoned hand at extracting gossip. He knew that the optimum route to attracting the deeply juicy tidbits was to be quiet and listen, even to feign indifference. People were always dying to spill the beans. All Joe had to do was sit tight and let them. While Joe was foremost a pickpocket and a gentleman of leisure, he had anointed gossip as his second career, his minor. He found little as richly satisfying in life as a secret revealed, a postcard shared, a fragrant morsel of intimate history dished up over the phone.

"Look at him," said Mrs. Reckler, glancing at her son. "He can't wait to hear. He loves gossip, it's awful."

"It's terrible," agreed Aunt Ida. "Joe, don't listen."

"Who's listening?" Joe protested.

"This isn't gossip," Aunt Pola decreed. "It's family history. Joe should hear it. He should know his roots."

"His roots?" said Aunt Ida. "What, did Mama come over on a slave ship? I never heard this."

"The comedian," said Aunt Pola, gesturing to Ida.

"Aunt Pola's right," Joe said earnestly. "This isn't gossip; it's educational. And besides, I suppose none of you like gossip? You don't pay phone bills every month?"

"I never gossip," said Aunt Pola. "It's an ugly habit and who needs it. Florence Gersten, she lives in the condo next door to mine in West Palm, all she does is gossip, all day long, yakety yakety yak, like a broken record. She gossips about the other people in Heritage Village. And she buys all those papers, those rags, like the *National Enquirer*. The last time I talked to her, she knew all about Madonna's marriage.

I wouldn't listen. I said, Florence, I beg your pardon, but I could care less.''

"So what about Madonna's marriage?" asked Aunt Ida. "Is it over?"

"Yes," said Aunt Pola. "They had a terrible fight, and she moved out, once and for all. She bought a new house, at the beach."

"I don't like him, the husband—who is he?—Sam Penn," said Aunt Ida.

"*Sean* Penn," said Joe, always mortally offended when people weren't religiously in touch on the gossip front.

"Sam, Sean," said Aunt Pola. "I feel sorry for him. That Madonna, she's a tramp."

"I think she's terrific," said Mrs. Reckler. "She's cute."

"Cute," scoffed Aunt Pola. "With the bra showing and the peroxide and the dress slit up to her *pupik*. If you ask me, that's not cute, it's something else."

All his life, Joe had heard his relatives refer to an organ called the *pupik*. Joe was never certain exactly what this organ amounted to, but both men and women were known to sprout one. *Pupik* seemed to be an all-purpose euphemism, a generic appendage or orifice. Joe had realized early on, however, that the *pupik* should never be exposed.

"I like Madonna," insisted Mrs. Reckler. "She does what she likes. She's sexy. I bought one of her records."

"You did?" said Aunt Ida. "Do you listen to it?"

"Sometimes," said Mrs. Reckler. "Once. It was nice; I vacuumed to it."

"You and your records," said Aunt Pola. "You see? You just buy records to upset people."

"Hoo boy, Mama had such a fit, do you remember?" said Aunt Ida. "Over those records you and Saul liked so much— what were they, the Rafters?"

"The Weavers," said Mrs. Reckler, referring to a popular leftist folksinging group of the fifties.

"The Communists," said Aunt Pola. "Real pinko."

"Pola, the Weavers were not Communists," said Mrs. Reckler. "Don't be ridiculous. They believed in unions; that's not communism. If Papa had belonged to a union, he wouldn't have had to work so hard.''

While Joe had no real memories of his grandfather, he had always found the garment center somehow epic. Joe's grandfather had cut the gabardine for men's suits, slicing through as many as fifty pieces of fabric at one stroke. A shaking wrist, and all the fabric would have been ruined. Joe thought of such arduous tailoring as an act of accomplished bravado, a master craft. Joe saw his grandfather as a breed of Jewish matador, cool and dashing under conditions of impossible stress.

''The records were the least of it,'' said Aunt Ida. ''It started much earlier. At birth, maybe.''

''What?'' said Mrs. Reckler. ''What started?''

''Your upsetting Mama,'' said Aunt Pola. ''But you know the worst thing? The thing that put a stone on Mama's heart?''

''Oh, she always said that,'' Mrs. Reckler recalled. ''It drove me up the wall. Everything I did, it put a stone on Mama's heart. Believe me, she lived to be eighty-two; she must have had a very strong heart.''

''When you cut school,'' said Aunt Pola, ''it killed her.''

''You cut school?'' said Joe, fascinated.

''Oh, I did not,'' said Mrs. Reckler. ''Maybe once or twice.''

''Half your senior year in high school,'' said Aunt Pola, ''and all through college. Mama would call me, she'd yell on the phone. Joe, your grandmother never understood the phone, she thought you had to yell through it or no one would hear. She'd call me up, she'd yell, 'Pola, what am I going to do? That Hedy, she cut again! She's a no-good!' ''

''I'm sorry,'' said Mrs. Reckler, remembering her teenage years all too resonantly. ''I hated school.''

''No you didn't!'' said Aunt Ida. ''You didn't hate school. You just never went.''

''I loved reading, I loved books,'' said Mrs. Reckler. ''But school was boring. I used to go with my girlfriend, Ruth Brocker. We used to cut and take the subway into Manhattan; we'd go to Central Park. We'd rent a rowboat for a quarter, can you believe that? We'd row out into the lake; we'd take turns. And once we were in the middle, we'd just drift. And we'd run our hands in the water and smoke cigarettes. It was . . . heavenly.''

Joe looked at his mother, who was almost in a trance state, recalling serious bliss. Joe could see her in that rowboat, floating lazily around the lake, taking dramatic drags on her cigarette, exhaling moodily into the hazy sunshine on a lovely truant afternoon. It was an ecstatic vista, a moment of pure youth. Joe was seeing his mother at a point of rebellion, of possibility. On that lake, Hedy Esker could be anything.

''And then you took that job on the newspaper,'' Aunt Ida recalled. ''Oh, did Mama hate that!''

''What newspaper?'' Joe asked, eager to hear more.

''That was still before I was married, before you were born,'' Mrs. Reckler said. ''I was just out of college; I thought I wanted to be a reporter. So I sent out, what, it must have been a hundred letters, to every newspaper on the East Coast, asking for a job. And the only answer I got, out of all the letters, was from this tiny local paper in Freehold, New Jersey. The Freehold *Transcript*.''

''That was it,'' said Aunt Ida. ''The *Transcript*. Mama never understood; she called it the *Gazette*.''

''She called it a lot of things,'' said Mrs. Reckler. ''I remember I had to beg her to let me take the job. But I went out to Freehold, I lived in a rooming house, all by myself. I'd never been away from home before. And I was a local reporter, like a trainee, the lowest of the low. They sent me out to cover fires and high-school graduations—everything nobody else wanted.''

''Did you like it?'' asked Joe.

''I loved it,'' Mrs. Reckler recalled. ''Well, I loved it and I hated it. The rooming house was lonely, and the men at the paper, the older men reporters, they gave me a hard time. But I wanted to be a glamorous journalist, like Margaret Bourke-White or Dorothy Thompson.''

''And so what happened?'' asked Joe. ''At the Freehold *Transcript*?''

''I stayed there for about ten months,'' said Mrs. Reckler. ''I knew they'd never promote me, and I missed people in

New York, and so I left. And then I met your father, and he was going to graduate school, on the G.I. Bill. We got married and I followed him.''

Mrs. Reckler recounted this development with a certain regret and an awareness. She didn't really wish she'd diligently slaved away and become a great reporter. She had not been seduced by the numbing grind of newspaper work. She was wistful not for lost opportunities but for her younger self, for that headstrong girl living alone in a dank rooming house in 1944. ''You know, I saw a picture of myself from back then,'' Mrs. Reckler said. ''And I was pretty. And I didn't even know it. But I looked great.''

Joe wanted to comfort his mother, but he realized that comfort was not the issue. He could neither restore nor erase her past. Mrs. Reckler's rue, her recognition of life's waywardness, was not to be usurped. All Joe could do was love his mother, both as she was and as she had been, as an uncompromising girl of twenty and as a woman nearing sixty, a woman who knew that life was not so simple.

''I was terrible back then,'' Mrs. Reckler told Joe, shaking her head. ''Just awful. I drove my mother crazy. Can you believe it?''

''Hey, Joe,'' said Aunt Pola, from the back seat. ''Believe it.''

23

The group navigated the Maine border by midafternoon. Their first stop was half an hour later, at the Maineway Outlet Store. Maineway had been a robe manufacturer for over a hundred years. Among the Esker sisters, certain brand names were holy writ, more than mere labels. Joe had been reared in Maineway robes.

Joe had never questioned his mother's cherished scroll of topflight brands. He assumed that these chosen products possessed some additional sorcery, some luster beyond mere quality. The finest knit shirtwaists were from Kimberly knits. The most esteemed little-girls' pinafores were from Polly Flinders. The summa men's outerwear was stitched with a rugged Mighty-Mac tag. Joe had no idea how these trusted brand names had been winnowed from the hundreds available. The recommendations seemed to derive not from experience or comparison jaunts but from some higher shopping authority, some Jovian being.

"Maineway robes are the best," Aunt Pola said, as Mrs. Reckler pulled into the outlet store's parking lot. "I always bought Nat a Maineway."

"Why are Maineway robes so good?" Joe wondered.

"They're beautifully made," Aunt Ida assured him.

"They're gorgeous," said Mrs. Reckler. "When you were little, I always bought you Maineway."

Joe did not press the issue. He honored his family's sacramental roll call of brand names. He did not need to learn the shrouded origins of the master list. He preferred some timeless mystery, some obscuring incense. He liked to think that at some long-ago juncture in the shifting tides of Judaism, or at least in the tides of the Esker sisters, the holy trademarks had been handed down, perhaps in a Dead Sea cavern, to avoid Pharaoh's prying minions. "Thou shalt buy only Karastan Carpet" struck Joe as a far more useful commandment than any of the usual, huffy ten. Joe liked to think that his family had inherited tribal knowledge, murky ancestral lore. He wanted Esker voodoo, drumbeats and skulls, not *Consumer Reports*.

The Maineway factory was a four-story rectangular brick edifice painted a flat barn red and occupying a scraggly block on the outskirts of Rockton, Maine. There was a clear stream running beside the building, a waterway whose flow had once powered the Maineway mill. Rockton was a dwindling backwater of perhaps four thousand residents. The Maineway factory employed several hundred of these townsfolk. Maineway was not an ambitiously extensive business, and its longtime owners had resisted being gobbled by a conglomerate. They preferred to retain hands-on control and to sell only to selected department-store chains in the East.

The outlet store was a flimsier structure thrown up alongside the factory, an afterthought constructed of white aluminum siding. There was a small, black-and-white tin sign reading MAINEWAY OUTLET STORE hung beside the metal door. The store resembled an overgrown garden shed or a miniature airplane hangar. The Esker sisters relished this near-anonymous, unassuming architecture. The lackluster facade spoke of secrecy, implying untouched bargains.

Within, the store remained bleakly spare and unimpressive. The walls were smudged panels of white plasterboard, and the merchandise was bunched haphazardly on chromium racks that rattled on a poured concrete floor. Cardboard signs were hand lettered with black Magic Marker: SAMPLES, IRREGULARS. The robes were grouped by size. Small plastic circles separated the racks into realms of Small, Medium,

Large, and XXL. There was a single, full-length, three-way mirror set up in a corner. The store had the practical, colorless air of a barracks, a temporary storage outpost. This utter absence of showmanship made everyone's mouths water. The outlet store was for the faithful.

The store was almost deserted, except for a few other well-informed travelers and a lone salesclerk, a bored, freckled teenage girl, a local who sat behind a cash register, chewing on her hair and paging through *People* magazine.

"We won't get any help from her," Aunt Ida commented, with some satisfaction. Experienced, even multiple sales help would only require more salaries, which would drive the prices up.

Maineway manufactured men's robes, so Joe was prepared to suffer, to single-handedly represent his gender. His mother and aunts ransacked the racks, slinging robes over their arms, possibilities for their various available men. The Esker sisters did not have to shop for themselves. Whenever the occasion arose, the Eskers shopped selflessly for busy neighbors, grateful shut-ins, anyone who needed a carton of milk or a new dining-room table. The Eskers were Nightingales, trained volunteers ready to lend their genius and keep in practice.

Joe had little interest in robes. He knew that at least once per year, his mother would box and mail him a robe. He would usually hate it but would wear it ceaselessly rather than shop for one himself. He would rarely launder the robe, so within a year's time it would fall to tatters and demand replacement. Joe did not like to acknowledge that he actually wore a bathrobe. Bathrobes were juvenile, nerdish, lacking nudity's verve.

Joe's obsession with style often made for discomfort. He was also convinced that toting an umbrella was hopelessly namby-pamby. A human of spirit would either bask in the downpour or race through it. Joe also rejected bedroom slippers, answering machines, putting his name over his doorbell, and any model of hat, earmuff, or glove. Style was morality. A decent person did not wear gloves. Only a cautious, small-minded, scurrying CPA wore such damning appurtenances. Joe was free and bohemian, his fingers naked and dancing. He was also usually freezing.

Joe roamed listlessly through the Maineway racks, snubbing every garment. A person who wore a robe would probably commit any number of style crimes. He'd probably wear a clean white V-neck T-shirt under his regular shirt. He'd undoubtedly sport slimy black nylon socks, without irony, and brass-buckled sandals. He'd own a turtleneck dickey. He would have lugged a briefcase to school in the third grade.

"Joe," Mrs. Reckler called out, from the vicinity of the three-way mirror. "You're needed!"

"Hey, Joe," called Aunt Pola. "Get over here!"

Joe trudged toward the three-way mirror as if to Calvary, knowing full well what fiendish torment to expect. He sighed noisily, so his mother and aunts would fully appreciate his afternoon's martyrdom. Joe thrust his arms out stiffly, completing the Crucifixion allusion.

"I'll go first," decided Aunt Pola. "Here, Joe, this is for Larry. He's about your size. Try it on, we'll see how it looks."

Larry was Aunt Pola's son-in-law, married to Alicia. Larry was a gangly, affable man. Joe had always admired him, for coping so graciously with his mother-in-law's shopping mania. Larry and Alicia lived in New Jersey with their four children, in a rambling restored farmhouse brimming with Aunt Pola's excess purchases. Aunt Pola's grandchildren, of course, adored her. Aunt Pola was a dream grandma, doting and patient and generous beyond even Santa's abilities.

Aunt Pola handed Joe a kimono-style robe, made of a bold floral cotton lined with white terry cloth. Joe slipped into the robe; it was ankle length, with billowing square sleeves. Joe knotted the matching belt and held his arms out, for the full Kabuki effect. The print was a jungly eye-popper of lime-green leaves, chili-red poppies, buxom yellow chrysanthemums, and some indeterminate, targetlike blossoms of a vibrating electric blue. Joe swiveled to look in the three-way mirror. He lurched and decided he was a ringer for a motel bedspread.

"Isn't that beautiful," clucked Aunt Ida.

"It's very . . . colorful," said Mrs. Reckler tactfully. "Does Larry go for that?"

"Larry, what does he know?" Aunt Pola said. "I love him dearly, he's made Alicia very happy, I have four grand-children, each one better than the next, but let me tell you something: Larry doesn't know from robes. I think this is very handsome. It wakes you up."

"It could wake the dead," said Mrs. Reckler.

"Joe, what do you think?" asked Aunt Pola. "Give us the man's opinion. Would you wear this, as a man?"

"Don't ask Joe," said Mrs. Reckler. "He hates robes; he's not a good judge."

"Joe, you don't have to answer," advised Aunt Ida. "You can take the Fifth."

"Stop nudging him," commanded Aunt Pola. "He's wearing the robe; I'm sure he has an opinion. Joe, be hon-est—what do you think?"

"Well," said Joe, staring at the headachy rainbow hallu-cination in the mirror. "If I went out at night in this, cars wouldn't hit me."

"You see?" said Mrs. Reckler. "What did I tell you?"

"No, that's a good point," said Aunt Pola. "Maybe Larry would go out, to the lawn or something. So, Joe, does that mean you like it?"

"I love it," Joe replied, auditioning a new strategy. "Buy it right now. Larry will love it. It's the perfect choice; look no further. This is the robe of Larry's dreams."

"He's just saying that," said Mrs. Reckler. "He just wants you to buy it so he doesn't have to try on anything else."

"Nice try," Aunt Pola told Joe, cackling.

"But no cigar," said Aunt Ida, laughing too. Joe grinned; he didn't really mind modeling the robes. Trying on robes made him feel somehow biblical; he thought he should be supplied with a flowing beard and a gnarled staff with which to cleave the Red Sea. Joe secretly enjoyed having his mother and aunts pick at him, rearranging a sleeve or checking a lining. He felt like the beloved Emperor, slavishly attended by his fussing tailors.

Joe tried on a series of robes in lieu of Aunt Pola's son-in-law. She ultimately selected two, the floral and a velvety brown shaving coat. "It's a little more dressy," Aunt Pola adjudged, and Joe wondered if Larry ever attended formal functions in his bathrobe. Next Joe was pressed into service as his cousin Kurt, Ida's son, the heart specialist from Monterey.

"Is this nice?" Aunt Ida asked, as Joe changed into a Prussian-blue robe with a thin burgundy stripe.

"It's gorgeous," said Mrs. Reckler. "Will Kurt wear it?"

"Who knows?" said Aunt Ida. "I'll send it to him. He'll throw it out for all I know. He's crazy."

"Joe," said Aunt Pola. "In your opinion, is this something a successful doctor would wear?" Before Joe answered, he pondered what seemed to be an auxiliary issue: Was there a specific robe that an unsuccessful doctor would lean toward? Perhaps an accursed dressing gown of some sort, or an unflattering style that might provoke malpractice suits?

"This is a very nice robe," Joe said. "Aunt Ida, buy it."

"Be serious," said Aunt Ida. "Are you serious?"

"What do you want?" Mrs. Reckler asked Aunt Ida. "A lie-detector test? Joe, do you really like that robe? Tell the truth."

"I really do," Joe replied. "Because it's dark. Kurt won't have to wash it very often."

"Wiseguy." Aunt Ida laughed. "He has a point. That's Kurt. I'll take it."

Joe then slipped into a progression of robes for his father. Mrs. Reckler was ignited by something in a lush pimento red.

"Isn't this a little bright?" Joe asked. "Does Daddy wear bright red?"

"He will now," said Mrs. Reckler. "We'll perk him up. As soon as I get home, I'm going to take his old robe and burn it. He wears this flannel thing, it must be ten years old, it's a rag. I can't even look at him, I get so angry. I always say, Saul, what's the matter, couldn't you find something a little more disgusting in your closet? He never knows what I'm talking about. Joe, your father is the most wonderful man in the world, but if I let him, he'd still be wearing his army uniform.''

Mrs. Reckler was correct. Her husband rarely gave a thought to his wardrobe. Since he hated to shop, he proved extremely resistant to acquiring fresh garments. The only solution lay in guerrilla tactics. Whenever Mrs. Reckler became truly appalled at the state of her husband's attire, she began torching things in the fireplace or smuggling shirts to the cleaning lady to be used for dusting.

"Just last week," Mrs. Reckler told Joe, "do you know what happened? Daddy asked me where his blue polo shirt was. It's a shirt he's had since graduate school; I threw it out ten years ago. All morning long he was wandering around, calling me at the office: 'Hedy, where's my blue polo shirt?' "

Joe smiled; he could envision his father doing this. Both Mr. Reckler and Clark were obsessively fond of "favorite" belongings—"my old blue shirt," "my good overalls." These esteemed possessions eventually disintegrated, but neither Clark nor his father could bring himself to abandon the shreds that remained. Such an action seemed heartlessly trendy. Neither Clark nor his father trusted new clothing; new clothing was always starch stiff, torturously itchy, tourniquet tight, medicine. This attitude infuriated Mrs. Reckler. Without new clothing, no one could ever "look nice."

"So what did you tell him?" Joe asked his mother. "When Daddy wanted his blue polo shirt?"

"I just said, 'Gee, Saul, I don't know where it is,' " Mrs. Reckler replied, and everyone burst out laughing. Mrs. Reckler's ingenuous reply was a shopper's revenge. Joe knew that at least once every five years, for the next millennium, his father would plaintively ask his mother for that polo shirt.

Joe finally deigned to choose a robe for himself, a well-cut design of regal burgundy terry cloth. He decided it was very Basil Rathbone, almost a smoking jacket, something that might be accessorized with a white silk ascot, a monocle, and a snifter of hundred-year-old brandy.

"Oooh, you look so nice," said Aunt Ida, fingering the sleeve of the robe.

"I love this," concurred Aunt Pola, smoothing a lapel. "This is a very good robe."

"Do you like it?" Mrs. Reckler asked her son, as she retied the belt. "Will you wear it?"

"I like it," said Joe. "And I will wear it." Joe tried to sound nonplussed, but he was taken with the robe. He and his mother exchanged a serious glance of agreement. Just to be certain, Mrs. Reckler tinkered with the robe a bit more, blousing the terry cloth over the belt. The three sisters stepped back to admire their handiwork, as if they had actually sewn the robe. Joe felt like a bride-to-be embracing a grandiloquent gown with train at the bridal shop. He turned with Balanchine hauteur, so his audience could applaud the robe from the back.

"That's it," said Mrs. Reckler. "Take it off."

"Congratulations," Aunt Ida told Joe. "It's one terrific robe."

"I hope you appreciate it," said Aunt Pola. "People would give their right arm for that robe. You're very lucky."

Joe wondered if he had chosen a robe or received a fellowship at Oxford. His mother approached him bearing a hopelessly beige robe, an oversize, ankle-length, hooded style, almost a camelmaster djellabah.

"Here," said Mrs. Reckler. "Try this on. For your brother."

"Mom," said Joe, "Clark doesn't wear robes."

"You never know," said Mrs. Reckler. "Just try it on."

"Mom," said Joe, tugging on the robe. "He's going to get mad if you give him this. I guarantee it."

"He'll get mad?" said Aunt Ida. "Why will he get mad? It's a lovely robe."

"You saw him with that shirt," said Joe. "Clark is allergic to nice clothing. He breaks out."

"Hedy, do you know what I would do about this Clark business if I were you?" asked Aunt Pola. "Do you want my opinion?"

Mrs. Reckler knew that this would be a difficult opinion to avoid. She took a deep breath. "Tell me, Pola," Mrs. Reckler said. "What's your opinion?"

"Well, if he was my child," said Aunt Pola, "first I would try and talk some sense into him. I would say, Clark, what's wrong with a nice bathrobe? If people see you in a nice robe, then they'll like you. They'll say, Look, that person has good taste. And if you own a nice robe, you can put it on after a shower and you don't get the dust from the furniture on your skin, not that the furniture should have dust on it to start with. Any human being appreciates a nice bathrobe. Without a robe, people would see everything, from the *pupik* to Toledo. To me, a nice bathrobe shows that man is not an ape. A man wears a bathrobe because he has a brain and has been through evolution. A monkey is a dumb animal, so he doesn't own nice things. It's all about civilization."

"What if that theory doesn't work with Clark?" Joe asked. "What if Clark prefers to be a monkey?"

"That's a good point," said Aunt Pola. "And you're probably right. Hedy, Clark will probably hate the robe, and he won't wear it, and he'll have bad feelings because you gave it to him. He'll think you want him to be something he's not, like a decent human being. And, Hedy, you'll feel bad because Clark feels bad, and you'll sit up nights wondering, Is he wearing the nice robe I bought him or is he using it to clean a carburetor. Any way you look at it, there's heartache. Hedy, if I were you, I would just not buy the robe. I would say, I have two fine sons, maybe they're both a little offbeat— and I'm being polite, believe me—but they're happy, so I'm happy. And if one of them is so nuts in the head that he won't wear a gorgeous Maineway bathrobe at below wholesale—at well below—then so be it. Hedy, don't drive yourself crazy."

Joe was impressed; Aunt Pola had thrown a curve. Joe had expected his aunt to approve of the robe and ignore the reality of Clark's life, but Aunt Pola had lived a long time. She had made her living by dealing with people, a few of whom were nearly as resolute as herself.

"You know, Pola," said Mrs. Reckler, "you're absolutely right."

Mrs. Reckler marched over to a chromium rack and returned to a plastic hanger the robe she had chosen for Clark. She felt as she had when she had forthrightly admitted stealing the tureen: liberated. She was freed from anxiety, un-shackled from worry over every aspect of her loved ones' lives. Mrs. Reckler felt somehow equal with Clark. She felt as if they had shaken hands and confirmed a truce. Mrs. Reckler was amazed at how simple life could be. All you had to do was put the robe back on the rack. She laughed.

"Life is full of surprises," said Mrs. Reckler, smiling.

"You know," said Aunt Pola, crossing her arms and studying Mrs. Reckler. Aunt Pola looked grave; an important new theory had occurred to her. "You know that business with the tureen? Hedy, it never would have happened if you hadn't moved to Jersey."

"What do you mean, if I hadn't moved to Jersey?" asked Mrs. Reckler, as the sisters hauled their many robes to the cashier. "What's wrong with New Jersey?"

"I'm just saying," said Aunt Pola, dumping three robes on the cashier's scuffed Formica Parsons table, "it might have had an influence." Aunt Pola turned to the languid cashier, who squeaked and reluctantly closed her magazine.

"These are very good robes," Aunt Pola informed the cashier. "You should be proud to work here."

"Uh-huh," said the cashier, as she rang up the purchases, slowly jabbing at the cash register's buttons as if inventing a lottery number.

"Do you get an extra discount?" Aunt Pola asked the cashier. Aunt Pola was smitten with employees' discounts. Every Christmas, she briefly toyed with signing on at the gift-wrapping department at Bloomingdale's, as part of the temporary holiday work force, in order to become eligible for an extra 10 percent off.

"Yeah, I think I get a discount," the cashier said, pulling some strands of lank, mouse-brown hair from her mouth.

"You must buy a lot of robes," said Aunt Pola knowingly.

"Nah," said the cashier, concluding the transaction. Aunt Pola turned to her group and shrugged, with a facial expression that clearly indicated that there were some people who just didn't appreciate things.

The cashier rang up the robe Aunt Ida was sending to her son, and then she rang up Mrs. Reckler's two robes. Ida and Pola scrutinized their sister as she paid for her purchases with cash.

"She's paying for these robes," Aunt Ida mentioned to the cashier anxiously.

"Right," said the cashier. She mulled, for a second, just what this trio of women might be afflicted with. "Are you from New York?" she asked the group.

"Some of us are from New York," Aunt Pola said. "And some of us are from New Jersey."

"Yeah," said the cashier, nodding.

"Thank you very much," Aunt Pola told the cashier, as the group layered their shopping bags. "When we leave, go buy your boyfriend a robe. Do you have a boyfriend?"

"Sure," said the cashier.

"He'll love it," promised Aunt Pola. "A nice bathrobe. Take my word. It will work wonders."

"Mama always hated that you moved to Jersey," Aunt Pola said, once everyone was in the car and under way again. "She used to say, Where's Hedy gone? Back to Europe?"

"I never understood that," said Mrs. Reckler. "I swear, you all gave me such trouble."

Saul and Hedy Reckler had moved to Piscataway in the late fifties. They had purchased and mortgaged an older de-

velopment home on a half-acre lot. The neighborhood had
been densely populated with other young marrieds, many
with new babies. There had been a pioneer spirit to the Jersey
suburbs at that time, an aura of homesteading. The streets
were wide, and there were trees and tubular swing sets and
a lake nearby. Piscataway had been a raw Eden with a shopping mall, although the malls of that era had been referred
to as "shopping centers."

Young Joe had been well served by growing up in the
suburbs. He had felt protected and cherished, as the suburbs
exist primarily to nurture children. Dr. Spock kids had been
the cottage industry of Piscataway. Joe had always yearned
to live in Manhattan, where the rooms had moldings, but he
had never disliked New Jersey. The state had been his Fisher-
Price playpen, a danger-free zone where he could ride his
three-speed bike and watch increasingly larger television sets
in the "TV room," where all the furniture was bunched
cozily around the Magnavox. Joe had known that New Jersey
was boring, but that had seemed appropriate. The very dull-
ness of the locale, the shady-carport-and-flagstone-patio uni-
formity of the houses, had implied security.

Mrs. Reckler had also found New Jersey appealing, at
least at first. As an urban child, she had thought the fresh air
and the diligently fertilized lawns to be intoxicating, a tempt-
ing narcotic. Mrs. Reckler had also liked being away from
her family, her mother and sisters. While she loved them,
she had not pined for their daily participation in her life. She
had not been a rising school administrator, like Pola, or an
adored librarian, like Ida. She had fulfilled few of her mother's dreams for her children. New Jersey had reminded Mrs.
Reckler of Central Park, on a more expansive scale. She had
pictured herself on a tartan blanket beneath a spreading elm,
reading poetry while her babies napped peacefully. This had
been the fifties, so Mrs. Reckler had even been able to in-
clude a cigarette in her fantasies of ease and art.

Mrs. Reckler's mother and her sisters had taken Hedy's
flight to the suburbs as a direct betrayal. When Joe was growing up, he had been under the impression that his aunts had
lived at least three days' travel from Piscataway. They had

always made such a fuss over any visit, setting out from Long Island at the crack of dawn, halting for a turnpike lunch midway, and phoning ahead at way stations. The journey actually lasted two hours, but Joe had always conjured covered wagons and brave scouts and fresh teams of horses.

"I used to feel so guilty," Mrs. Reckler told her sisters, turning back onto the Maine Turnpike. "Whenever I asked you folks to come and visit, for Thanksgiving or the Seder, you always made such a to-do."

"When you moved to Jersey," said Aunt Ida, "we thought maybe you didn't like us anymore. That's what Mama used to say. She'd say, 'I don't understand. What's wrong with here?'"

"And then you started taking those jobs," said Aunt Pola. "Those crazy jobs."

"What crazy jobs?" asked Mrs. Reckler, mystified.

Joe was confused as well. His mother had always worked, the family had needed the money. Mrs. Reckler had sought employment in or around fields that had interested her. For five years she had managed the office of a literary quarterly based at a nearby state college. She was now the director of public relations for the Garden State Ballet.

"You always had crazy jobs," said Aunt Pola. "You were very bright, you could have gotten your teaching certificate or gone into library science, but oh no. You wanted show biz."

"The *Delphine Quarterly* was show biz?" said Mrs. Reckler. "Two rooms and a Ditto machine? When I started work there, I thought, Won't this be heaven; I'll just read poetry all day long. Well, let me tell you, what I did mostly was type and tell poets why we hadn't paid them yet. Very glamourous."

"But what about the ballet?" asked Aunt Ida. "You love the ballet."

"As a matter of fact, I do," said Mrs. Reckler. "And I work very hard. Just last week I wrote four press releases, so I could go away with a clean conscience. I planned a fund-raising luncheon and I arranged the local interviews for the company's entire West Coast tour. And this was all by my lonesome, because the girl they hired to help me is more interested in her fingernail polish than in typing a letter. Believe me, it takes her three days to staple something. My job is backbreaking, but I'm not complaining. I love the ballet, and whenever I get sick to death of doing press releases, do you know what I do? I drag my little folding chair down the hall and I watch the rehearsals. There's a new prima ballerina, Yvette Dalle, she just joined the company; she's from Canada. I could watch her forever. She's gorgeous; she's so skinny you think she's going to break in two. I watched her rehearse *Coppélia*—oh, it was marvelous.''

Mrs. Reckler glowed. For her the ballet was poetry *en pointe*, a heightening of life. Mrs. Reckler believed, and Joe agreed, that a murderer was simply someone who had never been taken to see *Nutcracker* over the holidays.

''Watching dancers,'' said Aunt Pola, commenting on her sister's workday. ''It sounds very nice.''

''Pola,'' said Mrs. Reckler, ''I'm going to kill you. You never take what I do seriously. You act like it's my hobby. That's not a nice attitude.''

Joe knew that his mother was right. His aunts respected only professional people, toilers in law or medicine or education. The Arts were branded as suspect, unreliable, frivolous, no place to make a decent wage.

''Of course we take you seriously,'' said Aunt Pola. ''But look at the record. First you cut school, then you run away to that newspaper, then you marry Saul, then you move to Jersey, then you get the *meshuggeneh* jobs. It all adds up.''

''It all adds up?'' said Mrs. Reckler, outraged. ''To what?''

''You know what I've always wondered?'' said Aunt Ida, moving to cool things off. ''You never see any Jewish dancers. Nureyev, Baryshnikov, all those toothpick girls. They're always—I don't know—Lutherans or something. Hedy, you're in the field, tell me: Is it hard for Jews? Is there a restriction?''

Joe's mind reeled. He immediately began contemplating the concept of a Jewish ballerina, a Sandy Koufax in tulle, piously refusing to perform *Giselle* on Yom Kippur.

"Jews don't dance," said Aunt Pola. "And do you know why? I hate to say this, but it's because Jews are too smart. If you can be a surgeon, why put on the toe shoes? Those pretty little girls in the tutus, they don't have a brain in their heads. I love to watch them. One year I had a subscription at City Ballet, but I wouldn't want Jews dancing. If I saw a Jewish girl dancing, I'd know it was because she couldn't get her teaching certificate."

"Jewish girls don't dance," Joe added. "They might break a nail."

"You are all insane," said Mrs. Reckler. "Plenty of Jews dance. We have two Jewish girls in the company right now, and what about Jerome Robbins?"

"I knew Jerome Robbins," Aunt Ida said. "Pola, do you remember? I was sixteen, I was a junior counselor at Camp Kittatinny in the Poconos, and Jerome Robbins worked at the next camp over. Of course, back then he was Jerry Rabinowitz."

"You see?" said Aunt Pola. "You see what happens when Jews dance? I wonder, do you think he had the nose done?"

"I don't *care* if Jerome Robbins had his nose done or not," said Mrs. Reckler. "The man is a genius."

"*West Side Story* I liked," said Aunt Ida. "And *Fiddler*. The rest, it's a little fancy for me."

"All I'm saying," said Aunt Pola, "is that it's no surprise. Hedy, I could see it coming. You're my sister, and I love you more than my own life, but Mama was right. You're a hoodlum."

25

The atmosphere in the car grew decidedly frosty. Each sister catalogued the recent behavior and remarks of her siblings. "What can I say?" each sister silently concluded. "They're both crazy." Joe was at a loss. He enjoyed the fact that everyone was stewing. It always tickles children to catch their elders behaving childishly. Joe took an underhanded glee in watching his mother and aunts wrangling as they must have in their earliest years.

"Stop smiling," Mrs. Reckler told her son. "We're not fighting; we're thinking."

"Who's fighting?" said Aunt Ida. "No one's fighting. I'm not fighting."

"No one's fighting," Aunt Pola agreed. "Although believe me, there's plenty to fight about. But we're not fighting; we're watching the leaves change. See, even the leaves in Maine are changing. It's a wonderful thing."

Soon Mrs. Reckler turned off the interstate, at the green exit sign for Top Harbor, a coastal town. No one in the group had ever been to Top Harbor. Mrs. Reckler had often read about the town in magazines, and she had scheduled a stop-over.

Before nosing around the town itself, Mrs. Reckler drove out to a motel set into one of the grassy hilltops that ringed Top Harbor. The Land Ho Motel commanded a magisterial

view of the local crags and peaks, a panorama reaching down
to the rockbound coastline itself. The motel itself was modest, a hardy chicken coop for tourists, an elongated, narrow,
one-story whitewashed building offering only eighteen rooms
and no coffee shop. A friend had told Mrs. Reckler about
the Land Ho's stirring view and general cleanliness.

"This is lovely," said Aunt Ida, as the motel appeared.
"What a pretty spot."

"My friend Judy always stays here," Mrs. Reckler said.
"She says it's simple but very nice inside."

"It looks very nice," said Aunt Pola approvingly. "Who
needs luxury?"

The sight of the Land Ho and its nautical freshness cheered
everyone. The last hour's combat was forgotten.

Mrs. Reckler parked the car, and everyone stepped out
into the sweet, crisp air, inhaling deeply. Each breath restored the family members' good humor and perspective.

Mrs. Reckler went into the motel's front office and returned with three sets of keys swinging from plastic disks.
She had phoned ahead to avoid the close quarters of the
group's stay at the Grand Vermonter.

"Ida, you and Pola are in fourteen, I'm in fifteen, and Joe
is in sixteen," Mrs. Reckler explained, distributing the keys
and trying not to sound smug.

"Fine," said Aunt Pola, accepting her key. "So now we're
the Rockefellers."

"Live a little," Mrs. Reckler told Aunt Pola. "It won't
kill you."

"This is fun!" declared Aunt Ida. "My own room! Almost!"

Everyone retired to unpack and "freshen up." While Joe
loved his relatives, his single room felt like the Waldorf;
privacy is the most essential luxury. Joe's room was small
and bare, paneled in flat sheets of walnut veneer with dark
grooves, basement rec room paneling. The twin bed huddled
beneath a close-fitting brown corduroy spread. The only other
furniture was an office-supply, student-size metal desk with
a single drawer and a dented little metal chair. There was no
phone and no television. Joe did not mind forsaking TV; he

considered Maine to be a zone like Guatemala or Costa Rica, someplace where the reception would be scattered and little decent programming available. Somehow Joe imagined that Maine programs would not be in English.

The room had a single window, framed by limp, colorless fiberglass curtains, which Joe tugged aside. He could see all the way down to the Atlantic, across rocky fields and trees less colorful than those of Vermont. These trees were either staunch, dense evergreens, or they were less vibrant oaks, gnarled gray trees whose leaves went from green to brown to mulch with little fuss. These were Maine trees, not the preening Vermont orchards. Maine trees were hardier, taciturn specimens.

Joe drew the curtains. He did not want anyone peeking in at him, and he felt it was best to ration the view, rather than wearing it out and allowing it to become a cheap reproduction hanging on the wall. Joe poked around his bathroom, which was cubby-sized and functional, with a stall shower and no tub. The Land Ho provided only a supermarket bath-size bar of Ivory soap. It did not offer stationery, wrapped glassware, or even a postcard. The room was Soviet, something from a budget military academy. Joe decided that this eschewing of gimmickry was all very Maine.

Joe's conception of an archetypal Maine resident relied entirely on a lamp his parents had once owned. This lamp had a carved balsa-wood base depicting a grizzled fisherman in a flapping yellow slicker. The lamp's shade had been printed with silhouettes of fish and nets. Joe thought of Maine as a homey gallery of souvenir watercolors, amateur renderings of weatherbeaten piers with gulls perched on pilings. Joe had a gift-shoppe sense of geography. He identified states by their trinkets. Maine was a place, Joe knew, where the portholed rest-room doors at seafood restaurants would be outlined in hemp and marked "Buoys" and "Gulls."

Joe lay flat out on his bed and decided not to freshen up. He had no idea what freshening up consisted of. He usually assumed it was his mother's polite euphemism for using the bathroom.

There was a knock on the door. "Joe? Are you ready?" Mrs. Reckler asked from outside. "What are you doing?"

"I'm freshening up!" Joe called out, sitting up. He pulled himself to his feet and opened the door. "I'm fresh," he told his mother.

"You certainly are," said Mrs. Reckler. "Your room is even smaller than mine."

"It's not so small," said Joe. "We could all fit in here; we could set up a cot."

"Very funny," said Mrs. Reckler, as Aunt Ida's head bobbed in the doorway.

"Yoo-hoo," said Aunt Ida, coming into the room. "Isn't this nice. Joe, I like your room."

"Ida," said Mrs. Reckler, "wouldn't you like your own room? By yourself? It's very cheap here."

"Oh, I couldn't," said Aunt Ida. "Pola would never forgive me. I'd never hear the end of it. Thank God I remembered to bring extra shampoo. Pola keeps using mine."

"Hey hey," said Aunt Pola, standing in the doorway. "So, Joe, are you happy now? Now that you've got all this room, all to yourself? It's a sin. You watch, you'll be very lonely. Just remember, you can always move back in with us."

"Thank you," said Joe.

"So?" said Aunt Ida. "Are we going into town?"

"Is everybody ready?" asked Mrs. Reckler.

"I'm ready," said Aunt Pola. "Joe, are you ready?"

"I'm ready," said Joe. "Mom, are you ready?"

"Wiseguy," said Mrs. Reckler. Mrs. Reckler looked at her son. She jerked her head in the direction of the bathroom. "Have you . . . ?" she asked meaningfully.

Joe looked at his mother and aunts. He threw his head back and pretended to scream, soundlessly. Still screaming in this responsible manner, he grabbed his leather jacket and scarf and ran out of the room toward the car.

"What's his problem?" Aunt Ida asked calmly.

"He's very highly strung," said Mrs. Reckler.

"Like a violin," agreed Aunt Pola.

"Are we ready?" asked Mrs. Reckler, standing up.

* * *

Everyone piled into the car, and Mrs. Reckler started down the hill and toward the town.

"Top Harbor," said Aunt Pola, turning the phrase over. "What kind of town is it?"

"I don't know, Pola," said Mrs. Reckler. "I've never been here either. But I've always read about it. I think it's full of rich people."

"Rich people in Maine," said Aunt Ida. "Somehow it doesn't sound right. What are they rich from? Robes? Lobsters?"

Joe had also heard of Top Harbor. He associated the town with enclaves like Hyannis and Newport and Martha's Vineyard—Kennedy-style towns, gilded spas for American dynasties. These towns were the country retreats of the very wealthy, resorts once traveled to by private railroad car.

As the group drove along, Joe knew that they were in the land of the truly well-to-do, because he couldn't see any houses. All he saw were heavy iron gates, bounded by pillars of brick or carved limestone. These gates occurred at breaks in the roadside greenery, in the untended forest or in story-high boxwood. There were small plaques of brass or wood, either set into the masonry or nailed to stakes planted in the earth. These plaques all read PRIVATE DRIVE. Joe tried to look through the gates, but all he saw was winding road. Occasionally he glimpsed a mansard roof rising from the foliage far beyond the gates. The merely rich tend to live closer to the road, so their mansions may stagger all travelers. The thoroughly rich shun such common acclaim.

"So where are the houses?" asked Aunt Ida. "And the people?"

"They tuck them away," Mrs. Reckler said. "Somewhere back in there, so we can't see."

"That's ridiculous," said Aunt Pola. "I didn't come all this way to look at little gates. Hedy, go ahead, drive in. Go up one of the driveways."

"What?" said Aunt Ida. "Pola, are you crazy? We'll just drop in?"

"What?" said Aunt Pola. "We're not good enough to

look at a house? Hedy, pull over. Go right in there—see, where it says 'No Trespassers.' "

Left to her own initiative, Mrs. Reckler would have been too timid to approach the gateway. Fueled by Pola's thirst for adventure, she turned off the main road and drove between two crumbling granite columns, each topped with granite spheres overgrown with moss. The car crunched on the gravel drive.

"I'll drive very slowly," Mrs. Reckler told Joe. "They won't even know we're here. We'll just take a quick look."

"I'm so nervous," twittered Aunt Ida. "What if they have dogs? You know, those big black dogs that eat people?"

"We're not people," said Aunt Pola. "We're tourists. If we see anyone, we'll just say we're on the tour."

Joe stayed close to his window. Like his mother, Joe would have been loath to make this invasion without Pola's prodding. Joe was grateful to his Aunt Pola for owning more nerve than anyone else in the car and for ignoring the region's innate snobbery. Joe imagined that Columbus and Galileo must have been not unlike his Aunt Pola. They were all willing to charge ahead, regardless of public nay-saying or possible consequences. Aunt Pola was not a bully, Joe realized, but a true democrat, and a natural leader. She was a person who refused to accept obstacles.

"Oh my," said Aunt Ida, as the estate came into view. "Look at that."

After about half a mile, the gravel drive widened and became circular, looping before an outstanding Georgian manse. The house was two stories high, with single-story wings. The grounds were impeccably and subtly landscaped. The house was imbedded in greensward, now gray. The lawns were hemmed with sculpted islands of evergreens, poplars, and oaks. The main house must have had thirty rooms; the windows were all layered with draperies. The house was utterly formal and forbidding. The wealth of the owners was most clearly displayed in the upkeep. Joe imagined the many trained hands necessary to prune and weed and mow, to wax and dust and cook. The house was something out of a West End melodrama. When Joe detected some movement from behind a window, he assumed the shadow was Judith Anderson, or Alistair Sim, a Teutonic upstairs tyrant or a crook-backed retainer.

"Look at this," said Mrs. Reckler. "Isn't it something?"

"It's big," said Aunt Ida. "I wouldn't want to vacuum."

"Stop the car," said Aunt Pola, peering at the house.

"No," said Mrs. Reckler, who was very slowly rounding the circular drive. "Pola, are you crazy? We have to get out of here."

"Don't be silly," said Aunt Pola. "Stop the car. I want to take a look."

Once again buoyed by Pola's *chutzpah*, Mrs. Reckler stopped the car a few yards from the mansion's front door. Everyone leaned gaping toward the house.

"It's very beautiful," said Mrs. Reckler. "Joe, imagine living in a place like this."

"Yeah, imagine," said Aunt Ida. "It'd be a nightmare. All those rooms. All those beds. Who needs that?"

"Ida, I'm sure they have a staff," said Mrs. Reckler.

"Hoo, yesterday all she wanted was a cleaning lady," Aunt Ida said. "Now she wants a staff."

Aunt Pola opened the car door and stepped out.

"Pola, where are you going?" asked Mrs. Reckler.

"To take a look," said Aunt Pola. "Up close. It's a very nice place. I'm curious."

"She's crazy," said Aunt Ida. "They'll shoot her."

"Pola, get back in the car," said Mrs. Reckler.

Joe opened his door and stepped out.

"Joe," said Mrs. Reckler. "Joe, be careful."

Mrs. Reckler soon exited the car as well. She told herself that she was only getting out to retrieve her sister and her son.

"Ida, come on," said Mrs. Reckler a bit giddily, sticking her head back in the car, "We'll just take a peek."

"You go," said Aunt Ida, clutching her arms to her sides and settling more firmly in the back seat. "I'm fine here. When the police come, I don't know any of you."

"Ida, just for a minute," said Mrs. Reckler. "Come on."

"You go," said Aunt Ida. "Tell me all about it." Mrs.

Reckler realized that Ida would not be moved; Ida's caution was like iron. Mrs. Reckler dearly wanted to coax her sister onto the expedition, but she didn't want to miss out herself.

"I'll be right back," Mrs. Reckler assured Ida. "I'm just going to grab Joe and Pola."

Aunt Pola had stationed herself directly in front of the broad granite steps that led up to the mansion's portico. A stone canopy sheltered the front door, supported by smooth stone columns. Stone urns sat on the steps, harboring pyramidal topiaries. A curlicued wrought-iron carriage lamp swung on a wrought-iron chain from the canopy. Over the heavy, faceted oak door there was a massive fanlight, through which a glimmer of brass chandelier was visible. There were narrow windows to either side of the door, but the interior of the entryway was obscured by taut, ruched white drapes. Aunt Pola stood before all this splendor and nodded her head slowly up and down, frowning. This was Aunt Pola's most judgmental expression. She looked as if she were considering buying the house.

"It's nice," Aunt Pola said finally. "It's very nice."

"Pola, it's gorgeous," said Mrs. Reckler, who was more intimidated by the house than Pola was.

"Hedy," Pola said, "I've been to Europe, I've seen nice houses. I've seen palaces, I've seen Versailles. This is very nice, but it's not Versailles." Joe wondered for a moment if his Aunt Pola had stood before Versailles with her frown of possible acquisition.

The front door swung open about halfway. A young man leaned out, keeping one hand on the door. He was about Joe's age. He had blond hair, neatly parted and slicked back. It had a burnished quality, a sheen. His face was pinkish white, with a natural blush. He was wearing pressed khaki pants, a pale-yellow oxford-cloth shirt open at the neck, and a brown Harris tweed sports jacket. He also wore an alligator belt and Top-Siders, leather deck shoes, without socks.

"Hello," the young man said. "May I help you?" He spoke with a slur, almost a lockjaw; for a moment Joe thought he was kidding, affecting an overbred parody. He continued to lean out the door, without actually leaving the house.

"Hello," said Aunt Pola. "Don't worry, we're not trespassing; we're just looking."

"It's a beautiful house," said Mrs. Reckler.

"May I help you?" the man repeated, more severely.

"Is this your place?" asked Aunt Pola. "You're so young. Tell me the truth, the heating bills alone—is it a nightmare?"

"No," said the man. "And yes, it is my house. Actually, it belongs to my family. Who are you?"

"We're leaving," said Joe. "I'm sorry; we just wanted to take a closer look."

"Listen, a house like this, I bet it's on the market," said Aunt Pola. "Who can live like this? I'm from New York; I have an apartment, and a condo in Florida, and it drives me crazy. How many rooms?"

"This is not some sort of attraction," the man said. "I don't care where you're from. We really don't appreciate people gawking at the house. Is that your car?"

"We're going," said Mrs. Reckler; her tone was frosty, almost the equal of the young man's. "Come on, Pola. Joe, get in the car. Thank you very much; we're sorry we bothered you."

"Oh please," said Aunt Pola. "He's a nice man. He doesn't care. So what do you do for a living, to keep a place like this?"

"I have investments," the man said. "Excuse me, what would you do if I came to your . . . condo and started poking around?"

"I'd give you something to eat," said Aunt Pola. "But you won't come. My own family, they won't visit; it's like pulling teeth."

"I hope I don't have to involve the police," said the man.

"We're very sorry," said Joe, putting out his hand. "It won't happen again." The man was startled by Joe's offer of a handshake. He shook Joe's hand, as a reflex. Joe patted the man's elbow and then released him. By this time Mrs. Reckler and Aunt Pola had returned to the Oldsmobile. Joe trotted down the steps and hopped into the car. Mrs. Reckler released the emergency brake and began driving back toward the road.

"So what happened?" asked Aunt Ida. "Who was that guy?"

"The owner," said Aunt Pola. "He was very chilly." Joe turned for a final look at the house. The man was still standing by the door, keeping track of the interlopers' departure. Another man appeared from inside the house. This man was wearing a white apron over a white shirt and black pants. He appeared to be a servant of some sort.

"We were trespassing," said Mrs. Reckler. "But he really had a tone."

"He was a creep," said Joe. "He's a rich kid. When everybody dies, he'll inherit the place."

"I always tell Joe," Mrs. Reckler said, "that when Saul and I die, he and his brother can split the estate. One of them will get the electric fan and the other one gets the blender."

"Did you see inside the house at all?" Aunt Ida asked. "Was it nice?"

"I couldn't tell," said Aunt Pola. "Believe me, you couldn't pay me to live in a place like that. Who needs it?"

Mrs. Reckler had now reached the front gate. She swung the car back onto the main road. Joe tried to be objective. He knew they had been trespassing, imposing themselves on a private home. But still, the man really had been snooty.

"Ipsy-pipsy," said Aunt Ida. "I'm glad I didn't get out of the car."

The man had tried to make Joe and his family feel ashamed and envious. But the Esker sisters truly had no interest in becoming landed gentry. Even if they won the lottery, they would never pursue the glacial elegance of such an estate. The Esker sisters loved beautiful things, but they had a lasting suspicion of patrician glory.

"I don't think we'll look at any more private homes," Mrs. Reckler said, as the group neared the town itself.

"So far, I can take Maine or leave it," said Aunt Pola. "Except for the robes."

26

The town of Top Harbor was far from rustic. It suggested Southampton or Palm Beach more than any gull-ridden port. The group kept near the car windows as Mrs. Reckler drove through town.

"This is very nice," said Aunt Ida.

"It's very fancy," said Aunt Pola. "I don't see a super-market."

The town centered on a gold coast of fastidious boutiques and intimate restaurants, several polished blocks of high-rent retailing. The buildings were tastefully underslung, their architecture a tidy mingling of freshly scoured brick and Federal detailing. The windows tended to be small and reticent, framing only a few items, presented with jewel-like care, often against satin or velvet. There were diminutive branches of Cartier, Van Cleef & Arpels, Sea Island, Ltd., Gucci, Rogers Peet, and Charles Jourdan, along with an elfin outpost of Bonwit Teller. There were also specialty shops offering a regally edited mix of English antiques, lacy Victorian pillow shams, and tortoiseshell desk accessories. These shops had painfully genteel names like Hilary Beanbrook, Ltd., or the Lace Nook.

The town was immaculately kept. The sidewalks were free of gum wrappers. Here and there were small parks, poshly planted and lacking benches, so that no one could disturb the expressive hollyhocks. All of Top Harbor seemed to be the product of a single mind, a uniform taste. The town resembled an heirloom toy village beneath a Christmas tree, through which a valuable model train might puff. There was a private air to Top Harbor, an agreed-upon exclusivity. Everyone on the sidewalks had been matched to the shops. The strollers were all nattily turned out, in tweeds and melton and Burberry plaid. Top Harbor was less a town than a Ralph Lauren runway.

"I think we should park," said Mrs. Reckler, driving down a main street. "We can take a look around."

"I don't know that we'll find anything," said Aunt Pola. "But you know best."

Mrs. Reckler parked the car on a side street, and everyone walked to one of the avenues. The group moved along, window-shopping. They peered into shop windows, distrustfully, as if into aquarium tanks holding conceivably poisonous fish.

"So many beautiful things," said Mrs. Reckler, gingerly inspecting a window display of two highly polished Hepplewhite chairs. Joe knew that his mother was being appreciative rather than heartfelt. Mrs. Reckler took only a museum interest in Hepplewhite. She would not care to own priceless antique furniture because she would worry constantly, particularly when a new cleaning lady arrived. Mrs. Reckler knew that such furniture required costly, hard-to-locate English furniture waxes and electric humidifiers. She liked a clean house, but she preferred Lemon Pledge and Endust to anything in a small murky jar labeled "Mrs. Beeton's Bimonthly Maple Care."

"Mama had chairs like that," said Aunt Pola. "In the living room. When she died, I threw them out."

"Pola," said Mrs. Reckler. "Mama did not have Hepplewhite chairs. These are worth a fortune."

"To the *goyim*," said Aunt Pola.

The group strolled slowly down the block, rarely entering any of the shops. These stores were not inviting. Nothing begged to be touched or turned over or tried on in these stores. These were not hands-on establishments. They were designed to intimidate, to terrorize, to discourage casual browsing. Eventually the group stopped before a store called Sally Dale. The store's name was lettered in a lower corner of the plate-glass window. *Sally Dale* was scripted, in a finishing-school, ultrafeminine gold-leaf scrawl.

"Sally Dale," said Aunt Pola, appraising the name. "Who is she?"

"Sally Dale," said Mrs. Reckler. "It's the name of the store. I think I've heard of it."

"Sally Dale," mused Aunt Ida. "What was it before she changed it?"

"That's a beautiful coat," said Mrs. Reckler, regarding the sole garment in the store's window. This was a trench coat, of standard if luxurious design, lined with dark fur. The coat was not on a mannequin but hung from a knobby brass stand. The window was carpeted in white, and also held a few exquisitely strewn props: an antique globe in an oak stand, a brass telescope, also clearly antique, a collected Dickens, tooled in gold, and a pair of brass candlesticks, brightly polished and holding slim white tapers. The effect of the window display was restrained but expensive, the props suggesting the country retreat in which madame might don her mink-lined trench coat, her coiffure shielded from the elements by the Hermès scarf flowing across the white carpet in the Sally Dale window.

"So what are they selling here?" Aunt Pola asked. "Coats or candles?"

"I hope they don't light those things," said Aunt Ida. "That coat'd go up in a second."

"Ida, don't you need a coat?" asked Mrs. Reckler.

"What?" said Aunt Ida. "I have a coat. I'm wearing a coat."

"Ida, that's not a coat," said Mrs. Reckler. "That's a rag." Everyone stared at Aunt Ida's coat, which was a tailored style in beige cotton duck, with some brown leather trim at the pockets and buttonholes. It was well cared for but clearly several years old. The coat had a skimpiness to it and did not look particularly warm. The coat was just the sort of item Aunt Ida would choose. It was "good enough," the most modest purchase possible.

"This is a rag?" said Aunt Ida, of her coat. "It looks like a coat to me."

"Hedy's right," Aunt Pola decreed. "Ida, when did you buy that coat?"

"I don't remember," said Aunt Ida. "I truly don't. Seven years ago, at Abraham and Straus. Danielle made me buy it. Only 20 percent off; I still feel guilty."

"Ida," said Mrs. Reckler, demonstrating a tone not dissimilar to her sister Pola's. "You need a new coat. You're buying a coat."

"It's a very good idea," confirmed Aunt Pola. "We'll look in here. Sally Dale."

"In here?" said Aunt Ida, horrified. "This place isn't for coats. This is . . . Fort Knox."

"Ida," said Mrs. Reckler, "this is a store. They sell ladies' coats. You're a lady. We're going inside, and you will buy a coat, so that the rest of us won't be ashamed to be seen with you."

Mrs. Reckler pushed open Sally Dale's door, which had been pickled white. The interior was small, cocoonlike and hushed. The walls were painted a silvery white, a tranquil boudoir hue. The floor was carpeted in a thick cream-colored wool. Angled in a corner was a raised platform, also carpeted, with a curved edge. The walls of the corner were mirrored, and the mirrors were flatteringly lit by frosted bulbs recessed into the ceiling.

Little clothing was evident. Two racks were set into the wall opposite the platform. These racks held only a few garments. One rack was devoted to six lavish evening gowns. The other rack exhibited resort wear, crisp cottons in white or poster-color prints. There was a good deal of space between each outfit, allowing the clothing to breathe, to be properly adored. The clothes became haughty, standoffish. A single mannequin stood on a small, round, carpeted platform beside the row of gowns. It was pale and stylized. The facial features and hair were painted on, with chic dashes of black enamel. The mannequin arched languidly in a black satin gown, boned and strapless. Cerise taffeta was bunched along the neckline and about the hips. The taffeta was gathered in back, forming a near-bustle, with streamers of taffeta draping to the floor. The mannequin also wore elbow-length black satin opera gloves. A rhinestone bracelet glittered on one wrist. The mannequin's head was swathed in black cocktail net, dotted with tiny rhinestones.

"Get *her*," said Aunt Pola, jerking her thumb at the mannequin.

"What kind of store is this?" asked Aunt Ida, seeking an escape by the front door.

"It's like a dress shop," said Mrs. Reckler. "It's old-fashioned. Very exclusive."

"I don't think anyone's here," said Aunt Pola, but then everyone realized that there was someone else in the store. A woman was sitting at an antique desk toward the back of the store. The desk was clearly French, a Louis XIV excess of rosewood and ormolu, with curving spindly legs. The woman sat on a gilded armchair and was slumped over the desk, with her face hidden by her folded arms.

"Shhh," said Aunt Ida. "Maybe she's sleeping."

The woman raised her head, blinking, surprised to find herself surrounded by people. She was young, in her late twenties, with a sweet, tiny face. She wore little makeup, and her mouse-brown hair was short and ripply, in the dying stages of a permanent. Her eyes were reddened, and her cheeks were wet.

"Hi," the woman said, sitting up and wiping her eyes. She was wearing a black cotton turtleneck and a rust-colored corduroy jumper with patch pockets. Her outfit was homey, almost a slipcover, in sharp contrast to the jagged finery billowing from the racks of Sally Dale. "I'm sorry," she said. "Can I help you?"

"Are you all right?" asked Aunt Pola, with concern. The sisters all moved toward the young woman sympathetically. "Is something wrong?" Aunt Pola asked.

"No, I'm fine; I'm sorry," the woman said, trying to fix her hair. Then she gave up, and surrendered to her previous despair. "Oh God," she said.

"What's wrong?" asked Aunt Ida. "Is there anything we can do?"

"I'm sorry," the woman repeated. "I don't want to be a bother. You're very nice. Can I show you anything?" Then she clenched her fists and made a muted sound, a cry of stifled rage.

"Darling," said Aunt Pola in a businesslike manner, "you can help us in a minute. Right now we'd like to know what's wrong. Why are you crying? Are you Sally Dale?"

Joe had discovered a small gilt chair carved to look like bamboo. Its pink velvet cushion was anchored to the seat with pink velvet bows. Joe brought the chair over to the woman's desk, and Aunt Pola took a seat.

"Thank you, you're a nice boy," said Aunt Pola, and then, to the woman behind the desk, "This is Joe, my nephew."

Mrs. Reckler and Aunt Ida gathered around their seated sister.

"Hi, Joe," said the sniffling woman. Mrs. Reckler opened her bag and pulled out several pieces of Kleenex from a small travel pack. She held the Kleenex up to the young woman's nose. "Blow," said Mrs. Reckler. The young woman looked surprised, but she blew. She sighed, composing herself.

"No, I'm not Sally Dale," said the woman. "That's Mrs. Dale." The woman gestured to an oil portrait hanging on the wall behind her. It was framed in mildly rococo gilt and hung against a panel of pearl-gray Ultrasuede. The portrait was lit by a bronze picture light mounted on the top of the frame. The woman in the portrait was about sixty. The portrait was idealized, presenting a soft-toned vision of graciousness and beauty. Her ash-blond hair was upswept, and she wore a single strand of pearls and matching pearl earrings, against red silk. Sally Dale looked like the emblem on a box of Caucasian Good Taste, an upper-crust Betty Crocker or Breck Girl.

"She's attractive," said Aunt Pola, considering the portrait.

"Does she own the shop?" asked Aunt Ida. "Is she living?" At first Joe was startled by this second question, but then he thought again and decided that the woman in the portrait did seem already deceased, gazing out from some perfectly appointed heaven.

"Oh yes," said the young woman. "She's alive. She's my mother-in-law. I'm Kerry Rally."

"Rally?" said Aunt Pola. "If you're the daughter-in-law, why aren't you Kerry Dale?"

"Pola," said Mrs. Reckler, "just because all of us took our husband's names doesn't mean everyone else should take their husbands' names. She's modern; why shouldn't her husband take her name? Why should anybody take anybody's name?"

"Ipsy-pipsy," commented Aunt Ida.

"Uch," said Aunt Pola. "Hedy, you're crazy. You always get these ideas. I remember I looked for your name on the program for the ballet. I looked and looked, and there it was, right in front of me—'Hedy Esker Reckler.' Three names. I said, Who is this woman with the three names? John Philip Sousa?"

"If I had married Saul today," said Mrs. Reckler, "I would just stay Hedy Esker. It's my name; I'm proud of it."

"And then what would my name be?" asked Joe.

"If she married Saul today," said Aunt Ida, "you wouldn't be born yet, so there'd be no problem."

"So is that why you're—what?—Kerry Rally?" asked Aunt Pola. "You're being mod-ren?" Aunt Pola deliberately pronounced the word "mod-ren," for a satiric slant.

"Yes," said the woman. "I'm sorry."

"Don't be sorry," said Mrs. Reckler. "You're right."

"What sort of name is Kerry?" asked Aunt Ida. "Is it like Carrie, only wrong?"

"Sort of," Kerry agreed. "It's short for Kerrington, which is my mother's maiden name."

"All these names, you could go crazy just remembering them," said Aunt Pola.

"It's true," agreed Kerry, smiling.

Joe decided that he liked Kerry Rally immensely. She had just been subjected to a sample round of Esker logic, and she had survived. She had even appeared to enjoy the conversation. It had taken Joe years to accept the full entertainment value of such dialogues, but Kerry had plunged right in.

"So, Kerry," said Aunt Pola, "you're married to the son. What's his name?"

"Grey," said Kerry. "Grey Dale." There was a pause, as the group mulled this over. Kerry acknowledged everyone's doubting looks. "I know," she said.

" 'Gray'?" said Aunt Ida. "He's a color?"

"It's an old family name," said Kerry. "He's actually Grey Trouesdale Clarion Dale the Third; it's all Scottish or something. He has two brothers," Kerry continued.

"Blue and Green," suggested Aunt Ida.

"Stone and Barker," said Kerry, with a bit of satisfaction at topping Aunt Ida.

"Jeez," said Aunt Pola, and everyone nodded in agreement, including Kerry.

"So this Grey, what does he do?" Aunt Pola asked.

"He's an attorney," said Kerry.

"An attorney," said Aunt Ida, impressed.

"Very nice," said Aunt Pola, with a dignified nod.

"You poor thing," said Joe, and he and Kerry smiled.

"Grey is a wonderful lawyer," said Kerry, trying to be fair. "He works for his father's firm in Portland. He represents most of the major corporations in the state. He does very well."

"So you did very well," said Aunt Pola. "So what's the problem?"

"Grey is fine," said Kerry, her chin starting to quiver. "Mrs. Dale is fine. Everything is fine. It's just . . ."

"Just what?" asked Mrs. Reckler softly.

"It's just that I hate my life."

"Ah-hah," said Aunt Pola. "Now we're getting somewhere."

"You don't hate your life," soothed Aunt Ida. "I'm sure you have a very good life. You're a very pretty girl."

"Ida, that doesn't necessarily help anything," said Mrs. Reckler. "Pretty girls have problems too. Kerry, why do you hate your life?"

"Oh, I don't know," said Kerry. "Yes I do. Eight years ago I graduated from Harvard."

"Well, there it is," said Joe.

"He's Yale," explained Aunt Pola. "He's prejudiced."

"Yale is very nice," said Kerry, smiling. "But my grades weren't up there, so I had to go to Harvard. I was a history of art major. Do you know what that means?"

"Can you teach?" asked Aunt Pola.

"Not without my master's," said Kerry. "A bachelor's in history of art means just about zero. I just loved looking at the pictures. I thought I would do museum work; I thought . . . I don't know, I guess I was being a real ditz."

"A ditz?" asked Aunt Pola.

"A lamebrain," translated Kerry. "A dope. You see, I met Grey when I was a junior, and I just fell for him. I was just a goner. Everybody liked him, even my parents. I guess that should've told me something. But I was so happy, and when Grey started at Harvard Law, everything seemed so . . . easy. I just thought, Okay, Grey has more direction than me. I'll use the time to figure things out. So I worked at a day-care center, which was great, and Grey went to class, and I decided it was all just like *Love Story*, and I was Ali MacGraw, only I wouldn't die. And I knew I should be applying for museum work, or going back to school, but I just couldn't get myself together. We had this neat little apartment in Cambridge. Everything just . . . happened. I let it happen. Major ditz."

"Major," said Aunt Pola sagely.

"And then, once Grey graduated, we moved up here, to his family's house. It's an enormous place, and Grey's father is dead, so Mrs. Dale was living here all alone, although Stone and Barker both live in town. But anyway, I said, Well, why not? I thought, Who wouldn't want to live in Top Harbor, in a mansion? I'm just a Boston girl. I thought, How can I say no? And Grey started practicing, and then, three years ago, I had the twins."

"Twins?" said Aunt Ida. "Hoo boy. *Kineahora*."

"Kinna hera?" asked Kerry, confused.

"It's like . . . Holy Mary, Mother of God," Joe improvised.

"So you have twins," said Aunt Pola. "So that's terrific. Are they gorgeous?"

"Oh, they're the best," said Kerry, her face suffused with pride. "They're wonderful, but they deserve a better mother."

"Who doesn't?" said Joe.

"He's Ida's son," Mrs. Reckler assured Kerry. "I've never seen him before."

"You're not a good mother?" Aunt Pola asked Kerry. "Why not?"

"Oh, I love the twins, and I guess I'd better tell you their names," said Kerry.

"Beige and Aqua?" asked Aunt Ida.

"Toby and Molly," said Kerry, blushing.

"That's not so bad," said Aunt Pola. "It's cute. Those are real names. You did fine. But why do they deserve a better mother?"

"Because I'm hopeless," said Kerry. "Because I'm a bad person. I don't know why I'm telling you this, but . . . no, I shouldn't say it."

"Say it," urged Aunt Pola. "Get it off your chest."

"We're not from around here," said Aunt Ida. "Who are we going to tell?"

"Well . . ." said Kerry. "But you're going to hate me when I say it. I hate me for even thinking it. But . . . about a year ago, I woke up one morning, and I looked at Grey. And he was sleeping, and he looked very handsome and very successful, and I just thought . . . I just thought, I'm married to a jerk. See? Isn't that awful? I mean, that I thought that?" Kerry looked as if she was about to cry again. She looked ashamed and miserable because she had condemned herself so utterly.

"What is he like?" asked Joe. "I mean, what kind of jerk is he?"

"Joe, that's none of our business," said Aunt Pola. "That's Kerry's personal business, she shouldn't be telling it to strangers. Does he drink?"

"No," said Kerry. "Maybe he'd be better if he did. He's just . . . absolutely right about everything. Or on target— that's what he calls it. The right club to join. The right boarding school for the twins. The right nanny."

"You have a nanny?" said Aunt Ida.

"Mrs. Creely," said Kerry. "She's very nice. She's great. I said I would stay at home at least until the twins were in school, but Mrs. Dale wanted me at the store. And Grey said that he'd had a nanny and look at how well he'd turned out."

"Wait," said Aunt Pola. "This Mrs. Dale, she would rather have you here selling dresses than at home with your children?"

"She says she wants someone decent at Sally Dale," Kerry said. "It's loopy. The store doesn't really make any money. It's sort of Mrs. Dale's hobby. Her husband gave her the store. Mrs. Dale spends half the year in Europe, in Paris and Milan. She looks at all the collections. She buys a few things for the store, and then she can take the whole trip as a tax deduction."

"So she goes to Europe," said Aunt Ida, "while you sit here."

"And the nanny sits with the kids," said Aunt Pola.

"And your husband doesn't say anything?" asked Mrs. Reckler.

"No," said Kerry, in a tiny voice.

"Dear, you don't know me," said Aunt Pola. "You don't know me from Adam. For all you know, I could be a crazy woman."

"For all anyone knows," Aunt Ida said to Joe.

"Ida, what did you say?" asked Aunt Pola. "I didn't hear."

"Nothing, keep talking," said Aunt Ida.

"Like I was saying," Aunt Pola continued. "We're all strangers. But I have some advice, and I think you should listen. And do you know why? Because I have perspective. I'm outside. I can see your situation. And do you know what you should do?"

"What?" asked Kerry, mesmerized by Aunt Pola's self-assurance.

"Buy yourself a little something," said Aunt Pola.

"Buy myself something?" Kerry asked.

"At least try something on," said Aunt Pola. "There are all these nice outfits here, I'm sure there's something. Why not? You'll feel better."

"Really?" said Kerry, unsure but intrigued. "I should . . . shop?"

"It never hurts," said Mrs. Reckler, smiling.

"You don't have to buy," said Aunt Ida. "But look. You never know. You never know."

Kerry sat up straight, thinking. Aunt Pola's solution seemed absurd and yet . . . somehow satisfying. The notion of shopping, shopping as an antidote to despair, had apparently never occurred to Kerry. "This is going to sound awful," Kerry said hesitantly. "This isn't any of my business, but . . . who are you?"

"Don't apologize," said Aunt Pola. "You have a right to know. I'm Pola Berman, and these are my sisters, Ida Fleischer and Hedy Reckler. And that's Hedy's son Joe. We're just visiting Top Harbor. We're here to see the leaves change."

"Are you from New York?" asked Kerry intuitively.

"Ida and I are from Queens," said Aunt Pola. "Hedy is from Jersey. See, Hedy, I said it. I said it very nicely. Hedy thinks I don't like Jersey. I love Jersey. Till the day I die I'll never understand why Hedy lives there—except of course to punish people who shall remain nameless, namely our mother—but Jersey is just fine. I'm not saying a word."

"I live in New York," said Joe. "Who knows why."

"Gee," said Kerry, digesting all this. "I just want to thank you all, for listening to me. All my friends are in Boston, so there's really no one for me to talk to. So it all just sort of spilled out, the whole mess. I really shouldn't complain. I mean, I live in a beautiful house. I have two wonderful children. This job is really very easy. I probably should just shut up and stop complaining."

"Kerry," said Aunt Pola, reaching across the desk and putting her hand on Kerry's. "You're a lovely girl. You went to Harvard. I'm sure you're very bright, but right now you're not listening. Kerry, just try something on. For me.''

"I'm really not much of a shopper,'' said Kerry apologetically. "And the things here just aren't, you know, my style. They're very dressy.''

"I think,'' said Mrs. Reckler, standing up, "that we should look at coats. Ida needs a coat. That's why we came in here. Kerry, you'll show us some coats, and you'll get the hang of it.''

"I don't need a coat,'' insisted Aunt Ida. "I don't want a coat. But for Kerry's sake, I'll look.''

"These are selfless women,'' said Joe. "Shopping for peace.''

"Shut up,'' said all three Esker sisters simultaneously. This bull's-eye harmony caused everyone, Kerry included, to burst into laughter.

"Well,'' said Joe, in his most outraged Jack Benny impersonation. By now everyone was standing and gravitating toward the racks of clothing.

"We don't really carry that much outerwear,'' said Kerry. "We have some evening coats from Bill Blass. They're full length, in black satin.''

"Oh, perfect,'' said Aunt Ida. "Just what I need.''

"What about that thing in the window?'' asked Aunt Pola. "The trench coat; it looks very practical.''

"Well, it's lined with mink,'' said Kerry. "It's from our fur vault.''

"A fur vault?'' said Aunt Ida. "What, it's underground?''

"No,'' said Kerry. "It's right back here.'' There was a folding screen standing at the rear of the store. The screen had a wooden frame and five parchment panels, each daubed with *trompe l'oeil* trelliswork and cabbage roses. Kerry folded the screen back on itself, revealing a set of glass sliding doors. The doors led into a sort of closet, lined with gray wool. Inside the closet was a brass rack of fur coats. Kerry took a key from the pocket of her jumper and opened the lock on the glass doors, sliding one door open.

"Mrs. Dale keeps all the furs in here; it's safer, I guess, and it's thermostatically controlled.''

"That's very important," said Aunt Pola. "My stole, every summer I have it put into storage, so the skins won't rot."

"A fur?" said Aunt Ida, stopping dead several yards from the fur vault. "What are you, out of your mind?"

"Ida, fur is very warm," said Aunt Pola. "It makes a nice coat. I love my stole; I've gotten a lot of mileage out of it." Aunt Pola owned a white mink stole; she had bought it ten years earlier. The stole was a seven-and-a-half-foot highway of seriously fluffy white fur, backed in champagne satin. Aunt Pola's initials were embroidered in a corner of the satin. The stole was cumbersome and tended to swamp Pola when she wore it. She would sling the stole around her neck, with the square ends almost hitting the floor. The first time Joe had encountered Aunt Pola in her stole, at a second cousin's wedding reception, he had been convinced that she was wearing a white mink prayer shawl. Aunt Pola could have worn the stole more conventionally, draping the fur, allowing it to bunch in the crook of her elbows, but she chose not to. Aunt Pola figured that if she draped the stole, people would not get the full effect, they would not take in exactly how much white mink she had purchased.

"Ida, it doesn't have to be mink," said Mrs. Reckler, beginning to go through the fur coats on the rack.

"What's wrong with mink?" asked Aunt Pola, now working beside Hedy.

"Nothing's wrong with mink," said Mrs. Reckler. "But there are other furs in the world." Mrs. Reckler was trying to sound evenhanded. The truth was, she hated mink. She viewed mink as hopelessly suburban. A ranch mink coat was something to be won on an afternoon game show. Mrs. Reckler found mink coats oppressive. They were stunted goals, along the same lines as golf clubs, barbecue equipment, and built-in swimming pools. A mink coat lacked élan. It was a status acquisition, purchased more for the neighbors than for the woman herself. A mink coat was something Mrs. Reckler's mother would have approved of.

"These are all beautiful," Aunt Pola said, handling one

fur after another. "That Mrs. Dale sounds terrible, but she has very good taste. Kerry, get over here. Find a coat."

Kerry moved gingerly to a position beside Aunt Pola and Mrs. Reckler. She was awed by the two women, who were shopping with so little fuss and such military directness.

"Come on," Aunt Pola commanded Kerry. "Get busy." Without even thinking, Kerry put her hands out and began rifling the rack.

"Ida, here," said Mrs. Reckler, unleashing a coat from the rack. "Try this on."

"I'm not trying that on," said Aunt Ida. Aunt Ida had remained a few yards away. She stood with her arms folded, clutching her elbows.

"Joe," said Mrs. Reckler, "help your Aunt Ida." Joe took the coat from his mother and laid it across the desk. He then walked behind his Aunt Ida and touched her lightly on the shoulders.

"Joe, stop that," said Aunt Ida. "I'm not trying on that coat."

"Aunt Ida," Joe said quietly in his aunt's ear. "Do I have to get Pola over here?"

Aunt Ida tightened her lips in displeasure, but she began unbuttoning her canvas coat. She allowed Joe to take it, and she stood once again with her arms folded, in her navy shirt-waist dress and her white beads. Joe took the fur coat and stood behind Aunt Ida, holding the coat by the shoulders, exposing its lustrous black silk lining.

"You can stand there all day," said Aunt Ida. "I'm not getting in that thing."

"Aunt Ida," said Joe, "just try it on. Just for a minute. You don't have to like it. Pretend it's a housecoat."

"Some housecoat," said Aunt Ida, rubbing her elbows. "Housecoats don't shed."

"Ida," said Mrs. Reckler, who was still making her way through the rack of furs. "Stop being such a fool. You need a coat. Here, I'll try one on; I'll show you how it's done. Watch me."

Mrs. Reckler selected a lynx coat, a broad-shouldered, long-haired model, a bushy haystack of blond fur streaked with rust tones and silvery gray. Mrs. Reckler took off her own fuzzy beige wool coat, a beautifully cut garment with a full, swooshing look.

"I like your coat," said Aunt Ida. "I'll try on yours. Where did you get it?"

"Loehmann's, where else?" said Mrs. Reckler, as Kerry took the Loehmann's coat, put it on a hanger, and placed the hanger on a nearby rack. "Thank you, Kerry," Mrs. Reckler said, as Kerry helped her into the lynx. The lynx coat was almost full length and mountainously bulky. Mrs. Reckler bounced her shoulders a few times, insinuating herself into the hutlike garment.

"See?" said Mrs. Reckler, getting the feel of her lynx coat. "It's easy." She stood in the center of the store, her image reflected in the mirrors across the carpeted platform. "Look at me," she said. "I look like Bigfoot. I look ridiculous, but it's a very nice coat. All right, Ida, your turn."

Aunt Ida looked at her sister Hedy. Hedy did look a trifle comic in her bonfire of lynx. Mrs. Reckler was too straightforward for fur; it got in her way. She went for simpler luxuries.

"Aunt Ida?" said Joe, trying to coax his aunt into the coat.

"Ida," said Aunt Pola. "Go."

Reflexively, at Pola's directive, Ida slipped her arms into the sleeves of the fur, and Joe gently arranged the coat on his aunt's shoulders.

"I can't even find the buttons," said Aunt Ida, searching the front of the coat for some sort of closure.

"There's a loop and a button," said Kerry, who stepped to Aunt Ida's side and showed her how to secure the coat.

"Okay, I've tried it on," said Aunt Ida, as Kerry and Joe stepped back. "Am I done? Can I take off this nonsense?"

"Ida," said Mrs. Reckler, "stop being you. You haven't even looked in the mirror. It won't kill you."

"It might," said Aunt Ida. "Who knows?" This was the key to Aunt Ida's personality: while a wildly intelligent woman, she was positive that glancing in the mirror, that a second's vanity, that a moment's unchecked pleasure, might just kill her or, far worse, harm others. Aunt Ida was superstitious. She believed in evil eyes, a wrathful God, and knocking on wood. Aunt Ida pursued a safety that could be found in trusting only sorrow. Hope and joy were not to be trusted, or even welcomed. They could vanish in a second. Despair could be counted on; despair was a rock.

Aunt Ida believed that the minute a person was happy, God took notice and heaved down a thunderbolt. She believed that in resisting pleasure, she might keep the thunderbolts from her home, from her family, from all she held dear. Aunt Ida believed in the insurance of cloth coats and cheese sandwiches and gray hairs.

"Ida," said Aunt Pola, "look in the mirror. We don't have all day."

Aunt Pola's brisk command was reassuring. Aunt Ida turned to look in the mirror, to appease her sister. She caught a glimpse of herself across the store in the three-way mirror. Her body jerked involuntarily. She stared.

Aunt Ida looked glorious. Her fur coat was sable, in a brown as rich as the finest melted dark chocolate. Sable is a fur to drown in, to sprawl across, to snuggle beneath in a stallion-drawn troika charging across the Siberian snow-fields. The slaughter of animals in the service of fashion is an undeniable sin; still, the sables who had died to create Aunt Ida's coat were obviously decadent little beasts, courtesans and cocottes, starlets in depraved and wholly justified slavery to luxe.

Aunt Ida's hands slipped into the satin-lined pockets of the coat, and she swiveled slowly, modeling the coat. She put her hands beneath the coat's lapels and raised the collar. A fur coat overpowers most women, but Aunt Ida wore hers effortlessly, as if at any moment she might shrug the coat to the floor and kick it aside. On Aunt Ida, the coat had an irresistible slouch, a true noblesse. Aunt Ida looked as if she had been born in sable, as if her closet knew nothing else.

Aunt Ida continued to stare at herself in the mirror. Her gaze became almost clinical. She glided across the room, as if toward a lover, and stepped onto the platform in front of the mirrors. She nestled in the coat, tugging it around her, clenching her shoulders, playing hide-and-seek. Then she flung open the coat, thrust the fur aside, and stood with her hands boldly on her hips. Aunt Ida made the coat her own.

"This is a very nice coat," said Aunt Ida, still looking in the mirror. Her tone was matter-of-fact and speculative. She sounded almost like Aunt Pola, entertaining a sublet of Buckingham Palace.

"You look so beautiful," said Kerry.

"Of course," said Aunt Pola.

"Ida's always been beautiful," agreed Mrs. Reckler. Ordinarily this would have been the juncture for Aunt Ida to noisily oppose such praise and offer a *kineahora*, followed by a firm *poo poo poo*.

"This is a very nice coat," Aunt Ida repeated, nuzzling the fur collar with her cheek.

"So buy it," said Mrs. Reckler. "You need a coat."

"How much?" Aunt Pola asked Kerry. "In American money."

"Gee, that coat is Russian sable," said Kerry. "It costs—oh God—$25,000. Can you believe it?" Kerry asked apologetically.

"How much?" asked Aunt Ida, who had not been listening.

"Too much," said Aunt Pola. "Listen, for that kind of money, they should throw in a house."

"It's $25,000," said Mrs. Reckler, with great rue. "But it's a beautiful coat."

Aunt Ida wrenched herself away from her reflection. "$25,000?" she said. "For a coat?"

"I'm sorry," said Kerry. "Isn't that awful?"

"Look it over," proposed Aunt Pola, humorously. "Maybe there's a rip."

"A rip?" said Aunt Ida, gazing in the mirror again, now with melancholy. She savored her beloved, knowing they must part. "If there's a rip in the coat, can I get it for $49.00?"

"Aunt Ida," said Joe. "You look so great. I tell you what— let me buy it for you." Joe was sincere; he found the sight of his Aunt Ida in a $25,000 Russian sable coat supremely stirring. He had never seen his aunt knuckle under to pleasure. By all rights, the coat belonged to her. The coat clearly adored Aunt Ida; the sables were purring. If Joe could have his way, there would be a life-size bronze statue of Aunt Ida in her sable coat placed somewhere in Central Park. The statue would signal a wicked triumph, the victory of happiness. "Aunt Ida in Sable," a plaque would read. "Together at Last."

"You want to buy me this coat?" Aunt Ida laughed. "You want to buy me a $25,000 coat?"

"Sure," said Joe. "I'll put it on my charge."

"He'll put it on his charge." Aunt Ida chortled. "Big spender."

"You're a nice boy," said Aunt Pola, also chuckling.

"So let him," said Mrs. Reckler, who had some idea of what her son was up to.

"Let me," said Joe, fishing in the pocket of his jeans for his charge card.

"It's a beautiful coat," said Aunt Ida, striking a final pose in the mirror. "Oh well." While Aunt Ida's tone was wanly regretful, she was still not taking off the coat.

"Aunt Ida," said Joe, now clutching his plastic charge card. "I'll buy you the coat. I want to. It will make me happy—do it for me."

"Shut up," said Aunt Ida, good-naturedly. "But if it'll make you happy . . ."

"Go on," joked Aunt Pola. "He's such a sad boy."

"I'm serious," said Joe. He stepped up onto the platform beside Aunt Ida and held out his charge card. Aunt Ida leaned back and squinted at the card, as she was not wearing her reading glasses. "Get me my bag," said Aunt Ida.

Kerry brought Aunt Ida her handbag, and Aunt Ida unearthed the appropriate bifocals. She read Joe's charge card, which did not have Joe's name on it. The card was stamped with someone else's name.

"Aunt Ida," said Joe, trying to sound gruff, "if you don't let me buy you the coat, I'm going to be very upset. I mean it."

"Ida," said Mrs. Reckler, "you said yourself, it's a very nice coat."

Aunt Ida held the charge card. She thought about her life. She had been married for fifty years to a man she had loved dearly, a man who had died a year earlier. Aunt Ida's son was a heart specialist who couldn't clean a bathroom. Aunt Ida's daughter was a beautiful girl and an excellent teacher, but she had broken her engagement to a handsome Jewish medical student.

Aunt Ida thought about her forty-five years of employment in New York public school libraries. Aunt Ida loved her work, she brought children and books together, she shared her greatest passion.

Suddenly a scene flashed into Aunt Ida's brain, appearing vividly just behind her eyes. She saw three of her favorite characters floating out of children's books. The characters were Curious George, the mischievous monkey; the goony Cat in the Hat, from the Dr. Seuss series; and Eloise, the raucous little girl who lived at the Plaza Hotel. The three characters had their hands, or their paws, cupped around their mouths, or their snouts, megaphone style. *"Ida!"* the characters shouted.

Aunt Ida decided that she might as well plunge off the deep end, directly to hell. She turned to Kerry. "I'll take it," she said with a shrug.

"Ida," said Aunt Pola, staring at her sister in disbelief. "Are you crazy?"

"Leave her alone," said Mrs. Reckler. "She needs a coat."

"I'm so glad you're taking it," said Kerry, delighted. "It looks so wonderful on you. Shall I put it in a garment bag?"

"Nah," said Aunt Ida. "I'll wear it." Aunt Ida grabbed one last look at herself in the mirror and nodded at her reflection. She turned and stepped off the platform. "So?" she said to the group. "What are we waiting for?"

Joe followed Kerry to the antique desk, where he handed her the charge as she began to make out a receipt. Mrs. Reckler shed her lynx coat and slung it back on a hanger. "It's not for me," she said. "I'm no lynx."

Aunt Pola observed all this, tight-lipped. She had begun to suspect what was afoot; she had recalled her nephew's criminal history. "This is all very nice," said Aunt Pola ruefully. "A fine kettle of fish."

Kerry took Joe's charge card and ran it through the metal device that imprinted the raised lettering on the card onto the receipt form. Kerry picked up the form and checked the name on the card. Her head jerked up. She stared at Joe, stunned. He smiled back pleasantly.

The name on the card was Grey Dale. Joe had plucked the card from Grey Dale's Brooks Brothers wallet, which he had finagled from Grey Dale's khaki pocket earlier in the day. Joe and Aunt Pola had chatted with Grey Dale on the steps of his stately home, where they had been trespassing. Joe felt no remorse. Heisting the charge card of someone named Grey Dale was no crime. It was a moral imperative.

Kerry thought for a moment. Then she filled out the rest of the receipt. She handed the receipt to Joe. "Just sign right here," she said, as if she'd noticed nothing. "It's a beautiful coat."

As the group left Sally Dale, Aunt Pola arranged to take Kerry shopping again the next day. Aunt Ida was swaggering a bit in her sable.

"It's a gorgeous coat," said Mrs. Reckler, as everyone walked to the car.

"This rag?" said Aunt Ida, out of habit. Once Aunt Ida

had purchased something, she dubbed it old, a *shmatte*, a rag.

"Ida, I don't know what to say," said Aunt Pola, shaking her head. "From Hedy, I would expect such shenanigans. From Joe, well, look at the mother, look at the upbringing, what can you expect? But Ida, that business with the credit card—it's a terrible thing."

"It is," agreed Aunt Ida. She shut her eyes and hiked her shoulders so that the sable would tickle her earlobes. "It's a terrible thing."

"The only reason I'm not going straight to the police," said Aunt Pola, "is because you're my sisters and Joe is my nephew. And it is a beautiful coat. The skins are worked vertically. They're matched. I love that."

"So," said Mrs. Reckler, once everyone was in the car and headed back to the Land Ho. "What do we think of this Kerry business?"

"The poor girl," said Aunt Ida. "That mother-in-law."

"And that husband," said Mrs. Reckler.

"He's an attorney," said Aunt Pola, trying to keep things in perspective.

"Pola," said Mrs. Reckler. "So he's an attorney, so what? If he killed nine people, but he went to Harvard Law, would that make it better?"

"You know, that's something I'll never understand," said Aunt Pola. "Why a professional man would kill someone. I read about that man in the *Times*, that doctor, he was a surgeon, he poisoned half his patients. It doesn't make sense. And he was a Jewish fellow. Go figure."

Joe pondered this. Joe knew that in her heart, Aunt Pola considered Jews incapable of crime. The most a Jewish boy could be found guilty of, Aunt Pola believed, was unnecessary freshness.

"I think she should leave him," Mrs. Reckler announced. "I think she'd be much better off. Grey Dale."

"It sounds like a cemetery," mused Aunt Ida.

"Grey Dale," repeated Aunt Pola. "You know, I hate to say this, but with a name like that, he never stood a chance. The *goyim*, I'll never understand it, if I live to be a hundred.

All the kids are named Billy and Susie, no wonder they have no brains. Let's face it, if you marry a Saul, or a Jake, or an Aaron, you know where you stand. You married someone from history, from the Talmud. You marry a Tommy or a Timmy, you get what you pay for.''

"So you think she should leave him?" Aunt Ida asked, both titillated and horrified at the thought. "Just like that?"

"What, just like that?" said Mrs. Reckler. "We saw the man, at his house, he's very unpleasant. He makes her work in that awful store, and she can't see her children. She should take the kids and get out of there."

"You know who she might like?" Aunt Pola offered. "Irma's boy."

"Wait," said Aunt Ida. "She's still married, and you're fixing her up already?"

"Listen, she's got kids. She can't teach. What she needs is a better husband, so I'll find her one. What's wrong with that?"

Joe was fascinated. He imagined Aunt Pola tracking an appropriate fellow through the Home Shopping Caravan. "Who's Irma?" Joe asked, eager to hear more.

"Irma is a distant cousin," Aunt Pola explained.

"You've met her at funerals," Mrs. Reckler told her son.

"She's a redhead," added Aunt Ida. "Currently."

"She's a very nice woman," said Aunt Pola. "She lives out in Great Neck. Her husband's an osteopath. The son's a periodontist. He has a practice in Bayside. But you know, on second thought, we can't waste him on Kerry."

"What waste him?" said Aunt Ida. "She's a very nice girl. She sold me my coat."

"Of course she's very nice," said Aunt Pola. "But she's still a *shiksa* from Boston. If we give her the periodontist, then some Jewish girl won't get him. It's not right. It's not like there are so many periodontists in the world, like there's one to a customer. I like this Kerry, I feel for her, but we'll find her somebody more appropriate. Look, Joe's laughing. He think's I'm crazy. Joe, let me tell you, you're very lucky, a Jewish man is a very desirable commodity nowadays. But we'll find somebody. I'm very good at this. You watch, this

Kerry's going to thank me. She's going to say what everyone says. She'll say, Pola, at first I wasn't sure, but now I have to admit it, you knew best."

There was a pause. Then Aunt Ida, Mrs. Reckler, and Joe lost all self-control and began giggling maniacally. This did not disturb Aunt Pola in the slightest. She merely nodded and raised an open palm.

"You'll see," said Aunt Pola. "You'll see."

Everyone went to bed early that night, as Mrs. Reckler had scheduled a strenuous roster of activities for the next day. She had begun to feel guilty, because the group had been spending so much time shopping. From past experience, Joe knew that his mother's preferred antidote to shopping was museumgoing. Mrs. Reckler had always insisted that on all family vacations, Joe stumble through an appropriate passel of art and historical museums. Joe liked being forced to appreciate culture and history because he felt purified afterward, saintly. Joe was old-fashioned in this regard. He believed that it was all parents' duty to herd their children into such institutions, For Their Own Good. "You don't have to like it," Mrs. Reckler would always say, dragging Joe through yet another Winslow Homer retrospective or exhibit of Shaker furniture. "A little culture won't kill you."

The next morning everyone settled into the Oldsmobile and headed out for the Top Harbor Whaling Museum and Nautical Historical Society.

"It's a wonderful museum," said Mrs. Reckler, as she drove. "I read about it in *The New Yorker* once; it was fascinating."

"What, it's all about whaling?" asked Aunt Ida. "Will there be whales?"

"I don't know, Ida," said Mrs. Reckler evenly. "I've never been there. Maybe they have whales; I don't know."

"I think it sounds very interesting," said Aunt Pola. "Maybe we'll learn something."

"And maybe afterward," Joe suggested, "we can actually go whaling."

"Poor baby," said Mrs. Reckler, leaning over to pinch

her son's cheek. "He has to go to a museum. Listen, it won't kill you."

"You don't know that," said Joe. "There have been many documented deaths related to museumgoing. I might be overwhelmed by the exhibits. A whale might eat me. I might fall on a harpoon."

"We'll protect you," said Mrs. Reckler. "Don't worry, *bubbe*."

Mrs. Reckler drove up a winding, isolated stretch of road. A lighthouse tower was silhouetted in the distance. The lighthouse rose three stories and had been freshly painted, the lower half in red and the upper half in white. The whaling museum occupied a square wooden building at the base of the lighthouse. During the war this building had housed Coast Guard personnel. The lighthouse and the museum, anchored atop a sheer cliff dropping to the coastline, presented a postcard spectacle against the clear blue sky.

"Oh look," said Mrs. Reckler, as the car approached the museum. "It's next to a lighthouse. I love lighthouses. One of my fantasies has always been to live in a lighthouse in Maine."

"Hedy," said Aunt Ida, "I'm glad you didn't tell Mama."

Joe shared his mother's penchant for lighthouse living. The idea was dramatic, an American equivalent of solitude on the moors. A lighthouse was isolated, and battered by the elements. Whoever lived in the lighthouse played a vital role, keeping the lighthouse beam glowing to warn sailors from the treacherous shoals. Both Mrs. Reckler and Joe dreamed of slipcovered easy chairs in cozy, round lighthouse rooms, and reading books all day before a roaring fire, and switching on the big light whenever a storm threatened. This fantasy depended on an enormous degree of vagueness. When they gave the situation any serious consideration, they knew that lighthouse life would be unbearably tedious, clammy and claustrophobic. What Joe and his mother really wanted was a dazzlingly decorated beach house in the shape of a lighthouse.

"Isn't this pretty," said Mrs. Reckler, parking the car in a sandy lot beside the museum.

"So where are the whales?" asked Aunt Ida.

"Ida," said Mrs. Reckler, "Shut up."

Everyone left the car and crossed the parking lot. The day was brisk, so the sisters all pulled silk scarves over their heads, to keep their ears warm. Mrs. Reckler's scarf was a subdued beige, with a tiny dark-green houndstooth check. Aunt Ida's scarf was navy with a scarlet stripe. She was wearing her sable buttoned up to the neck.

"It's a good thing I got this coat," said Aunt Ida, tugging her collar up. "It's very practical."

"Don't talk about that coat," said Aunt Pola. "It's a coat from the devil."

"He does very nice work," said Aunt Ida. Aunt Pola had noticed that ever since obtaining her sable, Aunt Ida had been speaking up. Aunt Pola attributed this insubordination to Mrs. Reckler's influence.

"Ipsy-pipsy," said Aunt Pola, feeling a bit cowed. Aunt Pola tightened her own scarf, a splashy plaid in lime green, hot pink, and purple.

The group entered the museum via a small foyer. A local woman in a cardigan sold tickets to the museum, collecting the money in a gray-enameled tin box.

"That's one dollar and fifty cents admission," said the woman. "Welcome to the Maritime Museum."

"A dollar fifty," said Aunt Pola, taking off her scarf and smoothing her hair. "What's all the money for? Whale food?"

"The proceeds go for museum upkeep," said the woman. "Salaries and supplies."

"What if I give you a dollar," said Aunt Pola, "and some paper towels."

"She's joking," Mrs. Reckler told the woman. Mrs. Reckler bought admission for everyone.

"You're a fool," Aunt Pola told Mrs. Reckler, breezing into the display area.

The museum filled the airy, sun-washed interior of the clapboard building, which was basically one large, undivided room. Exhibits in glass cases lined the sides, and other whaling memorabilia hung from the walls and the peaked, beamed ceiling.

"So where is everybody?" asked Aunt Ida. There were only five or six other people touring the museum, a few elderly people and a couple pushing a well-behaved child in a stroller.

"It's nice; we can take our time," said Mrs. Reckler. Without even glancing at her son, Mrs. Reckler added, "Joe, don't roll your eyes."

"I wasn't rolling my eyes," Joe insisted.

"Joe isn't big on museums," Mrs. Reckler explained.

"I was rolling my brain," said Joe, shuffling toward the first display case.

The sisters followed Joe, and they gathered around the case. "A Map of the New England Whaling Territories," Aunt Ida read aloud from the filing card pinned beside a creased, almost indecipherably worn paper map lying in the case.

"This is very interesting," said Mrs. Reckler. "See, you can see where the whales were—right off the coast."

"So the whalers could find them and kill them," Joe said. "It's like a menu. Did people eat whale?"

"Not me," said Aunt Ida. "Just tuna."

"If we pay attention, maybe we'll find out," said Mrs. Reckler, and everyone, properly chastised, returned to the display cases.

"This is very beautiful," said Aunt Pola. "Look at this. It's scrimshaw." The scrimshaw case contained several examples of whale bones, which turn-of-the-century sailors had carved with lacy patterns and crosshatched scenes of demure courtship. Upon returning to shore, the sailors had donated the scrimshaw keepsakes to their pining sweethearts.

"Look at how intricate," Mrs. Reckler commented. "It must have taken forever to do that carving."

"They were on ships," said Aunt Ida. "They had time."

Even Joe was impressed with the pieces of scrimshaw. Scrimshaw struck him as a form of whaler's *tchotchkes*.

"Look at these," said Aunt Pola, moving along. "These are oarlocks. They keep the oars attached to the boat."

"Very nice," said Mrs. Reckler.

"Joe, what are those?" asked Aunt Ida. Joe was standing before a set of iron lances mounted on the wall.

"They're harpoons," said Joe.

"I'm glad I'm not a whale," said Aunt Ida, noting the sharp points of the harpoons.

"It's like *Moby Dick* in here," said Aunt Pola, joining the others at the harpoon rack.

"It says here," said Mrs. Reckler, skimming a pamphlet, "that they had to kill the whales, for heating oil and whale-bone for corsets and ambergris."

"Amber who?" asked Aunt Ida.

"Ambergris," said Mrs. Reckler. "It says it's used in making perfume. It's an essential ingredient."

"I knew that," said Aunt Pola, very blasé.

They all wandered through the museum at their own pace. Joe found he could absorb each exhibit in seconds, so he spent much of his time looking out the windows at the ocean. The sisters began with diligence, cooing over every water-logged captain's diary and tarnished brass sextant, memorizing every date and hurricane. Gradually, as they grew overly familiar with astral navigation, the Eskers moved more quickly, skipping labels and bypassing the shellacked board that boasted over forty subtle variations on the sailor's knot. Finally everyone had made a full circle and gathered in the center of the room, looking up at the ceiling. Hanging from thin steel wires was an enormous whale jawbone, set in what Joe decided was an eternal yawn. The jawbone opened to a span of over eight feet and sprouted ragged triangular teeth. The group stared up at the jawbone, mentally supplying the mammal that had once surrounded it.

"I wish they hadn't killed him," said Mrs. Reckler, pitying the whale.

"Maybe this was a very old whale," said Aunt Pola. "Maybe he died peacefully."

"Hello, Charlie," Aunt Ida told the jawbone.

"Imagine how big he was," said Mrs. Reckler. "I mean, he was a whale." Mrs. Reckler stared a while longer at the jawbone, and then she turned to her son. "Joe, have you been to the dentist lately?"

Mrs. Reckler was always worried that Joe didn't take care of himself, that he neglected his health. It was at moments like these that Joe knew his mother truly loved him. The unlikeliest things reminded Mrs. Reckler of her son.

"For your information," Joe said to his mother, "I went to the dentist just last week, and I had a root canal."

"Good," said Mrs. Reckler, brushing Joe's hair out of his eyes. "Keep it up." Mrs. Reckler was proud that Joe had independently had a root canal. She took this as a sign of his maturity. Joe knew that his having had a root canal would please his mother immensely. She had been his inspiration throughout the procedure. Joe smiled, knowing that his root canal tickled his mother as much as a bouquet. Joe found absurdity very touching.

The group finally descended upon any museum's most crucial element: the gift shop. The Whaling Museum's merchandising consisted of a single glass case, stocked with drinking glasses and key chains, and two minor revolving wire racks filled with postcards, pamphlets, and bumper stickers. The case also held sets of slides, featuring photos of drydocked whaling ships and the more pulsating scenes from film versions of *Moby Dick*.

"I'll send these to Kurt," said Aunt Ida, fingering some postcards. "Which do you like better, the lighthouse or the map?"

"Ida, go crazy," advised Mrs. Reckler. "Buy both."

"I like this," said Aunt Pola, holding a drinking glass up to the light. The glass was etched with a line drawing of a whale frolicking in the waves. The name of the museum was etched on the other side of the glass.

"Your father might like this," Mrs. Reckler told Joe, as she assembled a library of pamphlets on such topics as "Whaling: The First American Industry" and "Life on a Schooner." Mrs. Reckler rated pamphlets as intellectually superior to trinkets.

"Mom, you know, it's funny," said Joe. "Daddy has never mentioned whaling to me."

"Don't be fresh," said Mrs. Reckler, "or I'll buy you a pamphlet."

Joe approved of his mother's and aunts' fevered scrutiny of the meager gift-shop wares. Gift shops were by far Joe's favorite part of any museum. At Christmas, Mrs. Reckler had always bought each of Joe's teachers a Museum of Modern Art datebook. The Reckler home sported many museum exhibition posters, framed under glass. As a child, Joe had always collected postcards, hoarding his Monet Water Lilies and Unicorn tapestries the way others stockpiled their Mickey Mantles and Willie Mayses. Joe had always coveted the coffee-table books for sale at the larger museum shops. These ten-ton volumes, on Hockney's stage designs or the Treasures of the Prado, had always struck Joe as luscious. Shopping and museumgoing were closely related experiences. Both demanded curiosity and dedication and comfortable shoes. When Joe thought of his childhood, he thought of Lord & Taylor and *Guernica*. Mrs. Reckler had introduced him to both.

"Are we done?" asked Mrs. Reckler, after everyone had paid the woman in the cardigan for their gift shop haul. "You see, Joe, it didn't kill you."

28

The group plotted a course from the Whaling Museum to the Dale estate, on which they had trespassed the day before.

"It's still here," said Aunt Pola, as the car pulled into the circular drive in front of the mansion.

"It gives me the creeps," said Aunt Ida, retreating into her sable.

"Ida, with that coat you could own this house," said Mrs. Reckler.

"You think?" said Aunt Ida, toying with the notion. Her sable had led her to toy with all sorts of notions. "No," she decided. "It's too big. It's not for me. But I'll take a look."

Gathering her coat around her, Aunt Ida stepped out of the car.

"Look at her," said Aunt Pola. "Now she's a daredevil."

Everyone bunched at the front door, and Aunt Pola rang the bell. They composed themselves. Mrs. Reckler had freshened her lipstick in the car and blotted her lips with a Kleenex. Joe hoped that Grey Dale and his mother were at home; he was looking forward to some fireworks.

The front door opened and a man appeared, in black pants and a rough linen apron. This was the servant Joe had glimpsed the day before. "Good afternoon," the man said.

"So hello," said Aunt Pola. "We're expected."

"Whom shall I say has arrived?" asked the man.

"The Esker sisters," said Mrs. Reckler. "We're here to pick up Kerry."

"We're going shopping," said Aunt Pola. Aunt Pola said this grandly, as if she were announcing a polo match. She didn't trust the manservant. He was in the employ of Grey Dale and his mother.

"Very good," said the man. "Please come in."

Walking into the entry hall of the Dale estate was like invading a piece of Wedgwood. The walls were painted a matte jasper blue, and all the woodwork had been picked out in white. The ceilings were high, and there were matching Regency mirrors hung on either side of the hall. These large rectangles in gilded frames were topped by gilded eagles clutching batches of gilded arrows in their talons. Beneath each mirror was a narrow Chippendale mahogany table. Each table was graced with a sterling-silver bowl of stiffly arranged flowers, exact clusters of chrysanthemums, roses, and baby's breath.

"This is very nice," said Aunt Ida, standing near the front door.

"Very nice," said Aunt Pola, almost touching a chrysanthemum. Joe knew that neither his mother nor his aunts approved of such professional floral arrangements. Their choice would always be cut flowers, loosely bundled in a favorite vase. Arrangements were impersonal and reminiscent of funerals.

"Look at all this," said Mrs. Reckler, checking her appearance in one of the mirrors. "Joe, don't touch anything."

"Hello," said Kerry, appearing on the staircase at the end of the hall. "You came!" Kerry hurried down the stairs and kissed Aunt Pola, the nearest aunt.

"Of course we came," said Aunt Pola. "So this is where you live."

"Yes," said Kerry. "It's very . . . formal."

"It's elegant," said Mrs. Reckler, kissing Kerry. "Are you all right?"

"I'm fine," said Kerry. "I'm sorry about yesterday. I was such a total mess."

"You were," said Aunt Ida, kissing Kerry. "But don't worry."

"Hi, Joe," said Kerry, kissing Joe. "Welcome to Dale Dell."

"Dale Dell?" said Joe.

"Don't look at me," said Kerry, who, for a second, sounded like an Esker sister. "Come in," she continued. "Sit down. I'm just getting the twins. Can I get you anything?"

Kerry led the group through an archway, into a parlor. The parlor was sumptuous, in the imperial manner of an embassy receiving room. The room was so large that the furniture was grouped in at least three full conversational cliques. Kerry led her guests to the seating aimed at the imposing columned marble fireplace. Matched Ming vases were spaced on the marble mantel, beneath a massive painting, a murky English oil of two preening stallions being groomed amid a forest glade.

"Look at that painting," said Aunt Pola, moving closer to the mantel. "It's very beautiful. Do you know these horses?"

"Not me," admitted Kerry. "The painting belonged to Mrs. Dale's mother."

"Joe," said Mrs. Reckler, as Joe sat in a wing chair upholstered in taut chintz. "Be careful."

"Mom, it's a chair," said Joe, but he understood his mother's apprehension. The room had a mausoleum-like stillness and was clearly intended more for display than for rambunctious daily life. Joe found himself wondering if the chair he was sitting in was insured, in case he had a leaking Bic pen in his pocket.

"Doesn't it drive you crazy?" Aunt Ida asked Kerry, as everyone cautiously moved to a chair or settee. "This house is gorgeous, but aren't you afraid you'll break things?"

"All the time," confided Kerry. "I stay upstairs mostly; that's where Grey and I live. I don't know what I'll do when the twins get bigger."

Joe looked around the room. Many wealthy homes have an aura of Medici abundance, the rooms bursting with mammoth, overstuffed sofas churning with Aubusson pillows and cashmere throws. The end tables are jammed with zillionaire *tchotchkes*—ivory snuffboxes and priceless icons and silver-framed photos of celebrity cohorts. Joe found these homes obscenely inviting. They spoke of the dizzying languor, of the mad Arabian-nights plushness that money can buy. Dale Dell was expertly embalmed. There was an icy distance between the bunchings of furniture, and there was little fuss. All the surfaces were gleaming and bare, save for an occasional lamp fashioned from a Ming ginger jar. The room was not seductive. The decor was not the batty clutter of an English country home but the finicky spareness of a senate chamber.

"It must be nice when you have a fire," said Mrs. Reckler, teetering on the edge of a small, skirted sofa covered in the blue damask of the drapes.

"Mrs. Dale had the flues closed," Kerry explained. "She says a fire just smokes up the house and gets into the fabrics." Kerry tried to be fair to Mrs. Dale, but her heart wasn't in it. She sounded like someone who had spent far too long staring at an empty, spotless fireplace.

"Kerry?" came a voice from the hallway. A woman entered, and Joe immediately recognized her upswept hairdo: here was Sally Dale. "Kerry?" the woman repeated. "Oh. You have . . . people here."

"Mrs. Dale," said Kerry, "these are the wonderful sisters I told you about, and Joe. Everyone, this is Sally Dale, my mother-in-law."

Sally Dale came in and stood by the mantel. She had astounding posture. She was reed thin, in the stringy, drained manner of society women. She was wearing a tailored suit, in a bright flamenco red piped with black braid. The suit followed her parched frame; the outfit gave the appearance of a couture uniform, as if Mrs. Dale were some breed of haute bellboy. Mrs. Dale had the enameled air of a spokeswoman, a First Lady, a well-drilled figurehead.

"Hello, everyone," Mrs. Dale chirped. "So good to meet you." Her voice was thin and tinkly, as if any richer tones had been dieted off.

"So hello," said Aunt Pola. "So you're here. We like your store."

"Hello," said Mrs. Reckler, rising. "I'm Hedy Reckler, and these are my sisters, Pola Berman and Ida Fleischer, and this is my son Joe. It's so nice to meet you; you have such a beautiful home."

"It's gorgeous," said Aunt Pola. "We came by yester-day."

"Nice to meet you," said Aunt Ida.

"Is that sable?" Mrs. Dale asked, taking in Aunt Ida's coat. "Kerry . . . ?"

"Yes, Mrs. Dale," said Kerry. "Ida bought that just yes-terday. She's an important customer." Kerry grinned at Aunt Ida; Aunt Ida's eyes darted, but then she assumed a noncha-lant expression.

"I needed a coat," said Aunt Ida.

"Well, it looks marvelous on you," said Mrs. Dale, as if patting Aunt Ida on the head. "Kerry, dear, will you be in the shop this afternoon?"

"Mrs. Dale, if it's all right," interjected Mrs. Reckler, "we thought we'd kidnap Kerry for a few hours. She was so good to us at the shop. Can you spare her?"

Kerry looked frightened. She tried to speak, but couldn't, and stood intertwining her fingers.

"Kerry," said Mrs. Dale evenly, "you should have told me if you wanted the afternoon free."

"I did tell you," Kerry whispered. "Last night. And . . . this is my regular afternoon off."

"Oh," said Mrs. Dale grimly. Then her hostess charm resurfaced. "Well, then! How nice that you'll have a little outing."

"And . . ." Kerry continued, still whispering, "I'll be taking the twins. I won't be needing Nanny."

"Really?" said Mrs. Dale. "My, you're planning quite an adventure."

"Oh, we'll help out," said Mrs. Reckler. "We'll all pitch in." Joe noticed that his mother was using an overly polite, genial tone quite unlike her usual speaking voice. Aunt Pola and Aunt Ida were both being abnormally silent. Joe realized that even he was shutting up. The group was waiting for Mrs. Dale to leave. It was as if a headmistress or mother superior had entered a classroom, silencing the ordinary commotion. The group was not frightened of Mrs. Dale, simply wary.

"Well," said Mrs. Dale, smiling at everyone. "I suppose I'll have to look in at the shop. I do love my little shop."

"That's a pretty outfit you have on," said Aunt Pola. "Is that from Sally Dale?"

"This?" said Mrs. Dale, touching the fingertips of her right hand to her collarbone. "Oh no. I found this in Paris. It's Ungaro. Do you know Ungaro?"

"Not personally," said Aunt Ida.

"He's a dream," said Mrs. Dale. "So gifted. You know, I wish Kerry would try some of his things, but she has a more . . . country look. I always tell her, Darling, we're not in Maine, we're in Top Harbor. But she's our little bumpkin. You ladies are from Manhattan, I believe?"

"Queens," said Aunt Pola, gesturing to herself and Ida.

"New Jersey," said Mrs. Reckler. For once in his life, Joe wished he didn't live in Manhattan.

"I'm from New Jersey originally," Joe said, as a compromise.

"Oh," said Mrs. Dale. "Well, we're all from somewhere, aren't we? And you're all—what did Kerry tell me?—schoolteachers? Isn't that marvelous."

"I was a vice principal," said Aunt Pola, "and then an assistant superintendent. I'm retired."

"I'm a librarian," said Aunt Ida, "grades one through six."

"I'm in public relations," said Mrs. Reckler, "for the Garden State Ballet."

"The ballet," said Mrs. Dale, awarding Mrs. Reckler a half point.

"I'm a pickpocket," Joe said. There was a pause, and then Joe laughed.

"No, not really," Joe said. "I went to Yale."

"He's a real smart aleck," Mrs. Reckler told Mrs. Dale.

"My," said Mrs. Dale. "Such an accomplished group. We're all working women, aren't we? Except for Kerry, this afternoon. Doesn't it feel good to have something to really *do* with your life?" Mrs. Dale said this as if running her dress shop were less a sideline than a spiritual calling, on a par with founding a remote jungle hospital.

"Listen, forget feeling good," said Aunt Pola. "It's nice to eat."

"Oh, don't mention food to me," said Mrs. Dale. "I'm big as a house."

Joe watched his mother's right eyebrow rise. As far as Mrs. Reckler was concerned, Mrs. Dale had just sealed her doom. If there was one thing Mrs. Reckler abhorred, it was a bone-thin woman complaining about her weight.

"You look fine," Aunt Pola told Mrs. Dale.

"You're a toothpick," said Aunt Ida.

"Oh please," Mrs. Dale simpered. "You're very kind. Well, I must be off. A pleasure to meet you all. Enjoy Top Harbor. Good luck, Kerry. Shall we see you at dinner?"

"Yes, Mrs. Dale," said Kerry dutifully. "I'll have the twins back."

"Fine," said Mrs. Dale. "Ta, all!" Mrs. Dale waved, pivoted, and exited through the archway; as she passed into a farther region of the house, she could be heard calling, "Grey!"

"That's Mrs. Dale," said Kerry, breathing freely for the first time since her mother-in-law had appeared.

"She's not so bad," said Aunt Pola, being polite.

"She was very nice," said Mrs. Reckler.

"Hoo boy," said Aunt Ida.

"Exactly," said Kerry, slumping into a wing chair. Then she looked up; her face became suddenly radiant. "My babies!" she said, rising again.

A woman had arrived in the archway, holding the hands of two small children. The woman was middle-aged and solidly built. She smiled; she had a satisfied cook's grin.

"Here you go," said the woman, in a voice of much good humor. "Here are the brats."

The two children were dressed in matching down-filled parkas, with puffy hoods hanging out behind. They both wore knitted ski hats pulled down to their eyebrows. The children ran over to Kerry and started banging on her knees with their little mittened hands.

"Hi, Mommy!" said the little girl.

"Mommy," said the little boy, "do I have to wear my hat?"

"Hi, honeys," said Kerry, kissing each child. She turned to the group, with beaming pride. "This is Molly, and this is Toby. Molly and Toby, these are our new friends. This is Mrs. Reckler, Mrs. Berman, and Mrs. Fleischer. That's Joe."

The sisters crumbled as they met the children, from the mittens alone.

"Oh, they're adorable," cooed Mrs. Reckler.

"So cute," said Aunt Ida.

"Kerry, they're gorgeous," said Aunt Pola, and then she turned to the little boy. "Toby, wear your hat."

Molly and Toby clung to their mother, sucking on the tips of their mittens. They were shy, but fascinated by so many new faces.

"They're all ready," said the nanny.

"Oh, I'm sorry," said Kerry. "Everyone, this is Mrs. Creely. She's the twins' nanny, and she's the best in the world."

Mrs. Creely smiled wryly and curtsied. "How do you do," she said.

"Nice to meet you," said Aunt Pola. "You're doing a wonderful job."

"The nanny," marveled Aunt Ida. "I thought you'd be terrible."

"I am," said Mrs. Creely. "I made them wear their hats."

"I hate my hat," said Toby. He wandered over to Joe. "Do you have a hat?" he asked.

"No, I do not," Joe replied. "I hate hats too." Toby giggled and ran back to his mother.

"Toby, don't listen to him," advised Mrs. Reckler. "He catches colds."

"Will you be my nanny?" Joe asked Mrs. Creely wistfully. Joe now had a crush on Mrs. Creely; he decided he wanted her in his apartment, baking things.

"Not on your life," said Mrs. Creely. "You're a lost cause." The sisters all laughed, especially Mrs. Reckler.

"Bravo," said Mrs. Reckler, sharing a nod with Mrs. Creely.

"She's good," said Aunt Ida to Kerry.

"Mrs. Creely, I'll take them this afternoon," said Kerry. "Please, take the rest of the day off."

"Twist my arm," said Mrs. Creely. "I'll be back by dinner. Nice to meet you all." Mrs. Creely smiled again and left through the archway. "Good afternoon, Mr. Dale," Joe heard Mrs. Creely say, from the entry hall.

"Kerrington?" said Grey, striding toward the parlor. "Oh."

Grey stopped in the archway, appraising his wife's guests. He carried a camel's hair coat, a Chesterfield, over his arm, and he also toted a worn leather attaché case with a complicated lock. He was on his way out of the house. He stared at Joe and the Esker sisters, narrowing his eyes.

"Don't I know you?" Grey asked Aunt Pola.

"Yes, you do," said Aunt Pola. "We dropped by yesterday."

"We were trespassing," Joe added.

"Yes . . ." said Grey. "Kerrington, are these the people you told me about?"

"Yes, Grey," said Kerry. "They've been very sweet to me. We're going out shopping."

"Oh," said Grey. "Well. I suppose that's all right. Are you taking the children?"

"Yes, Grey. Molly, Toby, go say goodbye to Daddy." The twins ran happily across the room and hugged their father's legs at about knee height.

"Goodbye, Daddy," said Molly.

"We're going shopping," said Toby. "Daddy, can you come?"

Grey bent at the knees and squeezed the top of each child's head through the child's ski hat. This seemed genuinely affectionate, although Grey gave the impression of trying to unscrew his children's skulls. "No, I can't come shopping,"

Grey told the twins. "Daddy has to work. Kerrington, aren't you at the shop this afternoon? Where's Mrs. Creely?"

"She gave Mrs. Creely the afternoon off," Mrs. Reckler replied.

"Your mother is at the shop," said Aunt Ida.

"It's Kerry's regular afternoon off," added Aunt Pola.

"Oh," said Grey, taken aback by this volley of information. "So what will you be shopping for? Isn't shopping a nuisance?" Grey smiled at this attempt at charm, at finding a common ground with his wife's new companions. Joe felt almost sorry for Grey; Grey had no idea of the Waterloo scale of his error.

"You don't like to shop?" asked Aunt Ida mildly, smoothing her coat.

"No," said Grey. "Not really. I prefer classic things. I simply replace them over the years. In clothing and what have you. Shopping seems such a waste of time, don't you think? Perhaps that sounds odd; my mother does run a dress shop, but I really don't have a hand in it. Perhaps it's just a masculine trait." Grey addressed this last remark to Joe.

"I like to shop," said Joe, stretching. "I don't think it's gender related."

"Well, perhaps not," said Grey huffily.

"I think it's genetic," Joe continued. "I think there's a shopping gene that gets passed from one generation to the next. Grey, maybe you just didn't get the shopping gene. You got the corporate-law gene."

Everyone stared at Joe.

"Daddy, what did that man say?" Molly asked her father.

"I don't know, dear," Grey replied.

"Joe is very bright," Aunt Pola concluded. "He just makes no sense. So, Grey, why don't you let Mrs. Creely go, and Kerry can stay home with the kids. Let your mother get somebody else at the store. It's a much better idea."

Grey stared at Aunt Pola. He was appalled. Grey did not care for any public discussion of his marriage, and he was still not too keen on having yesterday's trespassers as today's house guests.

"Excuse me," Grey told Aunt Pola. "I don't believe this

is any of your business. Kerry and I discussed such matters, and we've done what's best.''

"Grey," said Aunt Pola, leaning forward. "I love that name. It must've been a lot of fun for you in kindergarten. Grey, let me tell you something: I'm a meddling old woman. But let me tell you something else: I know what I'm talking about. Kerry wants to be home with the kids, and she should probably go back to school part-time and get her teaching certificate. She's a lovely girl. You're very lucky. You look like a nice man. You make a good living. I don't know what you're doing still living with Mama, but that's your business. Grey, things are only going to get worse, believe me. Wake up. You don't have to listen to me; what do I know? But if you have a brain in your head, you'll do everything I say. I didn't get this old by being a dummy. That's all I have to say. And another thing—this isn't a good house for kids. They'll run around and knock things over, or they'll get very nervous. It's just a thought. Take it or leave it. These are adorable children, and they know I'm right. Toby, Molly, tell your daddy. Tell him to listen to Aunt Pola.''

"Listen to Aunt Pola, Daddy," said Molly and Toby in enthusiastic, singsong unison.

"Excuse me," said Grey, openly horrified. He gave each child another quick pat on the head. "Kerrington, I'll speak with you this evening." He turned and left hurriedly through the archway. A moment later, everyone heard the front door open and shut. Then there was the sound of a key in an ignition, and Grey's car was heard gunning down the drive, splattering gravel. The roar of the car faded as Grey reached the outer road.

"What?" said Aunt Pola. "Did I say something?"

"Where are we going?" Joe asked his mother, after everyone had been seated in the Oldsmobile. Kerry was scrunched between Joe and Mrs. Reckler in the front seat. Aunt Pola and Aunt Ida sat in back with the twins.

"I thought we would stop in at the Lady Carberry store," Mrs. Reckler told her son. "At least we'll start there." Mrs. Reckler started the car. "Is everyone settled?" she called to the back seat.

"We're fine," said Aunt Pola, and she tickled Molly, who was happily ensconced on her lap. "Except someone put a pretty little girl on my lap." Molly responded to this complaint by giggling and knocking on Aunt Pola's forehead with her fist. "Now she's hitting me," Aunt Pola said. "Molly, why are you hitting me? I'm a nice woman."

"Molly," said Kerry, turning to the back seat. "Don't hit. Pola, I'm sorry; let me take her."

"No, don't be silly," said Aunt Pola. "I'll just hit back." Aunt Pola tickled Molly again, and they both erupted into a fit of giggles.

"Ida," asked Mrs. Reckler, "are you all set?"

"I'm fine," said Aunt Ida. "Toby, how's by you?" Toby giggled and squirmed on Aunt Ida's lap. He took off his ski hat and tried to pull it onto Aunt Ida's head. "Oh, he's giving me his hat," said Aunt Ida. "He's very generous."

239

"Ida, I'm sorry," said Kerry. "I don't know why they're acting like this. Toby, give me your hat."

"Please," said Aunt Ida. "Now it's my hat." Aunt Ida pulled the hat more comfortably onto her own head. "It goes with my fur," Aunt Ida decided. Toby was dissolved in giggles.

"You're so good with them," Kerry said gratefully. She smiled shyly. "Aren't they great?"

"Not this one," said Aunt Pola, tickling Molly again. "She's the devil himself." Molly shrieked with pleasure.

"Mom, what's Lady Carberry?" asked Joe, as Mrs. Reckler headed out onto the road. "Isn't that shoes?"

"Of course," said Mrs. Reckler. "The factory is in Blue Mill; it's the next town over. I've never been there, but there's supposed to be an outlet."

"What's an outlet?" asked Kerry, calling out over her children's laughter.

"What's an outlet?" said Aunt Ida, and she mock-whispered to Toby, "Toby, what's wrong with your mother?"

"You've never been to an outlet?" asked Aunt Pola. "She's never been to an outlet?"

"An outlet is a store," Mrs. Reckler began.

"Only better," said Aunt Pola.

"Usually, when a manufacturer makes something," said Aunt Ida, "he sells it to the chains, to Macy's or Bloomingdale's or what have you. But sometimes he has things that don't sell, or he makes too many, or he has seconds."

"Seconds?" said Kerry.

"Uch," said Aunt Pola. "Molly, what are we going to do with her?"

"A second," said Aunt Ida, "is something that has a little something wrong with it. A rip, or no pocket, or a button missing. But the item is still perfectly good, so the manufacturer sells it at the outlet, at half off."

"Oh," said Kerry, nodding. "So an outlet is like a discount place."

"No," said Aunt Pola vociferously. "A discount place, anyone goes there. It's junk. But an outlet you have to know about."

"How do you find out about it?" Kerry asked.

"No one knows," said Joe. "The locations are passed on through the DNA of Jewish women."

"Oh, you are so anti-Semitic," Mrs. Reckler told her son. "You're disgusting."

"Well, excuse me," said Joe. "How *do* you know where all the outlets are?"

"My mother told me," said Mrs. Reckler, "when I was little."

"Listen," said Aunt Pola, "we can't give away all the secrets. Then everyone would find out, and the outlets would turn into discount places."

"This is fascinating," Kerry said sincerely. She felt like Margaret Mead, happening upon a fresh Samoan village.

"Outlet!" said Molly, bumping up and down on Aunt Pola's lap.

"Outlet!" repeated Toby, tugging his ski cap over Aunt Ida's eyes.

"They're adorable," Aunt Pola assured Kerry.

The Lady Carberry store possessed the promising anonymity of the other outlets the Esker sisters had besieged on their journey north. The store was located in a minor shopping mall on the fraying outskirts of Top Harbor. The mall comprised only four or five separate shops on a single level and included a Pantry Pride supermarket, a card and stationery store, and a dry cleaner.

"This looks good," said Aunt Ida, as Mrs. Reckler pulled into the parking lot. "It looks like Long Island."

"I've never been out here," said Kerry, checking the mall through the windshield.

"Of course you haven't," agreed Aunt Pola. "You've been locked up."

Mrs. Reckler parked, and everyone disembarked. "We're taking Kerry into Lady Carberry," Mrs. Reckler informed Joe. "You're taking Toby and Molly."

"I'm taking them where?" asked Joe.

"Oh, I'll watch them," said Kerry. "Joe, please, I don't want to be a bother."

"You're no bother," said Aunt Pola. "You need your hands free."

"Just take the kids and walk around," Mrs. Reckler told Joe. "Entertain them."

"Toby, Molly," Kerry told her children, kneeling to adjust their parkas. "You're going to play with Joe. Be good. Joe, don't let them talk you into anything."

"Come on," said Aunt Pola, leading the women toward the Lady Carberry store. "Let's get busy."

The women pushed open the plate-glass doors. Through the store's dusty glass facade, Joe could see cheap carpeting and functional metal shelving holding shoe boxes stacked to the ceiling. Joe and Toby and Molly stood outside, under the store's concrete overhang. Toby and Molly stared at Joe expectantly. They did not look particularly innocent. They looked like children who had been entertained before and had a basis for comparisons.

"Well, hey," said Joe, sizing up the situation. As a rule, Joe didn't care for children. He found them unformed, taxing. He had little use for anyone too young to gossip. Joe did not hate children. He just never chose to be around them.

"So," said Joe. "Hi, guys."

"I'm not a guy," said Molly. "I'm a girl."

"Excuse me," said Joe.

"She's a girl," said Toby. "You're stupid."

"Okay," said Joe, and this reply sent the twins into fits of giggles. Joe felt rather humiliated. Children rarely appreciated style. Joe comforted himself with a pet theory: twins were mere shadows, halves, and both twins were necessary to equal a whole regular, non-twin person. Joe considered sharing this insight with Toby and Molly.

"What would you like to do?" Joe asked instead. "Do you want candy?"

"We're not allowed," Toby said.

"Daddy says it's bad for you," Molly said. "You get cavities."

"That's not true," said Joe. "Candy is very good for you."

"No it's not," insisted Toby.

"No it's not," said Molly, sticking her chin out.

"They just found out," Joe improvised. "It's a recent discovery. I've seen the surgeon general's research; it was definitive. Come on."

Joe hated parents who forbade their children to snack on refined sugars, those nutrition-obsessed folks who encouraged their offspring to munch on wholesome carrot sticks or apple slices masquerading as sweets. Joe shuddered at the TV commercials that depicted frolicsome children popping individual servings of yogurt into their backpacks. Joe's mother had always slipped a shiny package of Yodels or Hostess Sno Balls into his plaid tin lunchbox. He took this as a sign that his mother wanted him to be happy. If Mrs. Reckler had tried dropping celery into Joe's lunchbox, he would have considered the act to be a form of espionage, an odious move intended to subvert his entire personality.

Naturally, Joe had a mouthful of cavities. This was a small price to pay for the ravishment of German-chocolate icing and Cracker Jacks and that most diabolical of all treats: rock candy—mouth-watering, jawbreaking lumps of pure crystallized cane sugar. Both Joe and Mrs. Reckler had noted the early death of Adelle Davis, the fabled health food advocate, a righteous woman who had keeled over in her sixties. While neither Joe nor his mother had wished an early demise on the whole-wheat pioneer, they both considered her passing to be an absolute refutation of her life's work. After all, Betty Crocker was still going strong, along with Sara Lee, Fanny Farmer, and Poppin' Fresh, the trademark Pillsbury Doughboy (Joe occasionally fantasized about honey-glazing Poppin' Fresh and downing him for breakfast).

Joe led Toby and Molly into Peterson's Save-Rite Stationery, another glassed-in storefront. Peterson's was lined with sloping racks of greeting cards and pegboard shelves of bestselling paperbacks. The aisles were narrow, and the store had an appealing helter-skelter quality, created by the availability of many products under four inches high, such as minijars of Liquid Paper and midget pads of Post-its. At the front of the store, beside the cash register, was a traditional terraced display of every known candy, a holy ziggurat of

Reese's Peanut Butter Cups, Tootsie blow pops, Chunkies,
Milky Ways, O. Henrys, and their brethren. Joe ushered the
children to this high altar of tooth decay.

"Okay, you can each choose something," Joe said. "My
treat."

"But we're not supposed to," said Toby, bobbing his head
and speaking slowly and deliberately, so that Joe would comprehend.

"I'm telling you it's okay," Joe said. "What do you do on
Halloween? Don't you eat your Halloween candy?"

"No," said Toby. "Daddy says we can eat the apples and
the raisins, and just one piece of candy."

"And what do you do with the rest of the candy?" Joe
asked.

"Daddy takes it away," said Molly.

Joe had already been near-convinced of Grey Dale's hei-
nousness, but now he gasped. The man took candy from
children on Joe's favorite holiday. Halloween had no unfortunate religious undertones. Halloween was the exaltation of
costume and candy, of homemade theater and store-bought
sugar, of unrefined pleasure. As a child, Joe had taken Halloween extremely seriously, hitting as many homes as possible before his midnight curfew. He would return home and
shake his pillowcase of goodies into a large ceramic mixing
bowl, which his mother stored in the refrigerator. Joe and
his brother guarded their mixing bowls zealously. Both were
always aware if any pilferage had occurred.

Joe hated anyone who handed out apples as Halloween
treats, or offered only paper napkins wadded with Unicef
pennies. Joe was all in favor of money for Unicef, and he
had gladly carried the little orange box for contributions, but
he had felt that Unicef money was intended as an additional
treat and not a candy replacement. Joe abhorred people who
twisted Halloween into something pious. Such people inev-
itably refused to glitz their homes for Christmas or purchase
chocolate bunnies at Easter. Commercialization was almost
always benign, Joe believed, and usually tasty. Religion was
all one had to watch out for.

"Toby, Molly," Joe said, squatting down to speak more

directly with his charges. "I talked to your dad. He said it was okay for you each to have candy today. He said he was sorry for taking away your Halloween candy."

"He didn't say that," said Toby.

"Yes he did," said Joe. "Ask your mom."

"Toby . . ." said Molly, "maybe Daddy said it."

Joe looked at Molly; Joe decided that he liked her, that she had real potential. They exchanged a glance similar to those Joe still exchanged with his mother. The glance said, We know we're not supposed to, but let's do it anyway. The glance admitted guilt but allowed joy. The glance was a great Reckler legacy.

"Daddy didn't say it," Toby continued to insist, with all the bossiness of a brother.

"*Toby,*" Molly said, impatiently.

"Toby," Joe echoed.

"No," said Toby. "I'm not going to eat candy."

Molly bobbed her head up and down and made an exasperated noise.

"Unless you make me," said Toby. Joe looked at Toby. Toby was not smiling. He offered no evidence of the masterful hypocrisy he had just spun.

"I said, Unless you make me," Toby repeated, glaring at Joe.

"Right!" said Joe, getting the point and standing up. "Okay, Toby, I'm making you have some candy. I'm the baby-sitter, and it's all my idea."

"Um . . . Three Musketeers," said Toby, grabbing a particularly fat candy bar. Joe approved. Three Musketeers was made of whipped milk chocolate, so it bulged.

"Nestlé's Crunch," said Molly, grabbing the larger, family-sized bar, not the ordinary fifty-cent size. Joe was pleased; he was amazed at how quickly Toby and Molly had become Esker sisters.

Meanwhile, the Esker sisters themselves were all staggering around the Lady Carberry outlet. The moaning trio resembled Greek widows keening at unkind fate, shaking their clenched fists at Olympus. Of course, they were trying on shoes.

"These are killing me," groaned Aunt Ida, rocking in a new pair of navy sling-backs with a beige accent. "I'm a cripple."

"I can't wear these," wheezed Mrs. Reckler, hobbled by stylish black pumps with a flat moiré bow. "I shouldn't even go near these shoes."

"I'm popping a blood vessel," whimpered Aunt Pola, with great satisfaction, modeling her white patent open-toe sandals in a low, floor-level mirror.

"Maybe you don't have the right size," Kerry ventured to Aunt Ida.

"It's never the right size," said Aunt Ida. "Oh, my legs are numb; I have to sit down."

"Ida, sit," said Mrs. Reckler. "Don't be crazy."

"She can sit at home," countered Aunt Pola. "Ida, walk in the shoes. Get the feel."

Kerry was astonished at this orgy of voluptuous masochism. For Kerry, finding shoes had always been an extremely lesser pursuit. She owned mostly Keds white sneakers or flats, uncomplicated footwear in the browns or dark greens that matched her soft corduroy skirts and Laura Ashley cottons. Kerry always bought the same shoes; she knew her size, and she rarely even bothered to try on duplicates of styles she'd worn all her adult life.

When the Esker sisters had entered the store, they'd fanned out along the wall on which the many available styles were displayed on wire racks. The sisters confronted almost every shoe, squeezing the toe and peering inside, as if they were cobblers evaluating a peer's workmanship. Ida and Hedy each settled on two or three styles. Pola gathered an armload. Then the sisters had summoned a clerk to hunt up their choices in the appropriate sizes. Once the precarious towers of shoe boxes had been trundled out of the stockroom, the moaning had begun.

"Kerry, what's the problem?" asked Aunt Pola. "Why aren't you looking?"

"Well . . ." said Kerry timidly, "I don't really need shoes."

The Esker sisters all looked at one another, as if Kerry had just uttered some incomprehensible foreign phrase.

"What, you don't need shoes?" said Aunt Pola. "You have feet, don't you?"

"Sure," said Kerry.

"Kerry, darling," said Aunt Pola, taking the Naugahyde-covered chair beside Kerry. "Kerry, this is an outlet. These shoes, some of them are sixty percent off. They're very good shoes. If you go into Manhattan, on Fifth Avenue, you'd pay a fortune. Take advantage; don't be foolish."

None of Aunt Pola's arguments really applied to Kerry's life. "But . . ." she began, "I usually just wear sneakers, or Top-Siders. What kind should I buy?"

"Kerry," said Aunt Pola, "listen to me. Listen carefully, because I'm going to be very rude, but I'm telling the truth. Your life is a terrible mess. You married the wrong man— hoo boy, is he the wrong man. Believe me, no one should get a divorce. It's a terrible thing. Everyone suffers. But if I were you I'd get busy. I'd call a lawyer. I'd figure things out pronto. You have two gorgeous children, but you never see them. A mother belongs with her children; not every minute of the day—they'll drive you up the wall—but you should be there. This mother-in-law of yours, she's a beautiful woman, she has lovely things, but she's an ice cube. If I lived in that house, by now I'd have frostbite. And now I'm only telling you this because I care about you and because I see things, but that husband of yours, he's his mother's child, he's the tundra, with the cashmere topcoat and the wing-tip shoes. He's not for you, he's not for anybody, except maybe a woman called Patricia or Mary, someone with a tennis racket. Kerry, somewhere you took a wrong turn, and you got stuck. But you're young, you're a pretty girl, you're a good mother, you can fix things. So get busy, get the show on the road. Do something for yourself. Say, 'My name is Kerry, and here I go.' And buy a pair of shoes."

Kerry stared at Aunt Pola. She was shocked. She wondered if she'd been insulted. This woman, whom she barely

knew, had just dissected her life and given her marching orders. This woman was a tyrant. For a split second, Kerry felt outraged. She wanted to deny everything, to insist on some alternative, happier truth. Then gratitude flooded her being. She wanted to take Aunt Pola's hand and kiss it. She felt a release, a wave of acceptance. Aunt Pola was not a dictator. She was an elemental being, a cleansing typhoon, the implacable voice of reason with a large handbag.

Kerry wanted to thank Aunt Pola, and she wanted Aunt Pola's acceptance. She realized that words would be inappropriate. Aunt Pola would dismiss them.

"Excuse me," Kerry called out to the shoe clerk. The clerk was an amiable fellow; his fine, pale-blond hair was parted in the middle and puffed back. He wore sky-blue double-knit pants with a broad waistband, and a nylon shirt with stripes and a raised diamond pattern.

"Yes, ma'am?" the clerk said to Kerry. "Can I help you?"

"I'd like to see those," said Kerry, pointing to the shoes Aunt Pola currently had on. "In a seven."

When Joe returned to the Lady Carberry outlet, with the twins in tow, Kerry was teetering through the shop in a pair of glossy white patent-leather open-toed high-heeled sandals, with gold lamé piping and a gold plastic hibiscus blooming on the instep. The sandals were garish, what Joe would term "pure Miami Beach," but he was in wholehearted sympathy with Kerry's choice. Joe knew that Kerry ordinarily went for penny loafers and deck shoes, blameless Maine classics. Such a wardrobe had deposited Kerry at Dale Dell. The white patent sandals were emblematic of fresh horizons and a halt to the tyranny of Good Taste. Kerry was cutting loose, and Joe couldn't wait to see her in a polyester tube dress with orange ball fringe.

"These are killing me," Kerry groaned to Aunt Pola. "How can you wear these things?"

"Don't ask," said Aunt Pola. "But believe me, they're very flattering. They lengthen the leg. They'll look beautiful with a tan."

Joe tried to resist an analysis of Aunt Pola's remarks. He tried not to predict the likelihood of procuring a tan on one's feet in Maine in October. While Joe was no stranger to shopping for shoes, he was aware that shopping for women's shoes was another upheaval entirely. Joe's mother, as far as he knew, had never purchased a comfortable, well-fitting pair of shoes. If the shoes were comfortable, they would undoubtedly be ugly, orthopedic in some way. Women suffered for their shoes. Women's shoes were designed to be antithetical to walking, let alone walking briskly. As a child, Joe had once stepped into a pair of his mother's high heels. At first he had welcomed the additional elevation, but then he had experienced only torture, via shooting pains in his shins. All of feminism, Joe knew, could be encapsulated in women's struggle to forsake the spike heel.

"Mommy, you have new shoes," Toby said to his mother. "With flowers."

"Aren't Mommy's shoes beautiful?" Aunt Pola prompted Molly.

"Uh-huh," said Molly. "Mommy, I can see your toes."

"I love these shoes," said Kerry, with heroic determination. "Grey is going to kill me."

"So who cares?" said Aunt Pola. "He doesn't have to wear them."

"Toby, what are you eating?" asked Kerry.

"Three Musketeers," said Toby.

"I made him eat it," said Joe. "He didn't want to. He wanted a carrot stick."

"My son the dietitian," said Mrs. Reckler. "Joe, what are you eating? What garbage?"

"A Hershey bar," said Joe, holding the half-nibbled bar out to his mother. "Be my guest."

"I don't want any," said Mrs. Reckler, breaking off a piece. "You're making me eat this."

"Aunt Ida," said Joe, "can I force some on you?"

"No, please," said Aunt Ida. "I don't like sweet things. I'll just have a little piece." Aunt Ida genuinely did not care for sweets. She took a chunk merely to be polite, to please Joe. She took a tiny bite of the tiny piece and handed the remainder to her sister Hedy. "Here, I can't finish this."

"Ida," said Mrs. Reckler evenly, "I'm going to kill you."

"I have Nestlé's Crunch!" happily trumpeted Molly. "Joe made me!"

"Good," said Kerry, breaking off an edge of the Nestlé's Crunch. "Joe, I'll send you the dentist's bills."

"Kerry," said Joe, "I leave you alone with these women for two minutes and look at what happens. Listen to you."

"What, listen to me," said Kerry, munching her wicked chocolate and admiring her festive new sandals in the mirror. "I'm just talking. Like a person."

Aunt Ida bought a pair of knee-high boots, in a deep-brown, butter-soft Italian leather, because the boots matched her sable. Aunt Ida had begun to think of her sable as someone she could buy things for, a child or a relative of some sort. Aunt Ida bought the boots not for herself but for her sable coat, so it would be happy. "The boots match my coat," Aunt Ida told the clerk. "It's like a set."

Aunt Pola had bought the sandals and two pairs of spectator pumps. "These are very good shoes," she had said. "I'll get a lot of wear out of them." She had also bought fat, ornate sneakers for all four of her grandchildren, and a pair of sleek black patent evening pumps for her daughter. "Aren't these gorgeous?" she had told the clerk, with regard to the evening shoes. "Now I just have to find her a dress."

Aunt Pola had also quizzed the clerk on his marital status

and then suggested various styles his wife might favor. "She's a very lucky woman, your wife," Aunt Pola had said. "Married to a man who works at a shoe outlet. She must think she died and went to heaven."

Kerry bought the white sandals and, in a burst of inspiration, the same sandals with silver lamé accents, a style that even Mrs. Reckler, watchdog of anti-Semitism, would have termed "pure bar mitzvah." Kerry did not buy these shoes for their gaudy beauty. She needed them because they were infused with supernatural powers, in a league with ruby slippers or Cinderella's glass heels. These shoes could walk out of Dale Dell.

Toby and Molly delighted in their mother's new shoes. Children exist in a pretasteful sphere, and if children ruled the world, Joe reasoned, there would be no beige.

Everyone jammed into the car, with the additional baggage of the plastic sacks of shoeboxes. Molly and Toby had grown restless and squirmy, crawling from the front seat to the back, and then returning.

"Molly," scolded Kerry, as Mrs. Reckler drove back toward town, "and Toby: make up your minds and stay in one place."

"I like it . . . here," said Toby, straddling the back of the front seat.

"Come," said Aunt Pola, dragging Toby onto her lap. "Sit. Hedy, I'm telling you, we should have taken two cars. I wish I still had my car; my life would be so much easier."

"Pola's car was stolen," Aunt Ida told Kerry. "Right from the street."

"That's awful," said Kerry. "Were you insured?"

"Sure," said Aunt Pola. "But it takes forever, they'll pay me *bubkes*, and meanwhile I don't have a car."

"*Bubkes?*" asked Kerry.

"It's Yiddish," explained Aunt Ida. "It means 'nothing,' zero."

Joe smiled. When he was little, he had resented his relatives' use of Yiddish. They would launch into rivetingly personal stories about other people, about a co-worker's affair or a cousin's divorce. As the tale heated up, Joe's mother and aunts would deliberately lapse into Yiddish. This strategy prevented Joe and the other younger relations from hearing the juicy stuff. Now Joe would wait for a mention of *bubkes* or *tsuris*. He found this second language exotic and helpful, for all sorts of emphasis.

"*Bubkes* means less than nothing," said Aunt Pola. "It means zip. So, Toby, why don't you buy Aunt Pola a car?"

"Okay," said Toby, as Aunt Pola tickled him.

"Pola, buy yourself a new car already," said Mrs. Reckler. "Stop talking about it. You deserve it, just do it. See, we could go right in there and get you a car." Mrs. Reckler was driving past a local car dealership, a low, airplane-hangar-style building set among the elms on the side of the road. Mrs. Reckler slowed the car to a crawl, so that everyone could ogle the cars behind the building's plate-glass windows. The vehicles were all shimmering tanks, outsize luxury roadsters.

"That's Bancroft Auto," said Kerry. "Everyone goes there. It's where Grey bought his Mercedes."

"A Mercedes." Aunt Pola sniffed. "A German car."

"They have all sorts of makes," said Kerry. "But everything's real big."

"We'll look," said Mrs. Reckler, steering into the Bancroft Auto parking lot. "Just for fun. Why not?"

"Are you crazy?" said Aunt Ida. "What, we're going to buy shoes and a car?"

"Stranger things have happened," said Mrs. Reckler, who was not even referring to Aunt Ida's sable.

"Very strange things," said Aunt Pola, who was.

Mrs. Reckler parked the car and everyone tumbled out onto the asphalt, like clowns squeezed from a tiny circus contraption.

"I want a car!" said Toby.

"He wants a car," said Aunt Ida. "Listen to him."

"Toby, we're just going to look at the cars," said Kerry. "Behave yourself."

"*Mom,*" whined Toby, Molly, and Joe. Joe joined in as an official child; he felt invigorated, pleased to be part of such a preadolescent chorale.

"Very mature," said Mrs. Reckler to her son. "You're setting a very good example."

"Do you remember when we were little," recalled Aunt Ida. "We never said Mom or Mommy."

"You said it," agreed Aunt Pola, as the group neared the dealership's twin plate-glass front doors. "We didn't have a mommy."

"So what did you have?" asked Joe.

"Maaaaaaa," the Esker sisters bawled, in jubilant nasal unison.

The interior of Bancroft Luxury and Foreign Vehicles recalled an MGM soundstage of the thirties, a stylized set for some sweeping Deco *Born to Dance* spectacular. The vast showroom had velvety black walls and a mirror-slick ebony-black linoleum floor, buffed daily. Cars were angled this way and that, both on the showroom floor and atop raised circular platforms carpeted in thick, spotless white wool. The cars' chrome and enamel were highlighted by the beams of many small spotlights, rigged from the high, dark ceiling. The cars were like Ziegfeld beauties, sinuous and pampered, flaunting themselves yet remaining aloof. All the showroom lacked was an orchestra in Stork Club white tie, under the nimble baton of Duke Ellington or Tommy Dorsey. Instead, Debussy was piped in, lending the premises a hushed gentility, a calm, almost nocturnal hauteur.

"Oh my," said Aunt Ida. "It's fancy in here."

"It's really neat," said Toby.

"Your brother fixes cars," Mrs. Reckler told Joe. "So how come his place doesn't look like this?"

Joe looked around, breathing deeply. The showroom smelled not merely of new cars nor merely of money; it had a potent musk all its own, the perfume of desire. This was what extravagance smelled like. This was excess of a very high, heedless order. Bancroft Luxury and Foreign was where shopping had been born, and nurtured, and adored; Bancroft Luxury and Foreign was a shopping cathedral. Joe watched the cars as they flirted and pouted, daring foolish mortals to possess them. My, thought Joe, this might be the entrance to hell, or to heaven, depending on one's moral perspective. Whichever it was, the showroom excited. Joe wondered if he was dressed properly.

"These are big cars," Aunt Ida whispered to Joe. "Like for the Mafia."

"Pick one," Mrs. Reckler challenged her sister Pola. "If you could have any car, which would you choose?"

Aunt Pola began to walk slowly among the cars, which glistened at her, vying for her attentions. Aunt Pola did not touch the cars; she wanted them to beg.

"Good afternoon," said a salesman, gliding over. The salesman glistened too. He could have passed for one of the showier, more overconfident machines that surrounded him.

"May I help you?" the salesman asked, in his self-conscious basso, his trained pitchman's beguine.

"We're just looking," replied Aunt Pola. "Thank you very much." "Just looking, thank you" could have been emblazoned on the Esker family crest. Joe had learned the phrase early in life, it could almost have been his first words. The phrase was armor, asserting the shopper's superiority to the merchandise. The phrase was a gauntlet flung. There was a shopping vocabulary that Joe had inherited from his mother and aunts: "Just looking," "What's the price on this?"—far more subtle than a crude "How much?"—"Not today," and, in crescendo, "I'll take it."

The group circled the cars, frowning and rating, protected by Aunt Pola's "Just looking, thank you." Mrs. Reckler stood back from a midnight-blue Rolls-Royce, with its signature hood and grillework, a modernized version of the legendary touring car.

"Isn't this pretty?" Mrs. Reckler murmured. "Joe, do you like this?"

Mrs. Reckler seemed lost in reverie, communing with the Rolls. "When I was little," she said, not looking at Joe, "the people who lived next door had an uncle, and he drove a car that was just this color. Midnight blue. Not black, not like a hearse. Midnight blue. It wasn't a Rolls, it was probably just a Buick, or a Packard. But I thought that was the most beautiful car in the world."

"That was Lou Karp's car, Uncle Lou from the Karps next

door,'' said Aunt Pola. ''He was a gambler. He was a terrible person.''

''Oh shut up,'' Mrs. Reckler told her sister jovially, breaking the mood. ''All right, Joe, don't get me this car. Lou Karp was a terrible person.''

''All the Karps were terrible,'' recalled Aunt Ida. ''The parents drank, and the children never bathed.''

''This is Grey's car,'' said Kerry, standing beside a deep-green Mercedes, a large blocky car that reeked of quality without romance, of Teutonic engineering. The car was a costly, finely made item, but Joe found it oppressive.

''It's very nice,'' said Aunt Pola diplomatically.

''You think so?'' said Kerry skeptically.

''No,'' said Aunt Pola. ''I was being nice, I'm a nice person. A car like that, first of all it's German, so forget it. And second of all, it does nothing for me. It's not roomy. My late husband, may he rest in peace, he used to say, 'Pola, I can live without a Mercedes. Pola, you know what a Mercedes is? It's a Volkswagen for rich people.' ''

''He sounds like he was very smart,'' said Kerry.

''Of course,'' said Aunt Pola.

Joe had fond memories of his Uncle Nat. Nat Berman had been a compact, muscular man, with a bristling steel-gray crewcut. He had been as joyously opinionated as his wife, if slightly less vocal. Nat had taught Physical Education, at the high-school level. Joe had always found this noteworthy. A Jewish Phys. Ed. teacher struck Joe as a rarity. In Joe's experience, Jews tended to emphasize the intellectual side of things and disdain the body. A Jewish Phys. Ed. teacher was an anomaly, like a Lutheran psychiatrist.

Uncle Nat had needed his stamina, to keep pace with his beloved wife. Both Nat and Pola were columns of energy, sparkplugs. They epitomized vigor. They had radiated sex, ruddy-cheeked adventure, and the pleasures of golf.

''You would have loved Nat,'' Aunt Pola told Kerry. ''Ida, wouldn't Kerry have loved Nat?''

''Of course,'' said Aunt Ida. ''He was very lovable. He was a terrific man.''

''Was he ever,'' said Aunt Pola, drifting for a moment,

caught up in thoughts of her husband. Uncle Nat had been dead for five years, but Aunt Pola still felt the loss sharply. Aunt Pola did not attempt to avoid grief, but she would not feed on it either. She believed in life, profoundly. She was, as she knew, a very smart woman.

"Oh my God," said Aunt Pola.

"What?" asked Kerry, concerned. "Pola, is something wrong?"

"Oh my God," said Aunt Pola. "Look at this automobile."

"Isn't this one a beauty?" said Aunt Pola. She was standing in front of a car parked on one of the raised, white-carpeted platforms. The car was blinding white and titanic. It was the widest, longest car Joe had ever seen, discounting limousines. Everyone encircled this car, standing back a few feet. The car gave off a glare, an arctic force field.

"Mommy," said Toby, "look at the car!"

"I like it!" crowed Molly.

"That's a very large car," said Aunt Ida, clutching her elbows. "Pola, what kind of a car is that?"

"This," said the salesman, swooping down, "this is from the Lincoln Continental Town Car Cartier Designer Series."

"Oh my," said Aunt Ida.

"It has a lot of names," said Mrs. Reckler.

"It ought to," said Aunt Pola. "It's a lot of car."

"You have a discerning eye," said the salesman to Aunt Pola. "My compliments. This is an automobile of unequaled distinction. By the way, I'm Bruce V. Dardone, Executive Vice-President for Sales here at Bancroft Luxury and Foreign."

"He has a lot of names too," Aunt Ida whispered to Joe.

"I'm Pola Berman," said Aunt Pola. "And these are my sisters, my nephew, and our friend Kerry and her twins. Now you know. This is a beautiful car."

"Top of the line," said Bruce V. Dardone. "Would you care to look inside?"

"Why not?" said Aunt Pola, with a rather calculated shrug. "Let's see who's home."

Bruce opened the car's left front and rear doors, with a practiced flourish. "The upholstery is the finest Titanium leather," he began. "Seen here in the Oxford White blended with a Cabernet accent. The hides have been tanned and matched for a suppleness and a luxury unheard of in an American sedan. You'll also note the Message Center with full digital readout, and the Ford JBL High-Fidelity Twelve-Speaker Audio System, with the Compact Disc option, for an acoustic perfection surpassed only by the finest concert halls."

"I'm noting, I'm noting," said Aunt Pola, refusing to be impressed. "Inside, it's like the London Philharmonic. Hedy, are you noting?"

"The Cartier Series Town Car is thermostatically controlled," Bruce continued mellifluously. "The twin Comfort Lounge seats provide six separate and distinct power adjustments. Rubber body mounts, placed throughout the interior, protect against road noise, vibration, and unnecessary harshness."

"That's good," commented Aunt Pola. "Who needs harshness? This is very interesting. Go on, Bruce."

"Pola—may I call you Pola?" Bruce asked, and Aunt Pola nodded. "Pola, the Lincoln Town Car is fully carpeted in outstanding thirty-ounce plush, for elegance plus durability. Moving to our rear seating compartment, you will find an

unprecedented fusion of space, design, and comfort inno-
vation.''

"Pish pish," said Joe and Aunt Ida, turning to each other,
like villagers critiquing a politician in a town square.

"Be quiet, you two," warned Mrs. Reckler. "Just pay
attention."

"All windows are tinted, eliminating glare and ensuring
privacy," said Bruce. "The Lincoln Town Car is the favorite
of crowned heads, statesmen, and celebrities the world over."

"Arabs?" asked Aunt Pola pointedly.

"Are you familiar with the sultan of Brunei?" asked
Bruce.

"Not me," said Aunt Pola. "Ida?"

"What are you talking?" said Aunt Ida. "He's a sultan?
Who's a sultan?"

"The sultan of Brunei," said Bruce airily, "is one of the
planet's five wealthiest private citizens. The sultan alone owns
fifty of the Cartier Designer Series Town Cars."

"I'll take fifty-one," said Aunt Pola, abhorring any form
of Arab supremacy.

"She's joking," Aunt Ida assured Bruce. "The Lincoln
Town Car represents an uncompromised summit in beauty
and product integrity," Bruce went on. "But the Lincoln
Town Car is so much more. Beneath the hood hums a five-
point-0-liter V-eight engine so advanced, it has been called
the state of the art by three leading automotive publications."

"Really?" said Aunt Pola, very offhand. "Very nice."

Bruce all but leapt to the front of the car. He reached
beneath the gargantuan chrome grille and released the car's
hood. Everyone huddled around the open hood, to meet the
engine.

"Oh my," said Aunt Ida. "Look at that."

"Ida," said Mrs. Reckler, "you don't know anything
about engines."

"I know," said Aunt Ida. "But it's so clean."

"It looks fine," said Aunt Pola, turning down the corners
of her mouth. "Big."

"This is a premium assembly," said Bruce. "Featuring
sequential multi-part electronic fuel injection and a four-

speed automatic overdrive transmission, all combined with the computer technology of the twenty-first century."

"What about the horsepower?" asked Aunt Pola. Joe had no idea what horsepower was. He suspected that Aunt Pola shared his ignorance.

"One fifty," said Bruce. "You know your engines."

"Of course," said Aunt Pola. "That's a very good horse-power."

"I like it," said Mrs. Reckler amiably.

"Suits me," said Aunt Ida. Joe stared at the engine. His father had often tried to explain engines to him, to elaborate on internal combustion principles and such, but the subject was light-years beyond Joe. He was convinced that the visible engine was actually a hoax, and that the car ran on some other force entirely, via hungry hamsters or gravity, something Joe could grasp. Mrs. Reckler watched Joe contemplating the engine. She shook her head.

"Joe," she said, "what are you looking for? You think maybe some candy fell in?"

"Excuse me," said Joe. "I'm looking at the engine. Aunt Pola, it looks great."

"Are you a car fanatic?" Bruce asked Joe, in a strenuous buddy-buddy manner.

"He doesn't have a license," said Mrs. Reckler.

"He can't fix a toaster," said Aunt Ida.

"But we love him anyway," said Aunt Pola. "He went to Yale."

"It's enough," said Joe, finishing the thought.

"A Yalie," said Bruce, shutting the car's hood with a choreographed slam. "You must be very smart."

"Of course," said Aunt Ida.

"I wish," said Mrs. Reckler, hugging Joe.

"This is a very nice car," said Aunt Pola. "Kerry, do you like this car?"

"I think it's . . . wonderful," said Kerry. "It's enor-mous."

Aunt Pola now fished out her reading glasses and put them on. She bent at the waist, searching out the price sticker glued to the car's side window; the sticker was a sheet of computer readout, listing the car's many possible options. Joe watched Aunt Pola reading this information, underlining the words with her forefinger. Joe wished that the sheet had been glued underneath the car, so that Aunt Pola could have turned the vehicle over.

"So," said Aunt Pola, straightening up. "So, Bruce, what's the real price?"

"The real price?" said Bruce, confused. "The Lincoln Town Car is a luxury sedan."

"Hoo boy," said Aunt Ida, pulling out her own reading glasses from her bag. She scanned the price tag. "Oh my."

"What is it?" asked Mrs. Reckler. "Joe, go look. I don't want to dig out my glasses." Joe went and looked at the price tag. He was mildly stunned. He returned to his mother's side and was about to relate the figure.

"Not out loud," said Mrs. Reckler. "Just whisper it to me."

"Why?" asked Joe. "Why not out loud?"

"It's a public place," said Mrs. Reckler. "Don't be crude."

Joe whispered the price into his mother's ear. She clutched her heart, through the fabric of her coat and dress. "For a car?" Mrs. Reckler said.

"What is this thing?" said Aunt Pola, gesturing to the Town Car. "Is it made of rubies and emeralds? Is it jet-propelled?"

Kerry was now dying of curiosity. She snuck a look at the price sheet. "That's crazy," said Kerry.

"Bruce, are you listening?" asked Aunt Pola. "Kerry says it's crazy. And she lives around here."

"How much, Mommy?" asked Molly, tugging on the hem of her mother's corduroy wrap skirt.

"How much?" piped Toby.

"Shhh," said Kerry, taking her cue from Mrs. Reckler.

"You see?" said Aunt Pola to Bruce. "She's ashamed to tell her own children. It's too horrible. You couldn't put it on TV."

"Ladies," said Bruce, on the defensive, "and young man,

this is a Cartier Designer Series Lincoln Town Car. Our figure is standard.''

"Standard," chortled Aunt Pola. "He says it's standard. Bruce, if it's so standard, you tell the children. Go ahead, tell it to Toby and Molly. They're innocent young children; see what they have to say."

Bruce then made a career-demolishing mistake: he listened to Aunt Pola seriously. He glanced nervously at the knot of people at his elbows. Everyone was watching him. They were like a hungry mob filling the bleachers at a championship tennis tourney. They were intensely focused, minutely critical. Bruce shook his head, to clear it. He was a car salesman after all. His forte was suave negotiation. He would not be cowed. He turned to the twins with a flair.

"It's $36,000," Bruce said, his throat suddenly dry. "It's a $36,000 car."

"He did it," said Aunt Pola. "Can you believe that? To children."

Joe had never seen his Aunt Pola haggle at this level. The term "hardball" came to mind.

"$36,000," said Molly, in a singsong. "Mommy, is that a lot?"

"Come," said Aunt Pola to her companions. "Let's go."

Aunt Pola hoisted her handbag higher on her forearm. She straightened her coat, pointed her chin, and headed for the door. The group followed in her wake, like obedient ducklings. Aunt Pola walked very deliberately, placing each foot down with exaggerated care. She walked the way the Queen Mother might, when reviewing the Royal Hussars. Aunt Pola walked to be seen.

"Mrs. Berman . . ." said Bruce, without thinking.

"Yes, Bruce?" said Aunt Pola, pausing and turning only her head, and only a fraction of an inch.

"Mrs. Berman . . ." said Bruce, still not certain why he'd opened his mouth. "Mrs. Berman . . . do you like the car?"

Aunt Pola now turned and strolled leisurely back to the Town Car. She surveyed the car, as if she'd never seen it before. "It's a beautiful car," she remarked. "If you're crazy."

"If you're crazy?" inquired Bruce.

"Bruce, listen to me," said Aunt Pola. "Because I'm going to talk to you. This is a very nice car. But it's a car, it's not the Hope Diamond. It's not putting four grandchildren through college and maybe, if there's a God in heaven, graduate school. It's not feeding the hungry and starving, and at a very nice restaurant. It's not world peace, may it come very soon, God willing. It's just a car. You put in Mobil unleaded. You get somewhere. Now, it's a big car. I'll grant you that, hands down. I like a big car, I like to see what I'm paying for. My late husband Nat, may he rest in peace, he liked a big car. He said it was safer. He'd say, If we sit in a big car, it's better in an accident, God forbid. It's like a fort. So it's a big car, and it's a pretty car, and it has power what-have-you and the radio works. But Bruce, I want you to look me in the eye and say, 'Mrs. Berman, give me $36,000 for this car.' "

"But . . ." said Bruce, almost plaintively, "that's what it costs."

"Bruce, please," said Aunt Pola. "Look at me. I'm an old woman. I wasn't born in a cabbage patch on the day before yesterday. The tag says $36,000. Do you listen to tags?"

"Mrs. Berman," said Bruce uncertainly. "Are you . . . haggling?"

"God forbid!" said Aunt Pola, mortally offended. "What are you, crazy? What am I, a Turk buying a rug at a bazaar? Haggling . . . Ida, did you hear?"

"I heard," said Aunt Ida, staying out of Pola's way.

"She heard," said Aunt Pola. "But she didn't believe it. Haggling . . . I'm seventy-seven years old, believe me, I don't haggle. I've got better things to do with what little time is left to me. All I'm doing is I'm looking at the car, and I'm talking to you, and I'm asking."

"You're . . . asking?" said Bruce. In some distant brain cell, Bruce knew just what was going on. Bruce was no slouch at turbocharged manipulation. But Aunt Pola was outclassing him, setting him spinning. He vowed to reassert himself, to honor his profession. He straightened his thin, expensive silk strip of Italian necktie. "Now, Mrs. Berman, what are you asking? Are you asking for a deal? Yes, that is a possibility. Are you interested?"

"A deal?" said Aunt Pola, as if encountering some perplexing foreign idiom. "What, a deal? Hedy, maybe it's me, maybe I'm out of touch, I don't live around here. Hedy, do you know what he's saying?"

"Pola," said Mrs. Reckler, stringing along, "I think he means he'll give you a discount."

"A discount . . ." said Aunt Pola, nodding her head slowly, as if she'd found a friend. "I see. A discount, Bruce, that's what you're saying."

"Say . . . $34,000," said Bruce, with a wazir's cunning smile. "Because I like you. And because you're a visitor to our state. As my guest."

"$34,000," said Aunt Pola, not showing her cards. "You don't like me very much. Joe, with friends like this one, I'll be dead tomorrow."

Joe wasn't certain how to respond, so he nodded, sagely, as if he were a fellow Justice on Aunt Pola's circuit court.

"Mrs. Berman," said Bruce gravely. "Pola. That was an extremely generous offer. We're running a business. You understand."

"You're right," said Aunt Pola, throwing up her hands. "He's right. The man is right. What am I thinking? Bruce, you're a very nice young fellow. I'm sure you sell a lot of cars. It's a very nice operation you have here. I'm sure it's the very best in the area. And you were generous, very generous, and I thank you. Come on everyone, let's go see some leaves. That's why we're here, Bruce, in the New England region. It's so picturesque." Aunt Pola began to once again herd everyone out of the store, shepherding her flock. She spoke to Kerry, in a mock whisper. "Kerry, did you hear? He's running a business."

"I heard," said Kerry, taking the twins' hands.

"Not for long . . ." said Aunt Pola, just as she placed her fingertips on the chrome door handle.

"Mrs. Berman!" said Bruce, jogging after the group. "Mrs. Berman!"

"Yes?" Aunt Pola drawled, turning. Everyone froze.

"Mrs. Berman," said Bruce. "I . . . uh . . . can't we talk?"

"We've been talking," said Aunt Pola, not moving an inch.

"$33,000," said Bruce. "Final and non-negotiable. Rock bottom."

"$30,000," countered Aunt Pola. "Make me happy."

"Mrs. Berman," Bruce wailed piteously.

"Mommy," said Toby, "is that man crying?"

"Not yet," said Aunt Pola. She moved a few steps back into the showroom, pretending mercy. She turned to her minions. "Just for a minute." Aunt Pola walked over to Bruce. She motioned with her head for him to follow her. She stood by the square, pristine front fender of the Town Car. She put her hand on the hood; she lacked only a bowler hat, sleeve garters, and a Tammany stogie. Bruce had trailed after her meekly. He stood very close, bending slightly. Everyone else remained at a respectful distance, a few feet off.

"She's got him," said Aunt Ida, nodding.

"She's amazing," said Joe.

"She's so good," said Kerry.

"That's Pola," said Mrs. Reckler. "I'm glad I'm not a car salesman."

"Bruce," said Aunt Pola, laying her hand on Bruce's shoulder. "I'm an old lady."

"Mrs. Berman," Bruce whimpered.

"I need a car. You've been very nice. Are you married?"

"No . . ." said Bruce in a tiny voice, wondering how the question applied.

"Get married," said Aunt Pola. "You deserve a little happiness. A little *naches*. Do you know what that means, *naches*? It's Yiddish, it means a little joy. You deserve it."

"Thank you," said Bruce, now utterly lost. He was like a sailor, alone in a dinghy, in the path of an oncoming destroyer. He was transfixed, terrified, prayerful.

"$30,000," said Aunt Pola.

Bruce could not form words. A strangled sound emerged

from his throat, something between an orphan's sob and a lonely death rattle.

"You can do it," said Aunt Pola. Her tone was both direct and caressing. Joe watched Aunt Pola deliver this final stroke. He realized that his Aunt Pola was a very sexy woman.

"Fine," mumbled Bruce, his knees buckling. His body went limp; his hands trembled at his sides and then fell, exhausted. "Fine."

"I can't," said Aunt Pola briskly. "It's ridiculous."

"Pola," said Joe, Mrs. Reckler, Aunt Ida, Kerry, Toby, and Molly. They were passionate theatergoers demanding a satisfying finale, a clinch and a sunset.

"All right," said Aunt Pola, making a clucking noise. She turned to Bruce. "Look what they're making me do."

"Thank you," said Bruce to Aunt Pola, with profound gratitude. He turned to the crowd, with the same humble moan: "Thank you."

"I'll take it," said Aunt Pola. "But . . . wait."

"What?" said Bruce.

"I love the car; we have a deal," said Aunt Pola. "It's a definite thing. But just to be 100 percent sure, just for my own peace of mind—could I take a test drive?"

32

"**What, I** should walk away from a bargain like that, when it's looking me right in the face?" Aunt Pola asked Joe, as they drove through Top Harbor. Aunt Pola sat behind the Titanium-leather-wrapped steering wheel of the Cartier Designer Series Town Car. Mrs. Reckler, Aunt Ida, Kerry, and the twins were following in the Reckler Oldsmobile.

Aunt Pola's head barely cleared the steering wheel. Passengers in nearby cars had to check twice, to be certain that someone was actually driving the Town Car. Aunt Pola was bouncing as she drove, keeping the beat of a rock tune blasting out of the Town Car's many sophisticated radio speakers. Joe was kneeling on the front seat, poking his head out of the car's moon roof. The wind was whipping Joe's hair back against his head and making his eyes tear. At Aunt Pola's insistence, Joe pulled himself back down into the car. "You'll catch cold," she predicted, closing the tinted-glass moon roof with the flick of a switch. "What is that song?" she asked, still bouncing. "It's peppy!"

"Aunt Pola," Joe inquired, "isn't this an awfully long test drive? We're pretty far from Bancroft Auto."

"Are we?" asked Aunt Pola, without real concern. "Listen, they have plenty of cars. They won't miss one."

"Aunt Pola," said Joe, impressed.

"That Bruce," Aunt Pola continued, "he was a nice boy. I think he learned something today."

"Aunt Pola?"

"What? Oh, I know what you're thinking. You're thinking that I'm like you and that mother of yours. You think I'm, what, stealing this car, don't you? You think that's why I told everyone else to get in your mother's car and follow us. Well, let me tell you something, college boy. You're dead wrong. I'm seventy-seven years old. I don't need to steal cars."

"Okay."

"So I'm just taking this beautiful vehicle for a nice long test drive. Just to make sure everything's in tip-top working order. The gauges and things."

"I believe you."

"Joe, I have to tell you something," said Aunt Pola. "It's a terrible thing, but I'm a happy woman. Isn't that awful?" With that, Aunt Pola floored the gas pedal, gunned the engine, and roared down the highway.

A few minutes later, both cars pulled up in front of Dale Dell. Everyone piled out, and Kerry stood on the steps with the twins.

"Do you all really have to go back tomorrow?" Kerry asked. She knew that Joe and the Eskers were planning to leave for New Jersey and New York.

"Tomorrow afternoon," said Mrs. Reckler. "We've all got to get back."

"To work," added Aunt Ida. "Uch."

"Don't even say it," said Mrs. Reckler. "I don't even want to think about that office and what's piling up."

There was an awkward pause. Everyone knew that a farewell was imminent. The Esker sisters did not care for maudlin goodbyes; they were not sentimental women. They kept their partings upbeat and bubbling with activity, with squeezes and gifts, so that any sadness could be held at bay.

"So long," said Aunt Pola, giving Kerry a kiss on the cheek. "I'm a terrible woman, but you know I'm right."

"Kerry," said Mrs. Reckler, giving Kerry a kiss. "You're a terrific girl; whatever you do, you'll be fine. Pola's given you plenty of advice, so I won't say a word. You have my address; send me a postcard. From wherever." Mrs. Reckler was trying to be fair, she was trying not to butt in, she was trying not to be her sister Pola. But she was still an Esker. She gave Kerry a searching look and made a quick hand gesture, mouthing the words "Get out!"

"Don't listen to either of them," said Aunt Ida, kissing Kerry. "What do they know? Live your life and be happy. Here, take this." Aunt Ida handed Kerry a crumpled paper bag.

"What is this?" asked Kerry. "Ida, I can't accept this."

"What, you can't accept it," said Ida. "It's garbage, it's nothing, take it or I'll be offended." Kerry opened the bag. Inside was a box of Estée Lauder White Linen dusting powder for Kerry and two sets of rainbow-hued Venus Paradise pencils for the twins. Kerry had no idea how Ida had found the time to shop for these items over the course of the day. Kerry was still not fully aware of Aunt Ida's stature as a *tchotchke* magnet.

"Ida, thank you," said Kerry, touched by the gifts. "Molly, Toby, say thank you."

"Thank you," said the twins, clutching their pencils.

"So cute," said Aunt Ida, pinching the cheek of each twin.

"I could eat them for lunch," said Aunt Pola, hugging the squirming children.

Mrs. Reckler tried to resist such hugging and pinching. Joe and Clark had often told her how much they had hated being mauled by every passing relative. "So what do you know?" Mrs. Reckler said to her son, and she proceeded to hug and pinch to her heart's content.

"Joe, you're very lucky," Kerry told Joe, giving him a kiss. "They're wonderful women."

"I know," said Joe. "And so shy."

"Get in the car," said Mrs. Reckler, swatting the back of Joe's head. "I'm so embarrassed."

Ida returned to the Oldsmobile with Mrs. Reckler. Aunt Pola climbed into her new chariot. Joe handed the twins two bags of Peanut M&M's and hopped in beside Aunt Pola. Joe felt like a G.I. airlifting out of Saigon.

"Bye-bye!" said the twins, waving furiously and munching their M&M's.

"Bye-bye!" said Kerry, waving wistfully. "Thank you! For everything!"

Joe and the Esker sisters all continued waving, even more ferociously than the twins, until both cars were well down the drive. Joe hung out the window, and he saw Sally Dale emerge from the house. She did not greet either Kerry or her grandchildren; she was focused entirely on Kerry's new shoes, on Kerry's silver lamé sandals, which Mrs. Dale had spotted from an upper window. Mrs. Dale stared at the shoes. Kerry retreated for a second, and then proceeded to proudly model her sparkly new footwear, as the twins giggled. Grey stepped out of the house, saw the shoes, and immediately stepped back inside. He had looked both ways, as if he was afraid that someone might have spotted him in the vicinity of such vulgar attire.

"Hoo boy," Aunt Pola told Joe. She had observed the Dales from her rearview mirror. "That Grey, he doesn't like those shoes."

"Do you think she'll leave him?" asked Joe.

"Who knows?" said Aunt Pola, steering out onto the open road. "Maybe he's not such a terrible person, and he's very wealthy, maybe things will work out. And maybe the mother isn't really so bad, maybe she has hidden qualities, maybe she's had a terrible life that we don't know about. But Joe, can I tell you something?"

"Please," said Joe.

"Those are beautiful shoes," said Aunt Pola, who was now doing seventy-five miles an hour.

Later that night, after a local dinner, the group returned to the room Aunt Pola was sharing with Aunt Ida at the Land Ho. The room itself was as simple as Joe's, although outfitted with twin beds. Little of the room's starkness was visible, however, as the premises were buried beneath Aunt Pola's and Aunt Ida's booty. Shoe boxes were stacked in a corner.

Dishes sat in newspaper nests on the steel desk. Odd sizes of still-wrapped packages had settled on the nightstand between the beds, and Aunt Ida's sable was laid carefully across one of the corduroy spreads. Aunt Pola's "extra" suitcase lay open across the other bed; this was a flimsy fabric valise that Aunt Pola had acquired a day earlier. The valise was used for accumulated bargains and now bulged with postcards, a set of hand-woven place mats, several cabin-shaped tins of souvenir maple syrup and many boxes of maple candy, nuggets in the shape of maple leaves and hatchets. Through the motel room's window, the view of the Maine coastline had been superseded by the lustrous aura of Aunt Pola's new car.

Aunt Ida sat on the bed beside her coat, scribbling more postcards to family members and co-workers. Occasionally her hand would wander and unconsciously stroke her fur. Aunt Pola sat in a curving Naugahyde side chair, her shoes off, her legs stretched out before her. Mrs. Reckler sat on the other bed, with her coat on, sampling a piece of maple sugar candy. Mrs. Reckler had been occupying the bed for almost an hour, but she had refused to relinquish her Loehmann's coat. Keeping your coat on was another Esker habit. Retaining outerwear implied that you were staying only "a minute," that you weren't wasting time, that you were about to run home and do the dishes. Mrs. Reckler also felt more comfortable eating in her coat. Keeping the coat on, she knew, reduced any food's calories by half. If she kept her coat on, she wasn't really staying and eating. She was at most nibbling.

Joe balanced on the little metal desk chair, leaning backward against the desk. This was a precarious position, designed to showcase Joe's bravado and upset his mother.

"Joe, if you sit like that, you're going to fall down and break your head," said Mrs. Reckler.

"I know," said Joe. "That's why I'm doing it."

"What is he doing?" asked Aunt Ida, looking up from her postcards. "Joe, don't do that."

"Let him do it," advised Aunt Pola. "So he'll fall and break his head. He'll learn his lesson."

"And I'll be stuck with the doctor bills," said Mrs. Reckler. "To buy him a new head."

Now Joe couldn't decide between continuing his perilous behavior or giving in. As he thumped the chair back on all four legs, he realized why there are so few Jewish acrobats. Joe took in the room. The place had come to resemble a pirate's lair, a shadowy grotto laden with treasure chests spewing ropes of pearls and cascades of doubloons. The bedside bullet lamp could easily have passed for a flickering torch. Aunt Pola, her hands patting her belly, could double for Long John Silver, with the addition of an eye patch and a macaw, and a simple relocation of her designer scarf. Rum would not be Aunt Pola's downfall, however; cream soda or Mylanta would be more the ticket. Joe polished this tableau, this Jolly Roger reverie. He imagined his family as a colorful ride at Disneyland, the popular "Jewish Women of the Caribbean."

"Well, I feel terrible," announced Aunt Pola. Joe was intrigued by this statement. He tried to predict the precise cause of Aunt Pola's downhearted mood. Did she feel terrible because she had spent the afternoon heisting a luxury vehicle? Because everyone in the room was now an experienced member of a crime syndicate? Because she had been instrumental in a possible divorce action? Because morality itself had become an extremely malleable conceit?

"Aunt Pola," Joe asked, "why do you feel terrible?"

"Why do I feel terrible?" Aunt Pola said. "Please. Look at me. I haven't bought a thing."

"Pola," said Mrs. Reckler, "what are you talking about? Tomorrow, when we leave the state, it's going to be empty."

"I don't know," said Aunt Pola reflectively. "I'm an old lady. On my last trip, I was in Geneva, just for a weekend. By the time I left, I needed two extra suitcases and a garment bag."

"Pola," said Aunt Ida, "what about the car?"

"The car," said Aunt Pola. "You know, I'll never believe that it's mine. For as long as I'm behind the wheel, for the next fifty years, I'll still consider it a test drive."

"Pola," said Aunt Ida, "don't feel bad. We've still got tomorrow."

"Tomorrow. That's very true," said Aunt Pola, brightening. "Our last day. So where are we going?"

"L. L. Bean?" suggested Aunt Ida. "We're right nearby."

"No," Mrs. Reckler hurriedly said. "That's a terrible idea. L. L. Bean—we don't need that."

"Why not?" asked Aunt Pola. "It's a terrific place. I always order from them. From the catalogue."

"Well, maybe," said Mrs. Reckler, to avoid suspicion. She glanced at Joe. "If we have time. There's lots to do. There's the Lauren outlet for linens. And the Hathaway shirt place. We can do Bean the next time around, on another trip. But right now I'm falling asleep. Come on, Joe, let's go back to our rooms."

"You can stay here," said Aunt Ida. "We'll make room. Look, poor Joe is dead on his feet."

"Ida," said Mrs. Reckler, "our rooms are two feet away. Believe it or not, we're all in the same motel. We'll see you in the morning. Don't eat any of this maple sugar candy, it tastes horrible."

"I know," said Aunt Ida. "I buy it for gifts. The secretaries at school, they love it."

"It tastes like sand," said Mrs. Reckler. "Very sweet sand."

Everyone said good night, and Joe and his mother left the room. They stood in the cool, starless evening air. They faced Aunt Pola's new car, in the parking lot.

"Look at this," said Mrs. Reckler. "I can't believe it. But you know something? We laugh at her, but your Aunt Pola is a very good person. She'd give you the shirt off her back."

"Wholesale," said Joe.

"Very funny," said Mrs. Reckler. "You know, I love your Aunt Pola dearly, but isn't this a ridiculous automobile? It looks like a lobby."

"In Vegas," said Joe. "It looks like there are going to be slot machines in the back seat. Or a lounge act."

"Be quiet. It's very beautiful. And . . . roomy."

"Excuse me. I wasn't the one who said it looked like a lobby."

"Well, I can say that—she's my sister. And you're a smart aleck. And remember, tomorrow morning we're going to L. L. Bean. Just the two of us. We have work to do."

"But what about Ida and Pola?"

"Don't worry; they won't suspect a thing. I'll send them off somewhere. They can go look at shirts, but you're coming with me."

"Mom . . ."

"Go get some rest; you look tired. And wake up bright and fresh, because tomorrow we're . . . we're going to redo the living room."

Joe was awakened the next morning by someone rapping on the door of his motel room. Wrapping the blanket around himself, Joe wobbled to the door. It was his mother, attended by his two aunts, all dressed for the day, with designer scarves draped inside their coats and Italian leather purses over their arms.

"I told them you weren't feeling well and couldn't go to the shirt place," said Mrs. Reckler. "I told them I would stay with you while they went. I told them you wouldn't mind."

"Right," said Joe, through a haze.

"So you're sick?" said Aunt Pola, standing on tiptoes to see over Mrs. Reckler's shoulder. "Why are you sick?"

"Pola, he's not sick," said Mrs. Reckler. "He just isn't feeling well. He's not up to running around. You two go ahead; don't let this spoil your day."

"Joe, what's wrong?" asked Aunt Ida, over Mrs. Reckler's other shoulder. Mrs. Reckler now appeared to have three heads, a common motif of Joe's childhood dreams. "Is it serious?" asked Aunt Ida. "Should we get a doctor?"

"Girls, don't be silly," said Mrs. Reckler, still barring the way. "Look at him—he's fine. He just doesn't feel well. He should stay in bed for the day and he'll be perfect. I'll be with him; I'll keep him company. You two go."

"We can't go," said Aunt Ida. "Not if Joe's sick. Joe, what's wrong? What hurts?"

"Um . . ." said Joe. "Everything. Everything hurts, but not very badly."

"Really?" said Aunt Pola. "That sounds very strange. Hedy, I'm coming in."

"Don't," warned Mrs. Reckler. "It might not be bad, but maybe it's catching."

"Hedy," said Aunt Pola. "Don't be crazy. I'll just take a look and I'll see and then I'll go." Aunt Pola nudged past Mrs. Reckler and into Joe's room. Joe ricocheted back into bed, pulled the covers up to his chin, and tried frantically to decide on a symptom or two.

"So hello," said Aunt Pola, standing beside the bed. "So you're sick."

"I'm fine," said Joe. "I'm just . . . I have a bug or something. Just a flu thing."

Bugs and flu things were standard Reckler illnesses; bugs and flu things were any conditions that could be cured by doses of Nyquil and afternoon soap operas.

"What," said Aunt Ida, also pushing past Mrs. Reckler and nearing the bed. "Is it like a twenty-four-hour thing? Like a truck hit you, but then it goes away?"

"That's it," said Mrs. Reckler. "It's a twenty-four-hour thing, maybe less; maybe it's just a twelve-hour thing. You two go; I'll time it." Before Mrs. Reckler could shoo her

sisters from the room, Aunt Ida expressed an eternal concern, a question dear to mothers throughout the cosmos, an
amateur physician's creed.

"Does he have a fever?" asked Aunt Ida. "Is he hot or
cold?"

Aunt Pola immediately slapped the palm of her hand across
Joe's forehead. Then she tried using the back of her hand.
"He's fine," said Aunt Pola. "He's average."

"Let me try," said Aunt Ida, repeating the hand-
thermometer routine. "I can't tell," said Aunt Ida. "He feels
fine, but I could be wrong. Hedy, you try."

Mrs. Reckler came to the bed and applied her hand. "He's
burning up," she concluded. "But it's all right. Don't worry.
I'll buy him some aspirin, and he'll drink some orange juice.
He'll be fine. Why should you two miss out on Hathaway
shirts at half off?"

"Should I call Kurt?" asked Aunt Ida. "He could tell us
something."

"Half off?" asked Aunt Pola. "Really?"

"Kurt's in Monterey," said Mrs. Reckler. "I'm sure he's
got better things to do. At the hospital."

"I'll call him," said Aunt Ida, reaching for the phone.
"Maybe he'll suggest something."

"Ida," said Mrs. Reckler, beating her sister to the phone.
"Don't call."

"What's going on here?" demanded Aunt Pola. "Joe, are
you sick, or what? Do you just not want to go look at shirts?
Tell the truth."

"Okay," said Joe, improvising. "I don't want to see the
shirts. I just should've said it."

"What?" asked Aunt Ida. "Why don't you want to see
shirts? What's wrong with shirts?"

"I don't know," said Joe. "Shirts are just so . . . I don't
know. I guess I'm just tired of shopping."

Aunt Pola slammed her palm back onto Joe's forehead.
"Still fine," she decided. "Go figure."

"So we won't go shopping," said Aunt Ida. "So we'll do
something else. We'll find another museum, we'll go see
some leaves. Maybe there's one of those restored villages

around here—I love those—where everyone wears costumes and there's a blacksmith. We'll go to one of those.''

Mrs. Reckler leaned against the small metal desk. ''Ida,'' she said, ''I don't want to go to a restored village.''

''Hedy,'' said Aunt Pola, ''I'm not blind. If you and Joe don't want to go to the Hathaway place with Ida and me, for whatever *fachacta* reason, be my guest, don't go. Believe me, it's no sweat off my nose.''

''Pola, don't be ridiculous,'' protested Mrs. Reckler. ''Joe and I would love nothing better than to go to the Hathaway place with you and Ida. It would be sheer heaven. It's just that . . . well, we have other things to do.''

''So fine,'' said Aunt Pola. ''So go. So do them. I won't ask. What things?''

''Just . . . things,'' said Mrs. Reckler. ''Don't ask.''

''I won't,'' insisted Aunt Pola. ''So, Joe, what things?''

Joe looked up, taken by surprise. Joe had not been paying attention. He had been fixated on Aunt Pola's use of the expression ''no sweat off my nose.'' This phrase sounded like a timeworn cliché, or several timeworn clichés, but Aunt Pola had given the words a zest all her own. ''What?'' Joe repeated, a bit lost.

''So what things are you and your mother going to do today?'' said Aunt Pola. ''What terrible things that you don't want to discuss?''

''Pola,'' said Aunt Ida, ''leave him alone. It's none of our business. Joe, you don't have to tell.''

''Of course not,'' agreed Aunt Pola. ''Of course he doesn't have to tell. It's a free country; he's an American. If he wants to keep secrets from his own flesh and blood, that's his right. And if he wants to jump off the Brooklyn Bridge at high noon, that's his right too, but I wouldn't recommend it. Now, I'm just guessing here—what do I know?—but, Joe, are you and your mother up to no good? If you know what I'm saying and I think you do very much.''

''I don't feel well,'' said Joe, dropping his head back onto the pillow. ''I think I have a fever.''

''Pola, we're not doing anything wrong,'' said Mrs. Reckler. ''All right, we're doing something terrible, but it's in a good cause. All right, so it's not such a good cause, it's not curing major diseases, but it has to be done."

"What?" said Aunt Pola. "Speak English. What has to be done?"

"The living room," said Mrs. Reckler. "It has to be done over."

There was a pause, as Aunt Ida and Aunt Pola absorbed this fresh information.

"Oh," said Aunt Ida. "Now I understand. I mean, I think I understand. So what's wrong with your living room? I was there last month; it was gorgeous."

"Gorgeous?" said Mrs. Reckler. "Ida, what, do you have rocks in your head? I only let you into my house because you're my sister and I love you and I know you won't talk. The walls need painting, the carpet is so dirty it makes me cry, and the couches are ready for the Goodwill. I'm embarrassed to have people over; it's like a slum. And now that Saul is retired, I want him to have a nice room."

"All right," said Aunt Pola approvingly. "That makes sense. If the room needs redoing, you should redo it. I couldn't agree more; it's only right. But, Hedy, I don't know how to tell you this, but your living room is in Jersey. We're in Maine. So how are you going to redo your living room this morning?"

"Well," said Mrs. Reckler, "it's not so easy, redoing a room. On a budget, I might add. I don't have the money. And it's breaking my heart. So while you and Ida are at the Hathaway place, Joe and I are going to rob L. L. Bean." Mrs. Reckler said this very simply, to put an end to the discussion.

There was another pause, as Aunt Ida and Aunt Pola looked at each other.

"Bean?" said Aunt Ida finally. "You're going to rob Bean?"

"Just a little," said Mrs. Reckler. "Don't worry about it. It's an errand."

"You're robbing L. L. Bean?" said Aunt Pola. "My sister Hedy and my nephew Joe? Joe, do you know about this?"

"My stomach aches," said Joe, scrunching down farther beneath the sheets.

"Oh please," said Mrs. Reckler. "Joe always does this. Whenever we ask him to help around the house, that's when his stomach aches. Joe, get up and get dressed, and use the facilities."

"Bean?" said Aunt Ida. "Pola, I don't think they should do this, do you?"

"Listen," said Aunt Pola. "I'm not one to butt in. It's their funeral, believe me. But if I were Hedy, I would ask me to help."

"What?" said Mrs. Reckler.

"I'm not saying a word," said Aunt Pola. "Not one word. But I was a vice-principal for thirty years and an assistant superintendent for twenty; I know how things should run. Hedy, I'm not saying you're incompetent. I would never say that, even if you can't knit or hold a normal job. And I'm not saying that Joe isn't very bright, even if he doesn't have a driver's license and only eats candy. But believe me, if I was robbing L. L. Bean, before I'd ask you or Joe to help out, I would ask me. I'm just thinking out loud, and no one should listen. Unless they know what's good for them."

"You always do this," said Mrs. Reckler. "Ida, she always does this. She never trusts me. Because I didn't get my teaching certificate, and because I moved to Jersey, she thinks I'm a dunce."

"That's not true," said Aunt Pola. "You're my sister, and I love you and I respect you. I would lay down my life for you. But I'm just saying."

"Ida, can you believe this?" said Mrs. Reckler. "Doesn't she always do this? Am I right?"

"Ida, you don't have to answer," said Aunt Pola. "She's your sister; you don't have to tell her she's wrong. Even if she is, and any fool knows it."

"Ida?" said Mrs. Reckler.

"Ida?" said Aunt Pola.

"Ida?" said Joe, just for symmetry.

"What?" said Aunt Ida. "What is this? Suddenly I'm Solomon? Suddenly I'm a Supreme Court Justice, with the black robes? Look, you're both my sisters and I love you like anything, even if you're both acting crazy. Hedy, I don't think anyone should be robbing L. L. Bean. I think it's awful. But if the living room is a problem, then I understand. You don't want to rob L. L. Bean, but you have to. Fine. Pola, your living room is perfect, so you don't need to rob anything. But if you think you can help out, with Hedy and Joe, then be my guest. Hedy, let her help, or you'll never hear the end of it. And that's what I think. Those are my words of wisdom.''

"What?'' said Aunt Pola.

"I didn't say anything,'' said Aunt Ida. "Not a word. Both of you, do what you please, leave me alone. Joe, guess what? I think I have a stomachache too.''

"All right,'' said Mrs. Reckler, standing up. "As usual, Ida is the only one around here who makes any sense. Pola, if you want to come, come. If you don't want to come, don't. I appreciate your help, but I can live without it. It's up to you.''

"Hedy,'' said Aunt Pola. "I don't go where I'm not wanted. Believe me, I can live without robbing L. L. Bean on my last day of vacation. So I tell you what I'll do. I'll come along, but I won't say a word. I'll be like a little mouse. You won't even know I'm there. Joe, I'm putting you in charge.''

"In charge? Of what?'' asked Joe, peeping out from beneath the covers.

"Of me,'' said Aunt Pola. "You're in charge. If I start to get pushy, if I start to say one word, if I so much as open my mouth, just give me a pinch, and I'll shut right up. I'll be very good. I'll be like the wind, just a little ocean breeze. And, Ida, if Joe isn't watching, then you watch. You pinch. Hedy, you see? No problems.''

"I watch?'' said Aunt Ida. "I pinch?'' Aunt Ida was horrified, not at the idea of participating in the robbery of L. L. Bean but at the notion of monitoring her sister Pola.

"I'll watch,'' Joe assured Aunt Ida. "I'll pinch.''

"Uch,'' sighed Mrs. Reckler. "It's crazy. I've gotten everyone involved—what a mess. But it shows we're a family.

We do things together. So let's go. Joe, get a move on. We'll leave you alone, to get dressed and use the facilities.''

"So we're robbing Bean?" said Aunt Ida, as the sisters left Joe's room. Aunt Ida's tone was skeptical but not unhappy.

"Why not?" said Aunt Pola. "And maybe afterward we'll get to the Hathaway place."

Joe joined his mother and aunts in the motel parking lot.

"Come on," said Aunt Pola. "We'll take my car."

"Pola, don't be silly," said Mrs. Reckler. "Why should we take your car? It's new, let's not get it dirty. My car is fine."

"Hedy," said Aunt Pola, "I have to tell you. We've been riding in your car for almost a week now. I'm getting claustrophobic. Ida, isn't driving in Hedy's car enough already?"

"It's a beautiful car," defended Aunt Ida. "Not that Pola's car isn't beautiful too."

"Ida," said Aunt Pola, "stop being so nice. Tell the truth, wouldn't you like to ride to L. L. Bean in a brand-new Lincoln Continental Town Car? Wouldn't that be a dream come true?"

"Ida," said Mrs. Reckler, "you don't have to answer that. She's just trying to win."

"Oh, what, so now I'm Mussolini?" said Aunt Pola. "All

right, fine, I'm the bossy one, I've got the big mouth. Joe, isn't that what they're saying, that I'm the big bully?''

"Do I have to answer that?" Joe asked Aunt Ida.

"Okay, I'm very sorry, excuse me," said Aunt Pola. "Like I said before, I'm turning over a new leaf. From now on, I'm a little mouse. Here's what we'll do. We'll go in my car, but Hedy, you can give me gas money. We'll share. I'll watch the mileage.''

"It's like a whole new person," marveled Mrs. Reckler.

"Pola won," adjudged Aunt Ida. "Let's go."

Everyone boarded the Town Car. Joe and his mother were stowed in back, and Aunt Ida sat up front with Aunt Pola.

"This car," said Aunt Ida. "It smells so good. Like a casserole."

"It's a beautiful car," said Mrs. Reckler, rolling her eyes so only Joe could see. Joe and his mother leaned back into the thick white leather upholstery, which had been tarted up with welting and leather-covered buttons and chrome-plated plastic crests. As with most bloated, overdone, kitschy locales, the interior of the Lincoln Continental was extremely comfortable, a bowling league's Xanadu.

"You know the only thing this car needs," said Aunt Pola, "the only thing I miss? My cushion. That nice woven cushion I bought in West Palm, for the driver's seat. Those car thieves, I hope they're enjoying it. I guarantee you, they don't have any lower back problems. So Hedy, how do we get there? To Bean?''

"Hold on, let me get the directions," said Mrs. Reckler. She rummaged in her pocketbook for an envelope that had contained her last month's phone bill. Mrs. Reckler had used the back of this ragged envelope to jot down directions to L. L. Bean given to her over the phone by a helpful store employee. The backs of envelopes were Mrs. Reckler's true stationery; Joe had grown up amid these shards.

"Here it is," said Mrs. Reckler, digging out the envelope in question. "We take Route One, until we hit I-95. We stay on that until the second Freeport exit, and then it's two blocks south.''

"Very good," said Aunt Pola. "We're on Route One. Ida, you watch for the I-95 sign, that's your job."

"Joe, you watch for it too," said Mrs. Reckler. "You help Ida."

"Listen," said Aunt Ida. "I'll watch for I-95, I'll do my best. But I have a question. Once we get there, to L. L. Bean, then what do we do? Just go in and ask for money?"

"No, don't be silly," said Mrs. Reckler. "First we show them the gun." Mrs. Reckler opened her purse and took out a revolver.

"Mom," said Joe, "where did you get that?"

"Back in Piscataway. At the sporting goods store."

"What?" said Aunt Ida, craning her neck. "You've got a gun?"

"She's got a gun?" said Aunt Pola. "Let me see it."

Mrs. Reckler handed the weapon to Aunt Ida, who held it gingerly. "Is this a real gun?" she asked. "A gun that goes bang?"

"Hold it up so I can see," said Aunt Pola. "That's a very nice gun. How much?"

"$49.50," said Mrs. Reckler.

"You paid that?" said Aunt Ida.

"Reduced from $75.00," added Mrs. Reckler. "Plus tax."

"Did they have any more?" asked Aunt Pola.

"You guys," said Joe, his jaw dropping. "It's a gun. A real gun. Mom, I don't think you should be carrying it around. Someone could get hurt."

"Calm down," said Mrs. Reckler. "It's not loaded. I didn't even buy any ammunition. What do you think, I'm crazy? I bought it so we could show it to the salesclerk, just to make the point."

"How much is ammunition?" asked Aunt Pola. "Is it by the bullet or the box?"

"I don't know," said Mrs. Reckler. "I didn't ask."

"Ipsy-pipsy," said Aunt Ida.

"So we only have one gun?" asked Aunt Pola. "To go around?"

"Pola, I'm very sorry," said Mrs. Reckler. "I thought it

was just going to be Joe and me. I didn't know we would have special guest stars."

"I wasn't criticizing," said Aunt Pola. "I was only commenting. So who's going to carry it?"

"I thought Joe," said Mrs. Reckler. "Because he's the boy."

"What?" said Joe. "Mom, I've never touched a gun in my life. I'm a pickpocket. Guns make me incredibly nervous. How come I carry the gun just because I'm the boy?"

"Can you believe this?" Mrs. Reckler asked her sisters. "I ask him to do one little thing. It's always like this. We used to beg him, Please rake the leaves, please take out the garbage. We would pay him."

"You would pay him?" asked Aunt Ida. "To take out the garbage?"

"How much?" asked Aunt Pola.

"Excuse me," said Joe. "You are not asking me to take out the garbage. You are asking me to walk into L. L. Bean and terrorize people with a revolver."

"Five minutes out of your day," said Mrs. Reckler.

"Don't be a baby," said Aunt Pola.

"It's for a good cause," said Aunt Ida soothingly. "Joe, don't worry. You'll make your mother so happy."

Joe stared, first at his mother and then at his aunts. He held up the palms of his hands in resistance. He shut his eyes tightly, hoping to eliminate the entire debate. *Who are these women?* Joe pleaded with some Higher Intelligence. *Who are these women, and what do they want?*

Then, for the first time in his young life, Joe let go. He severed the last tenuous threads, the struggling filaments, that bound his brain to reason. He felt his brain drift high, like a shiny, inconsequential pink balloon, off into the stratosphere; he felt it leave his skull. And oddly, Joe found that he did not miss his brain one whit. He entered a state of exceedingly pleasant acceptance, of Esker bliss. Joe loved his mother and aunts ferociously, not in spite of their insanity but because of it. Perhaps, Joe thought, this is what love truly is. Love is robbing a store at gunpoint for your mom, so that she can redo the living room. Fair enough, Joe decided.

Page

"Fine," said Joe, opening his eyes.

"Fine," said Mrs. Reckler approvingly.

"He's a good boy," said Aunt Ida.

35

Freeport was a sleepy little town that had become a shoppers' Valhalla. The road to L. L. Bean was lined with outlets hawking crystal, decorator fabrics, shoes, skiwear, and bridal gowns. Freeport had the air of a boom town, a ragged Klondike village slapped together overnight.

"Keep driving," Mrs. Reckler told Aunt Pola. "We'll stop at these places later. If we have time."

L. L. Bean had once been a small, country-store sort of establishment, a way station for fishermen, hunters, and other serious New England sportsmen. Over the years, as Bean became a mail-order empire, the dimensions of the flagship store had doubled and then quadrupled. Bean now resembled a hardier, more plainspoken Macy's. The store was enormous and ringed by parking lots. It was open twenty-four hours a day and always busy.

"I haven't been here in years," said Aunt Ida, as Aunt Pola located a parking space. "They've expanded."

"It's a big business," said Mrs. Reckler. "Millions of dollars, maybe billions. But the quality is still there."

"I love their things," said Aunt Pola. "You know, part of

me wishes we weren't robbing the place. Then we could browse.''

"No," said Mrs. Reckler. "No browsing. When you're home, you can order from the catalogue. We have work to do.''

"Joe, have you got the gun?" asked Aunt Ida.

"Did he lose it?" asked Aunt Pola. "Already?'

"Joe, keep a firm grip," advised Mrs. Reckler. "I should tie it to your jacket sleeve with yarn, like I used to do with your mittens. He used to lose everything; it was endless.''

"I have the gun," Joe said evenly.

"I was only asking," said Aunt Pola. "He has such a tone.''

Aunt Pola parked, and everyone left the car and began walking across the parking lot. "Now what are you going to ask for?" Mrs. Reckler prompted.

"$10,000," Joe replied.

"What if they don't have it on hand?" worried Aunt Ida.

"What, of course they have it," said Mrs. Reckler. "They make that much in ten minutes. Maybe they'll have to go to the safe or something, but believe me, they have it.''

"What if the police come?" asked Aunt Ida.

"Ida," said Aunt Pola, "where were the police when those thugs stole my car? I love the police, I think they should be very well paid for what they do, but they're never in the neighborhood. By the time the police get here, we'll be back in Queens.''

"This is very exciting," Aunt Ida concluded, deciding to be optimistic. "Joe, are you excited?"

"What's so exciting?" said Mrs. Reckler. "We're doing a terrible thing, but it's fine. There's nothing exciting going on.''

"L. L. Bean," said Aunt Pola, as they reached the store's entrance. "What a smart man. I'll bet when he opened this store, way up in Maine, everyone laughed at him. And now who's laughing? I wonder if he's still alive.''

"He's not," said Mrs. Reckler. "But the family still owns the business.''

"What's the L. L. for?" asked Aunt Ida. "I've always wondered."

"Larry?" suggested Aunt Pola. "Or maybe Lou?"

"Aunt Pola," said Joe. "I don't think he was Jewish."

"You never know," said Aunt Pola. "He was very smart."

"Oh my God," said Aunt Ida, as everyone entered the building. "Look at all this."

"Don't look," said Mrs. Reckler. "We're not here to look."

"So who's looking?" asked Aunt Pola, heading toward a counter covered with merchandise.

"Stop it," said Mrs. Reckler, grabbing Aunt Pola's sleeve and reeling her in. "Joe, do you see the cash register? That's where we're going. No more shopping. Do you have the gun?"

"He's lost it?" said Aunt Ida.

"Again?" echoed Aunt Pola.

"I . . . have . . . the . . . gun," said Joe. "It's in my jacket."

"All right, don't get all wrought up," said Mrs. Reckler. "We were just asking. Now, before we go over to the cashier, do you have to do anything?"

"You mean, do I have to use the bathroom?" asked Joe incredulously.

"Don't be crude," said Mrs. Reckler. "Do you?"

"No," said Joe, trying to remain calm. "I do not."

"Okeydoke," said Mrs. Reckler, trying to lighten Joe's mood. "Then let's get busy."

"Stand up straight," advised Aunt Pola.

"You'll do a wonderful job," said Aunt Ida.

"Don't embarrass me," said Mrs. Reckler.

Joe stood up straight. He reached into his jacket; he had tucked the revolver into the waistband of his jeans. With his hand concealed, he walked over to the cashier's counter, which was set near a stairway, beside the tents and other larger camping equipment. A middle-aged woman with short, steel-gray curly hair stood behind a register. She was stout and wore a dark-green canvas smock. She also wore eye-glasses with oversized pinkish plastic frames, hooked to a chain around her neck. Pinned to her smock was a plastic name tag that read "Frances."

"Yes, young man?" the cashier said, as Joe approached. She spoke with the harsh, no-nonsense lilt of the native Maine resident.

"Um . . ." Joe began. "Um . . . hi."

"Yes?"

"Um . . . well . . ."

"Speak up," coached Aunt Pola, standing at Joe's elbow.

"Hi," Joe began again. "I have to ask you something. And I have a gun."

"Pardon?" the cashier said, as Joe had been mumbling.

"Frances," said Aunt Pola, "he has a gun."

"I have a gun," Joe repeated, quite clearly. "And I need money."

"Who doesn't?" commented Aunt Ida philosophically, at Joe's other elbow.

"He has a gun?" said the cashier skeptically.

Joe felt his mother's elbow in the small of his back. He tugged the gun from the waistband of his jeans. He attempted to brandish the gun dramatically. In midbrandish, the gun slipped from Joe's fingers and clattered to the floor.

"Uch," said Mrs. Reckler. "Joe."

"Wait," Aunt Pola told the cashier. "Be patient."

Mrs. Reckler and Aunt Ida both crouched to retrieve the gun.

"Oh my," said the two women simultaneously, from a mutual pang of arthritis in the knee.

"Hedy," said Aunt Ida, "we're not sixteen."

"Ida," said Mrs. Reckler, "we're not forty."

Aunt Ida reached the revolver first. Both women stood up, groaning. "Here," Aunt Ida told Joe, handing him the gun. "Please, don't do that again."

"Is that an actual gun?" said the cashier.

"Yes," said Joe firmly, pointing the revolver at the cashier. "Don't make me use it."

"Oh please," said Mrs. Reckler. "He's such a hambone."

"*Mother,*" said Joe, without turning.

"He's doing very well," said Aunt Ida, patting Joe's shoulder. "Don't pick on him."

"I need $10,000," Joe told the cashier. "And I need it fast."

"It's like *Dragnet*," said Mrs. Reckler, rolling her eyes.

"Young man," said the cashier, "am I to understand that you are robbing me?"

"Not robbing," said Aunt Ida, worried. "Just asking."

"You're just asking for $10,000?" the cashier asked Joe.

"No," said Joe. "I'm demanding $10,000. Open the register, or the safe, or wherever the money is."

"Excuse me," said a woman standing on line behind Joe and the Esker sisters. The woman was carrying a pair of ski poles, a Hudson's Bay blanket, and a canvas tote of some sort. "Excuse me, but there are people waiting."

"Keep your clothes on," Aunt Pola told the woman. Aunt Pola's phrase caused Joe to squint.

"We'll just be a minute," Aunt Ida told the woman. "What is that—the canvas bag?"

"It's not really a bag," the woman explained. "It's more like a sling, with handles, see? It's for carrying firewood."

"Isn't that handy," said Aunt Ida, examining the tote. "Pola, did you see this?"

"It's very nice," said Aunt Pola. "Does it only come in the green?"

"Aunt Pola," said Joe, "you don't have a fireplace."

"So what?" said Aunt Pola. "I can still carry things. It would also make a lovely gift."

"Excuse me," said the cashier. "Young man, what is this nonsense?"

"It's for carrying firewood," Joe said. "Oh. I'm sorry. Give me the money." Joe once again pointed the gun at the cashier.

"Is he robbing the store?" asked the woman on line. "He's robbing Bean?"

"Excuse me," Aunt Pola told the woman. "This is a family matter, if you don't mind."

"He's robbing Bean," the woman told the woman on line behind her. This second woman was laden with two sets of bright-red thermal underwear and what appeared to be a carved wooden duck decoy.

"What is that?" the first woman asked the second. "Is that a duck?"

"It's a telephone," the second woman replied. "You see, the head and the back lift off, it's a receiver. It's an extension phone."

"That's adorable," said Aunt Pola. "Where did you get it?"

"Right there," said the woman, pointing to a table stacked with mallard phones.

"Hedy, do you want one of these?" said Aunt Pola, taking a decoy phone. "Aren't they something?"

"I don't think so," said Mrs. Reckler firmly. Novelty phones would never appear in the Reckler home.

"We want $10,000 and we'll take two of these," Aunt Pola told the cashier, depositing two ducks on the counter. "I'm giving one to my daughter, for her family room, the kids will love it. And the other one's for Ida."

"What?" said Aunt Ida.

"You want $10,000 and two phones?" said the cashier, who had been on her feet all morning.

"And this," said Aunt Ida, adding a set of thermal underwear to the ducks. "It's for my son, in case he's chilly."

"Ida, are you crazy?" asked Mrs. Reckler. "Kurt lives in California. He doesn't need long underwear. Joe, could you use a pair? It's very practical. During cold weather, do you wear layers?"

"Mom," said Joe, "I'm trying to rob the store."

"Give me that," said Aunt Pola, taking the revolver from Joe. She moved in front of Joe. She pointed the gun at the cashier and kept her other hand on her hip. "Frances, I'm sorry, he's a very bright boy, but he gets confused. He can't even drive—can you believe that? Frances, let me talk to you. I hope you'll understand, and I'm sure you will. How long have you worked here, at Bean?"

"Nineteen years," said Frances, "come November."

"Good for you," said Aunt Pola. "I hope there's a pension plan. What do you get, 10 percent off on all purchases?"

"Yes, ma'am," said Frances.

"You're very lucky. It's a wonderful operation they have here. Now Frances, I hate to do this—it sounds crazy, I know. But my sister Hedy, she lives in Jersey—why I'll never know, but that's her business, you know what I'm saying. Frances, she has a beautiful home and two terrific kids, and her husband is retired, God bless him. It sounds like heaven, but there's a problem. There's tumult in paradise, isn't that what they say? Joe, isn't that the saying?"

"Yes," said Joe.

"It's the living room. Hedy, don't listen. Her living room's a mess. The walls, the couches, the wall-to-wall, it's a disaster area. It's like she should get assistance from the government. She's embarrassed to have people over, even family, who would look the other way, or at least try to. She needs to fix up the living room, and maybe the kitchen while she's at it. And maybe the half-bath. Hedy, why don't you redo the half-bath, off the TV room? You could repaper, maybe use a nice foil or a vinyl. Anyway, that's the situation. And Frances— That's a pretty name. My mother's sister was Frances. Aunt Fran, Ida, do you remember?"

"Of course," said Aunt Ida. "Tante Fran, with the bad wig."

"But a wonderful woman. And I'm sure you're wonderful too, Frances, even though I don't know you from Adam. Frances, Hedy needs $10,000 for the living room. She doesn't have the money, although she works very hard. Don't ask me what she does, I'd tell you, but I'd get yelled at. And she doesn't want to bother her husband, who's had two heart attacks but is doing great, knock on wood. And her children are no help. Don't ask what they do for a living either, believe me, you don't want to know. So Frances, we need the money. Frankly."

"You need $10,000 to redo the living room?" said Frances.

There was a pause, as Frances and the women on line reviewed this request. Joe wondered if Frances might have already pushed some hidden button to summon a platoon of burly security guards. He wondered if, within a few seconds' time, he and his relatives would be apprehended and shipped off to grim penitentiaries or harrowing mental institutions. He wondered if a jittery guard might assume the revolver was loaded and strafe the whole group. Joe looked at Frances, who had donned her eyeglasses and was studying the sisters.

"She needs the money for the living room?" Frances said. "Well, why didn't you say so?" She turned to a fellow cashier, a woman toiling at a register a few feet away. "Gretchen, do you have big bills?"

"Will $10,000 be enough?" asked the woman with the duck phones. "What about window treatments?"

"Levolor miniblinds are very attractive," said the woman with the thermal underwear. "If you're going contemporary."

"When you have the painters in," added a woman standing on the neighboring cashier's line, "watch them like a hawk. I left for ten minutes, and when I got back—well, I wanted Ivory, but I'm living with Bone."

"Here you go, Frannie," said Gretchen, the other cashier, passing Frances a stack of bills with a paper wrapper.

"Have you been to the Lauren place?" another shopper asked Mrs. Reckler. "They have marvelous throw pillows. They really warm up a room."

"The pillows," asked another woman. "Are they down-filled or foam? Down is more expensive, and sometimes it goes flat, but in the long run it's worth it. Those foam pillows are like rocks."

"Tell me," Aunt Pola asked the woman who had recommended the Lauren outlet. "Do they have bedspreads?"

"They have duvets," the woman replied.

"Do what?" asked Aunt Ida.

"Duvets," said Mrs. Reckler. "It's a cross between a quilt and a bedspread. You sleep under it but you can smooth it out during the day and it looks like a spread. It's very convenient."

Joe looked around the store. Everywhere he saw women shoppers, juggling sleeping bags and attacking tables full of Shawl-Collar Ragg Sweaters, Weekender Wrap Skirts, and cozy flannel sheets. Most of the women seemed to be from out of state; this was made obvious by the intensity of their shopping. Many of the women were wearing oversize pinkish eyeglass frames. Somehow, this vision of shoppers from the fifty states prowling L. L. Bean struck Joe as rousingly patriotic. America, Joe realized, was a land of Esker sisters.

"Here you go," Frances told Joe, passing him an envelope full of large bills.

"What do you say?" Mrs. Reckler prompted her son.

"Thank you," Joe told Frances, and, to his mother, "I was going to say it."

"Thank you very much," Mrs. Reckler told all the assembled shoppers. "I hate to do this."

Joe and the Eskers left L. L. Bean with their cash, their duck phones, the thermal underwear, and a canvas-and-mesh bait bag, which Aunt Pola had selected for a grandchild's high-school graduation gift.

"That Frances," marveled Aunt Ida, in the Town Car on the return trip to the motel. "She couldn't have been nicer."

"I should send her a note," said Mrs. Reckler.

"Or a plant," suggested Aunt Pola, as she drove. "Maybe a rhododendron. Joe, have you counted it? The money?"

"No," said Joe, who was holding the envelope that Frances had passed to him. "I thought it would be rude."

"Rude, listen to him," said Aunt Pola. "Count it. Just to make sure. It's the living room. You don't want to get half the job done and then run out. Count so I can watch."

Joe took the many bills out of the envelope. He held the bundle up near the dashboard, so Aunt Pola could certify his calculations. "It's mostly in fifties," Joe said. "Here we go. Fifty, one hundred, one hundred fifty—"

"He's very good at that," commented Aunt Ida.

"Two hundred, two hundred fifty, three hundred—"

Just then the Town Car hit a pothole. The bills lurched out of Joe's hands and fluttered throughout the car, blizzarding all four passengers.

"Whoops!" said Aunt Pola. "This is a terrible road. You could have an accident."

"Look at all this!" said Aunt Ida, pulling bills out of the air. "It's like the leaves."

Everyone gathered up the money. "Joe, give me the envelope," said Mrs. Reckler.

Joe and Aunt Ida passed Mrs. Reckler their wads of bills. She combined the bunches into a single stack. "Look at all this money," she said, straightening the stack. "I don't think I've ever held this much money in my hands before. I feel like Chase Manhattan."

"It's like Monopoly," said Aunt Pola. "Only better. So? Is it all there?"

"I don't like carrying a lot of cash," said Aunt Ida. "It makes me nervous. I always think somebody will come along and steal it."

"It's a problem," Joe agreed.

"Hedy, count again," advised Aunt Pola. "I'll avoid the bumps."

Mrs. Reckler licked her forefinger, in preparation for counting the bills. Then she put her hand down. "You know," she said, "this isn't my money."

"No kidding," said Aunt Pola. "Keep counting."

"It's not my money," Mrs. Reckler repeated.

"Mom?" said Joe.

"Ida, do you have a pen?" Mrs. Reckler asked.

"Of course," said Aunt Ida, digging a pen out of her handbag.

"Thank you," said Mrs. Reckler, taking the pen and addressing the envelope.

"What's she doing?" asked Aunt Pola. "I can't see."

"She's addressing the envelope," reported Aunt Ida. "To Frances, at L. L. Bean. Hedy, are you sending a note?"

"No," said Mrs. Reckler, slipping the bills into the envelope and sealing it, before she could change her mind or be talked out of it.

"What are you doing?" asked Aunt Ida. "Pola, she's sending the money back."

"What?" said Aunt Pola. "Hedy, what's wrong? Did you hit your head?"

"Mom," said Joe, "what's going on?"

"Joe," said Mrs. Reckler, "and all of you. It's just a living room."

"Hedy?" said Aunt Ida.

"Is she hot or cold?" asked Joe, reaching for his mother's forehead.

"I'm fine," said Mrs. Reckler, brushing Joe's hand aside. "I'm sorry. I can't do it."

"What?" said Aunt Pola. "After we came all the way to Maine? Now you can't do it?"

"No," said Mrs. Reckler. "Pola, I'm sorry. I can't knit, I can't sew, and I can't steal $10,000. It's a character flaw. A bracelet, fine. A bracelet is . . . my friend. But all this money—it's too much."

"But what about the new rug?" asked Aunt Ida. "And the lamps?"

"I'm not going to lie," said Mrs. Reckler. "My living room looks like a tornado hit it. It's not fit for human consumption. But you want to know something else? Who cares?"

"What're you talking?" said Aunt Pola. "Hedy, make some sense."

"You know," said Mrs. Reckler, "I got it into my head, I thought that if I could just get the money, for my living room, everything would be fine. My life would be complete.

I'd be happy. All for $10,000. But you know something? Everything is already fine, even without the $10,000. My life isn't half bad. And I hate to say this, but I'm very happy.''

"*Kineahora,*" said Ida.

"*Poo poo poo,*" said Joe, Aunt Ida, and Aunt Pola.

"I have two wonderful sisters," Mrs. Reckler continued. "Ida and Pola."

"Well, that's certainly true," Aunt Pola admitted.

"And I have two weird children, who are also wonderful. Clark, who I'll never understand if I live to be a hundred. And Joe, who I understand completely because he's just like me, and that's even scarier."

"I'll say," said Joe.

"And I have a wonderful husband. Who's at home right now, probably eating nothing and doing a crossword puzzle in the middle of a filthy living room that he doesn't even notice. And on top of all this, I have a job where they drive me crazy. But I can still take my chair down the hall and watch *Coppélia.*"

"*Coppélia?*" asked Aunt Ida. "Which one is that? The doll who comes to life or the peasant girl who dies?"

"The doll," replied Mrs. Reckler. "So that's my life. And you want to know something? I love my life. Even if sometimes I think it would be better with a new couch in it and a decent rug. But I don't need $10,000, not to be happy. Ten million, that's another story. But this trip was very nice, and I'm glad I came. I'm glad we all talked and looked at a few leaves and a few robes. And I'll send the money back. They can give it to someone who has no couch whatsoever."

By this time, Aunt Pola had pulled into a parking space at the Land Ho. She stopped the car. Everyone sat for a moment.

"This car," Aunt Pola said finally. "You know, I'm not sure it was such a bargain."

"But Pola," said Mrs. Reckler, "it's beautiful."

"Eh," said Aunt Pola. "Who needs beautiful? I'm thinking maybe the test drive is over. You know what I think I'll do? To save time? I think I'll just leave this car right here. Somebody will find it, and they'll return it to the dealer.

Because you know something? I'll tell you, I'll confess it. I'm feeling a little guilty.''

"Because you stole the car?" asked Joe.

"Maybe," said Aunt Pola. "Maybe I cheated. I like to earn my money, and I like to spend my money. When I'm not spending, I don't feel the savings. If I wait until the end of the year and go to my dealer in Queens, I can get a real buy. They have to give the cars away, they beg you to take them. If I was smart, I'd wait a few months and then make my move."

Aunt Pola left the keys in the ignition. "It was a test drive," she declared. "I was entitled."

Aunt Ida made a whimpering sound. She turned up the collar of her sable, nuzzling the lapels.

"I'm not saying a word," said Aunt Pola. "Not one word. I'm the little mouse, remember?"

"Ida," said Mrs. Reckler, "it's a gorgeous coat. It looks marvelous on you."

Aunt Ida made the whimpering sound again and shut her eyes. Gingerly, almost surgically, with her eyes still shut, she opened the coat, holding each lapel with only the tips of her fingers. She made a high-pitched piping sound, a toot of longing. She took a deep breath. Her chin held high, she slowly slid the coat off her shoulders.

She opened the car door and climbed out. Reaching back within the car, she folded the sable carefully and returned it to the back seat, arranging it just so, like Moses' mother surrendering her babe to the bulrushes. Aunt Ida took one last ardent look at the sable, its dark folds rippling across the car's white leather upholstery. Joe could swear he heard the sables themselves cry out; they had been loved.

Aunt Ida shut the car door slowly, as if not to wake the now slumbering, innocent coat. Aunt Pola, Mrs. Reckler, and Joe now also left the car and stood in the parking lot.

"I don't need a coat," said Aunt Ida. "It's crazy."

"Ida, you were very brave," said Mrs. Reckler.

"Tell me about it," said Aunt Ida, taking another deep breath.

"Don't you feel better now?" asked Aunt Pola. "Now that you're an honest woman?"

"Not particularly," said Aunt Ida, rubbing her upper arms. "I feel chilly. I'm going to the room; I'll find my old coat. But you know, once I'm back home, I think I'll go to Loehmann's. I'll find something."

"Ipsy-pipsy," said Mrs. Reckler approvingly.

"Ipsy-pipsy," agreed Aunt Ida.

"Come on," said Aunt Pola. "Let's get our things."

Aunt Pola and Aunt Ida headed back to their room. "Joe," said Mrs. Reckler, staying near the car. "Wait. Help me with something."

"What?" said Joe.

Mrs. Reckler walked over to the Oldsmobile, which was parked beside the Town Car. She unlocked the trunk. "There," she said to Joe, pointing to a large bundle, an army blanket wrapped around something, cushioning it. Joe lifted the bundle, which was fairly bulky. He pulled back a corner of the blanket; he was lifting the egg-shaped tureen from the Bennington Pottery.

"Put it in Pola's car," instructed Mrs. Reckler.

"Are you sure?" asked Joe, hoisting the tureen.

"Yes," Mrs. Reckler sighed. "It's breaking my heart, but I'm sure."

Mrs. Reckler opened the rear door of the Town Car. She unwrapped the tureen as Joe held it. Joe deposited the tureen on the back seat. He nestled it in Aunt Ida's sable, so the back seat of the car assumed the allure of a sumptuous advertising layout, a full-color spread of some grand luxury picnic, promoting diamonds or mustard.

"Things are so beautiful," said Mrs. Reckler regretfully.

"You said it," Joe agreed.

"We're terrible people," said Mrs. Reckler. "Every one of us, and especially me. And especially you."

"Thank you," said Joe.

"Shut the door," said Mrs. Reckler. "Now go get your things. And remember, we'll be driving for quite some time. We won't get to Long Island until the middle of the night."

"Gee," said Joe. "So I guess I'd better use the facilities."

''Wiseguy,'' said Mrs. Reckler, tugging on her son's hair. ''This trip wasn't so bad. It didn't kill you.''

Mrs. Reckler gave her son a kiss and then returned to her room, to assemble her belongings. Joe leaned against the Town Car for a moment. He tried to make sense out of his past week in New England. Morality had asserted itself, Esker morality. Joe thought about his mother's relinquishment of a new living room; this struck him as an entirely agreeable sacrifice. If Joe could replace a new couch in his mother's affections, he felt truly loved. Joe so wanted his mother to be happy, and he now suspected that she was. Mrs. Reckler might always be dissatisfied, she might always tug at the leash of family life, but she would also know happiness, a lightness of spirit. She had decided to be happy.

As for thievery, Joe knew that it was not really in his Aunt Pola's or his Aunt Ida's vocabulary. They had wanted to fly the dizzying ozone of bourgeois crime, but their hearts hadn't been in it. Mrs. Reckler, Joe suspected, was also through with Zen kleptomania.

Joe wondered about his own life. He knew that the most important thing was not to compare it to anyone else's. Joe decided that he wanted more than anything to be an Esker sister, or at least to honor the Esker virtues. He wanted to be strong, like his Aunt Pola, and infinitely kind, like his Aunt Ida. Above all else he prized his mother's restlessness, her questioning, her refusal to settle. Joe knew that whatever else happened in his life, he would keep shopping. Shopping meant that you were curious, that you were alive, that there was always something to look forward to. And, as an Esker sister, Joe might even find bargains.

About the Author

PAUL RUDNICK is the author of a novel, SOCIAL DISEASE, and the plays POOR LITTLE LAMBS, for which he won an Outer Critics Circle Award, and COSMETIC SURGERY. His work appeared in *Esquire*, *Vanity Fair*, *Spy*, and *The New York Times*. He is a graduate of Yale University. He lives in New York City.